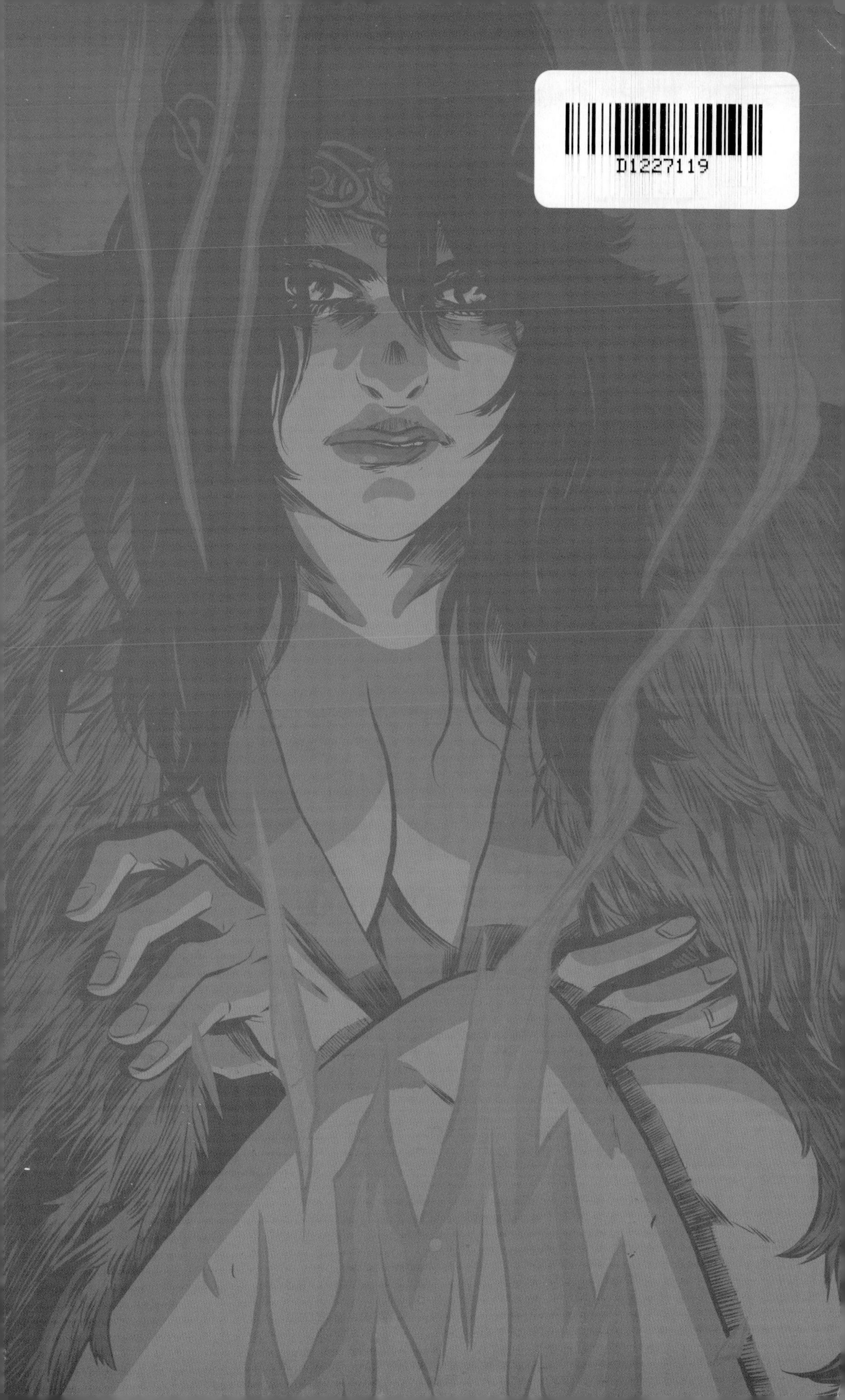

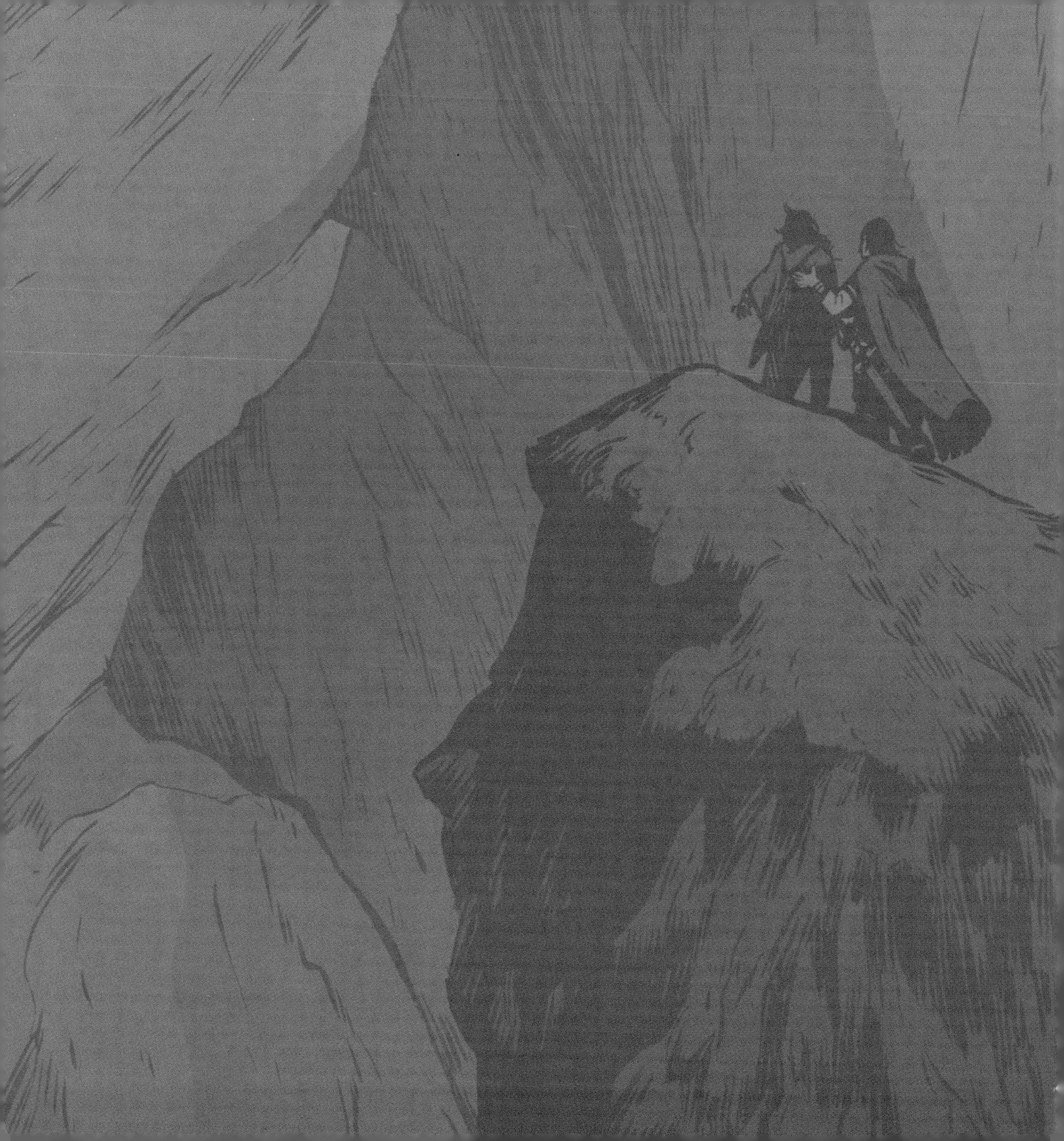

CONAN

THE DEATH

Writer BRIAN WOOD

Art by BECKY CLOONAN (chapter 1)
VASILIS LOLOS (chapters 2–3)
DECLAN SHALVEY (chapters 4–6)

Colors by DAVE STEWART

Letters by
RICHARD STARKINGS
and COMICRAFT'S JIMMY BETANCOURT

Cover and Chapter-Break Artist
MASSIMO CARNEVALE

Creator of Conan
ROBERT E. HOWARD

DARK HORSE BOOKS®

Publisher MIKE RICHARDSON Designers KAT LARSON with ADAM GRANO Digital Production CHRISTIANNE GOUDREAU Assistant Editors SHANTEL LAROCQUE and IAN TUCKER Associate Editor BRENDAN WRIGHT Editor DAVE MARSHALL

Special thanks to FREDRIK MALMBERG and JOAKIM ZETTERBERG at CONAN PROPERTIES.

This volume collects issues #7 through #12 of the Dark Horse Comics monthly *Conan the Barbarian* series.

Published by Dark Horse Books
A division of Dark Horse Comics, Inc.
10956 SE Main Street
Milwaukie, OR 97222

DarkHorse.com

Library of Congress Cataloging-in-Publication Data

Wood, Brian, 1972- author.
Conan : the death / writer, Brian Wood ; art by Becky Cloonan (chapter 1) Vasilis Lolos (chapters 2-3) Declan Shalvey (chapters 4-6) ; colors by Dave Stewart ; letters by Richard Starkings and Comicraft's Jimmy Betancourt ; cover and Chapter-Break Artist, Massimo Carnevale ; creator of Conan, Robert E. Howard. — First hardcover edition.
pages cm
"This volume collects issues #7 through #12 of the Dark Horse Comics monthly Conan the Barbarian series."
ISBN 978-1-61655-122-3
1. Graphic novels. I. Cloonan, Becky, illustrator. II. Lolos, Vasilis, illustrator. III. Shalvey, Declan, illustrator. IV. Howard, Robert E. (Robert Ervin), 1906-1936, creator. V. Title. VI. Title: Death.
PN6728.C65W69 2013
741.5'973—dc23
2013008531

International Licensing: (503) 905-2377
To find a comics shop in your area, call the Comic Shop Locator Service toll-free at 1-888-266-4226

First softcover edition: December 2013
ISBN 978-1-61655-123-0

10 9 8 7 6 5 4 3 2 1

Printed in China

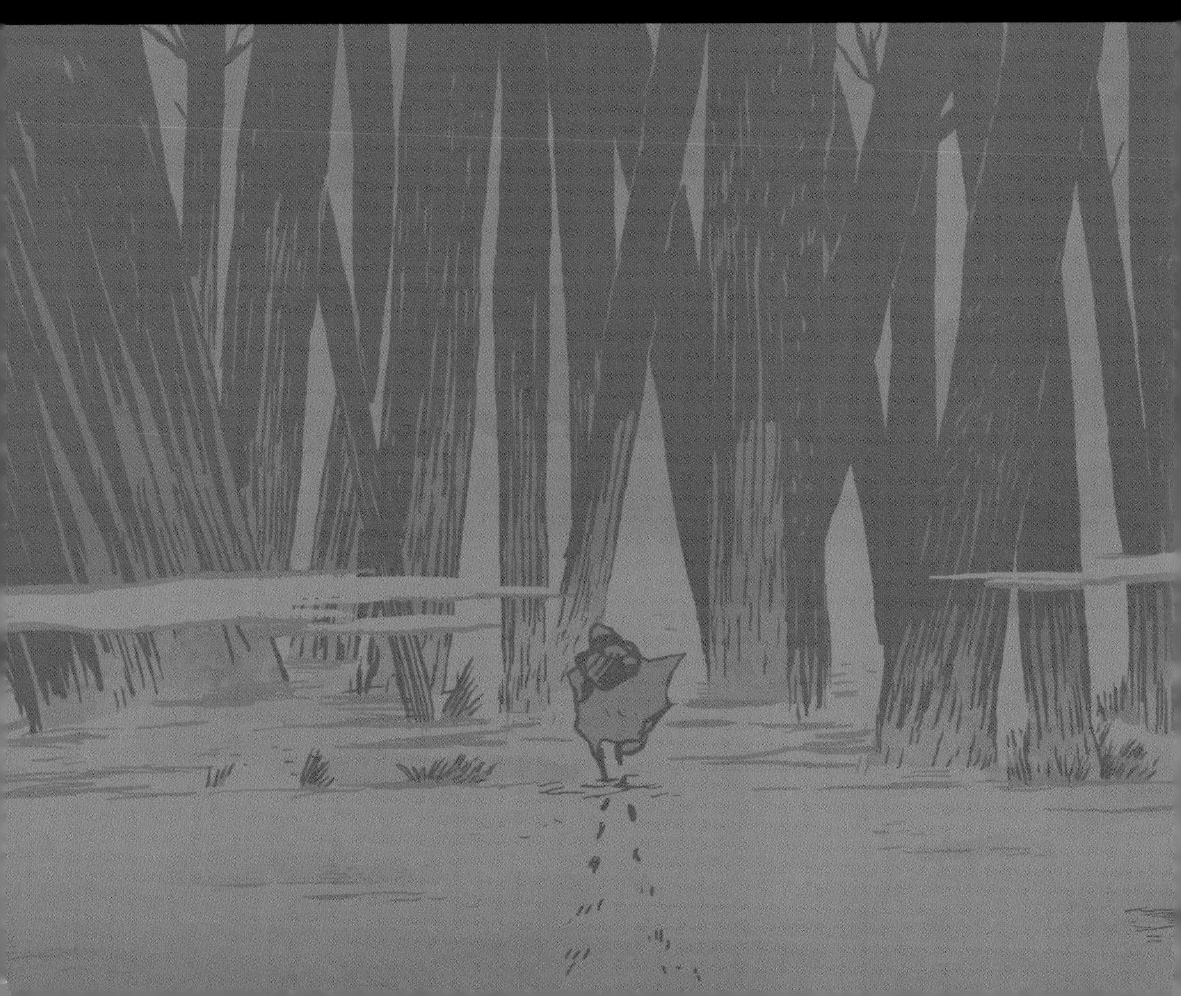

CHAPTER ONE

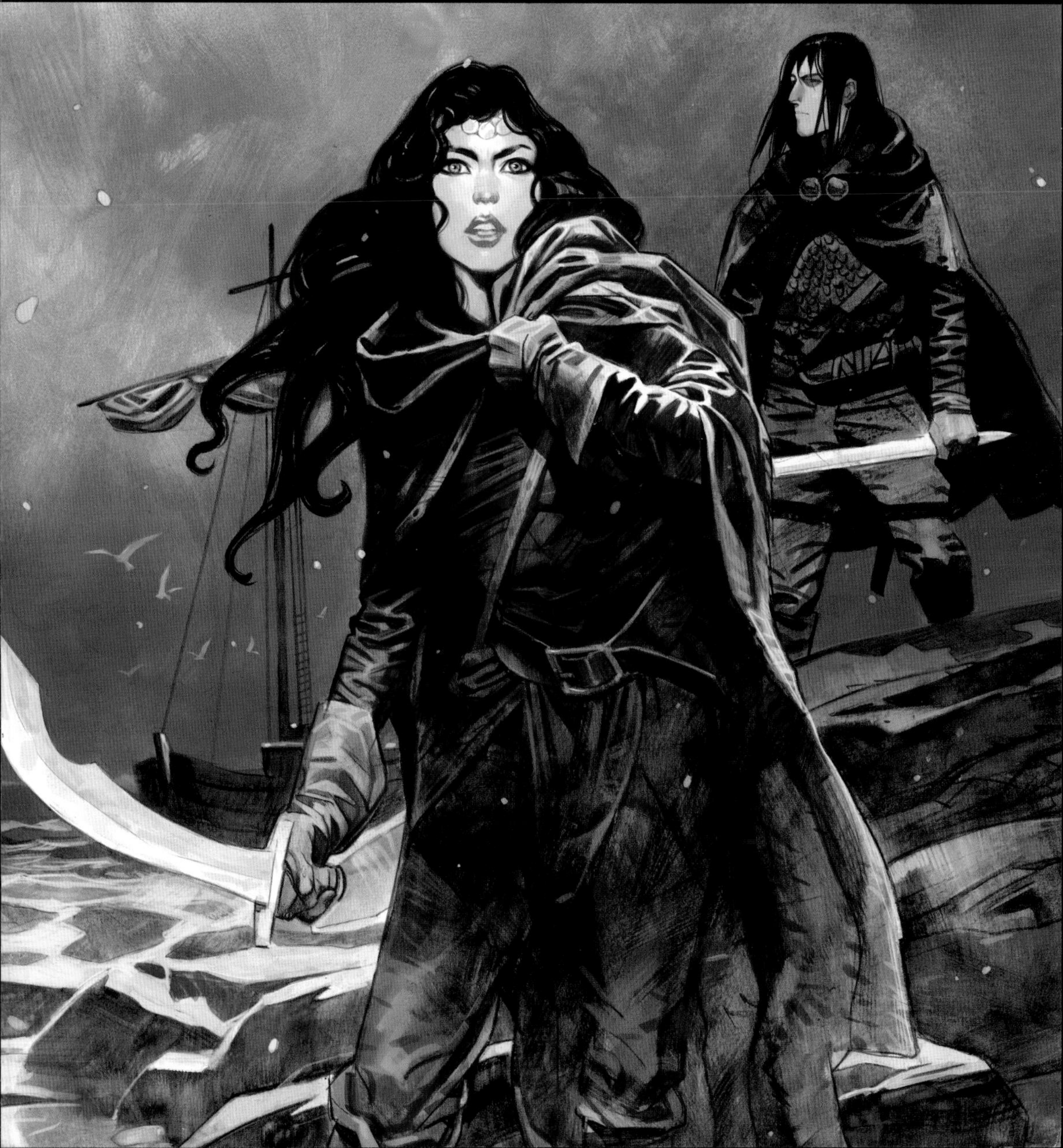

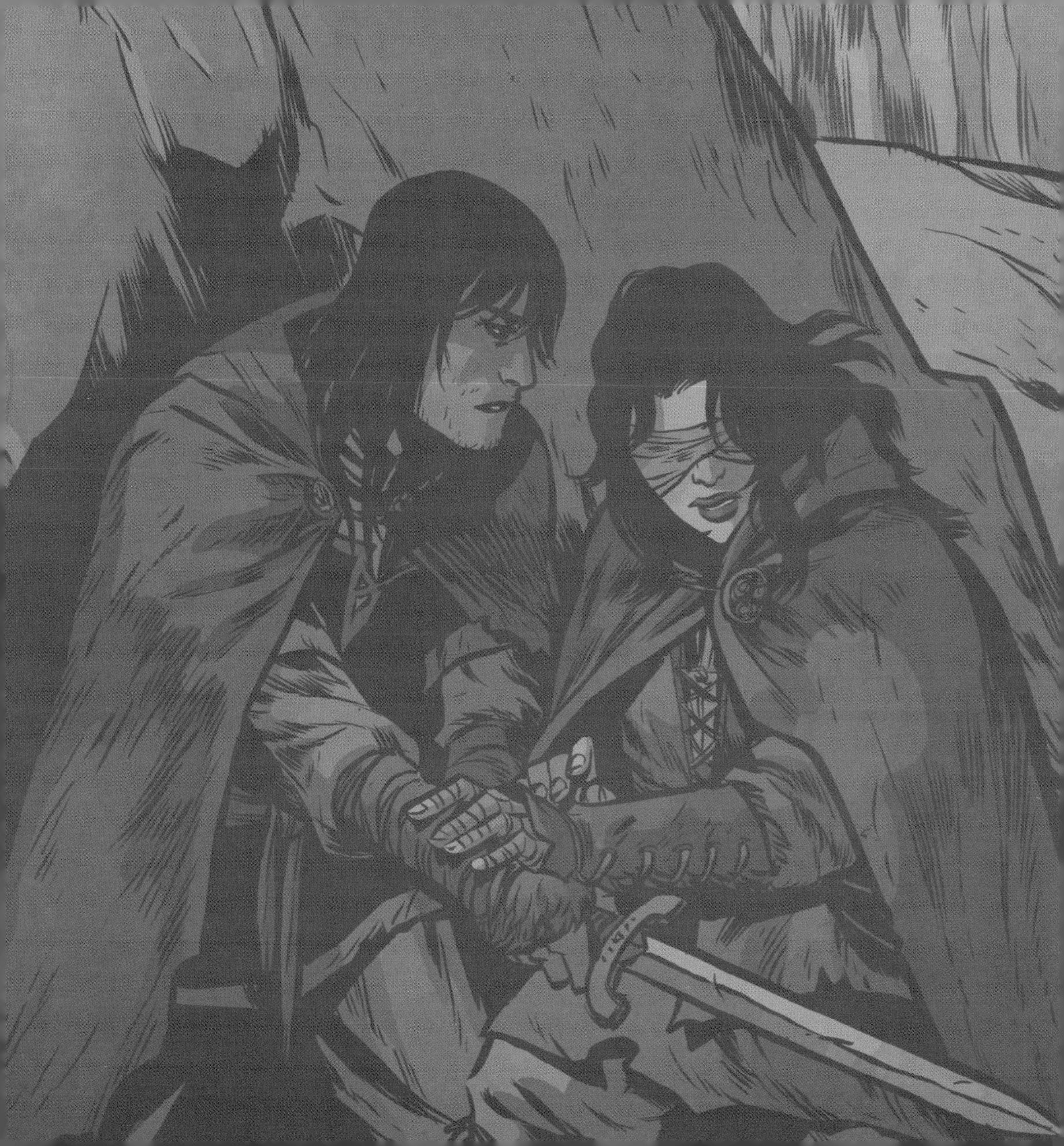

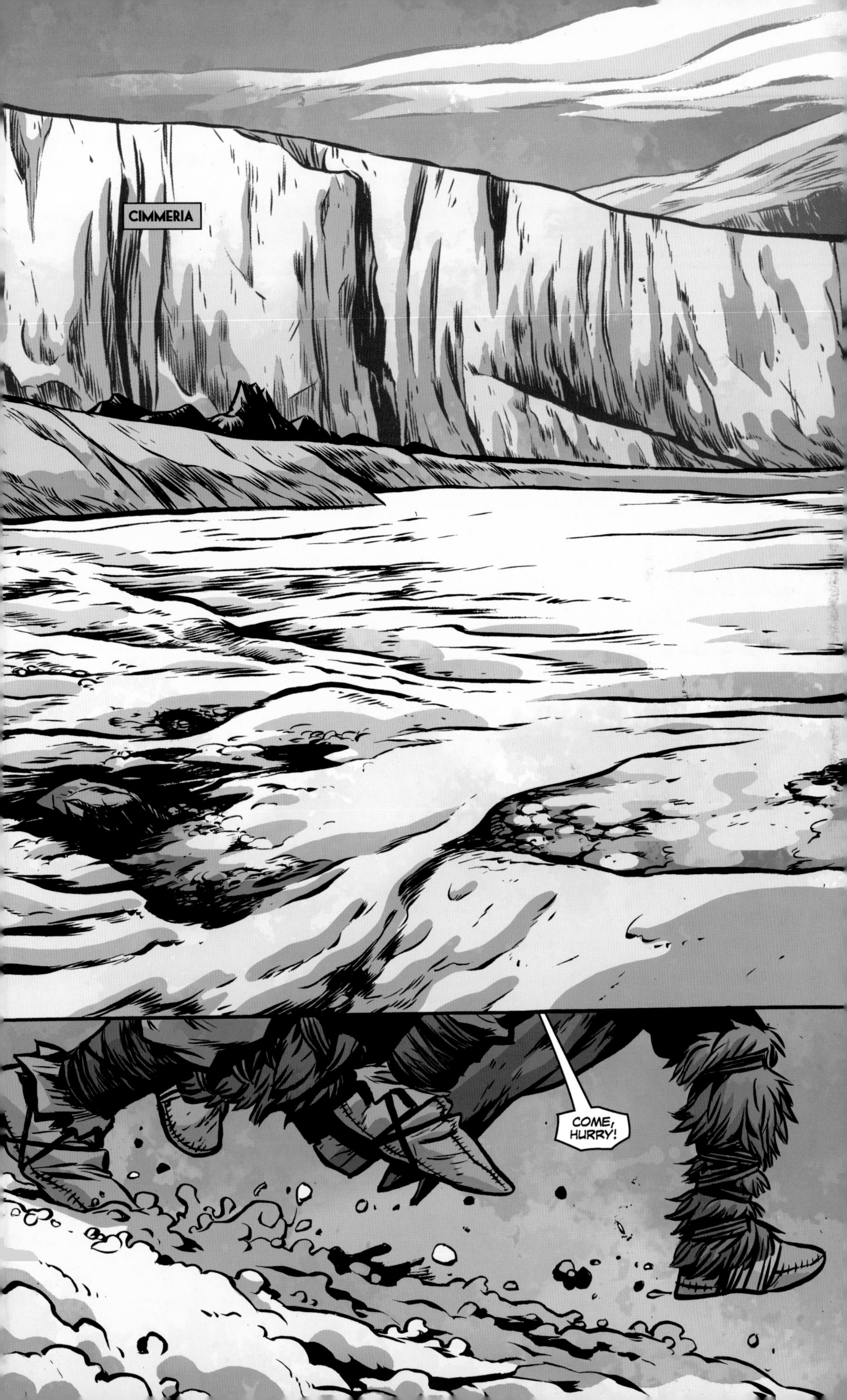
CIMMERIA
COME, HURRY!

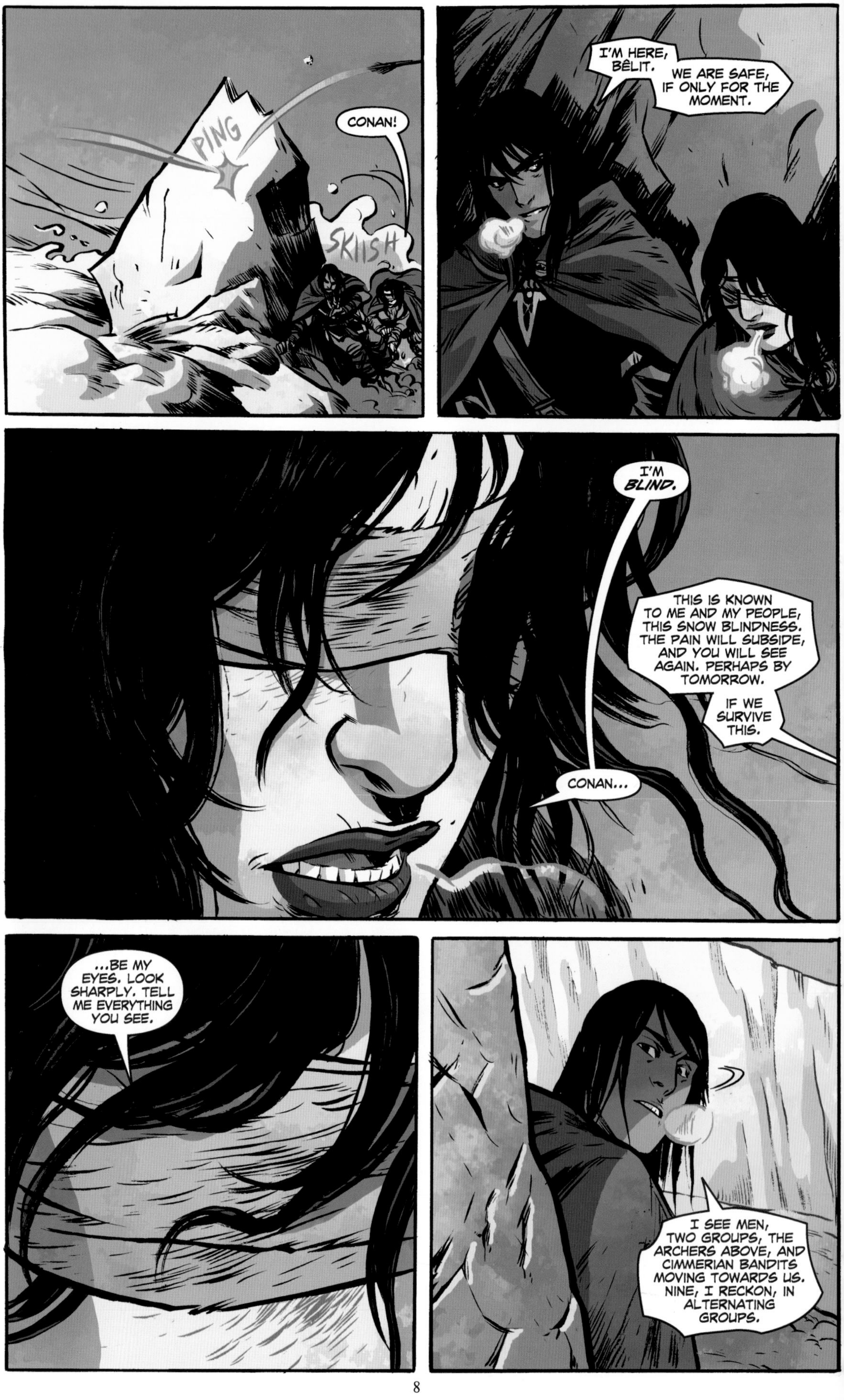
PING
CONAN!
SKIISH
I'M HERE, BÊLIT.
WE ARE SAFE, IF ONLY FOR THE MOMENT.
I'M *BLIND.*
THIS IS KNOWN TO ME AND MY PEOPLE, THIS SNOW BLINDNESS. THE PAIN WILL SUBSIDE, AND YOU WILL SEE AGAIN. PERHAPS BY TOMORROW.
IF WE SURVIVE THIS.
CONAN...
...BE MY EYES. LOOK SHARPLY. TELL ME EVERYTHING YOU SEE.
I SEE MEN, TWO GROUPS, THE ARCHERS ABOVE, AND CIMMERIAN BANDITS MOVING TOWARDS US. NINE, I RECKON, IN ALTERNATING GROUPS.

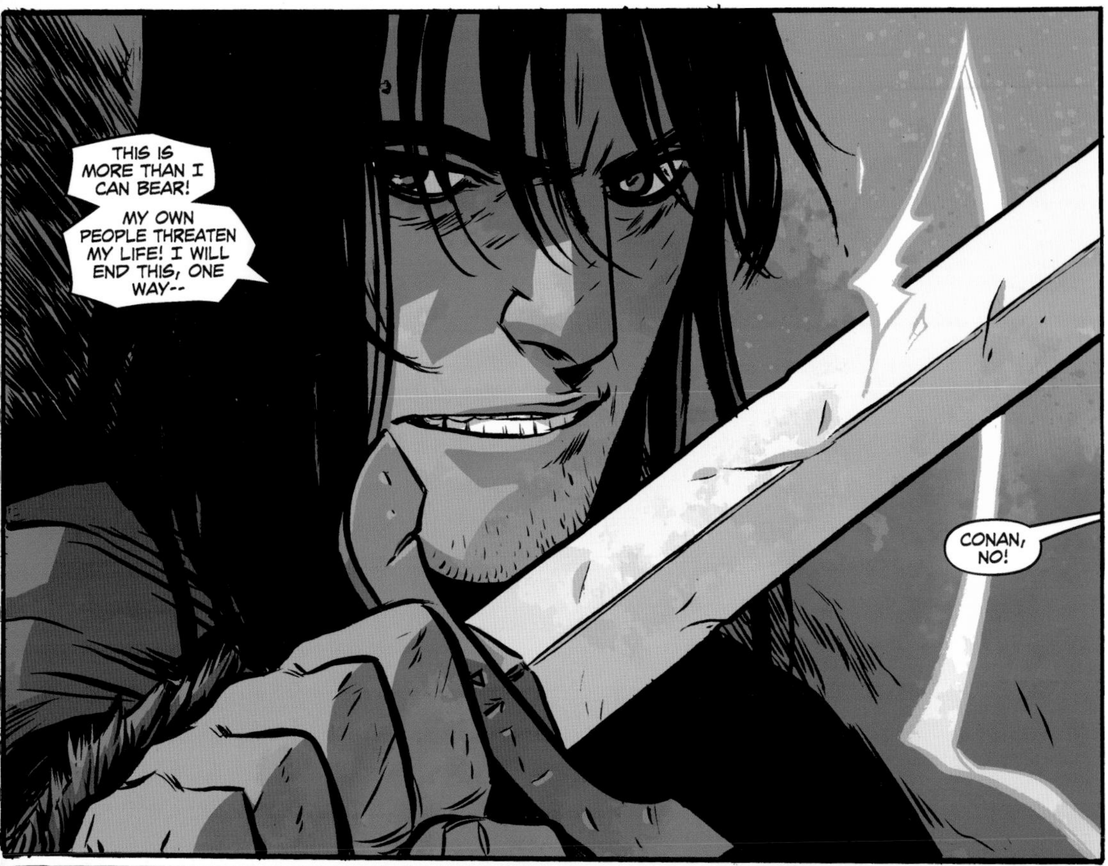

THIS IS MORE THAN I CAN BEAR!
MY OWN PEOPLE THREATEN MY LIFE! I WILL END THIS, ONE WAY--
CONAN, NO!

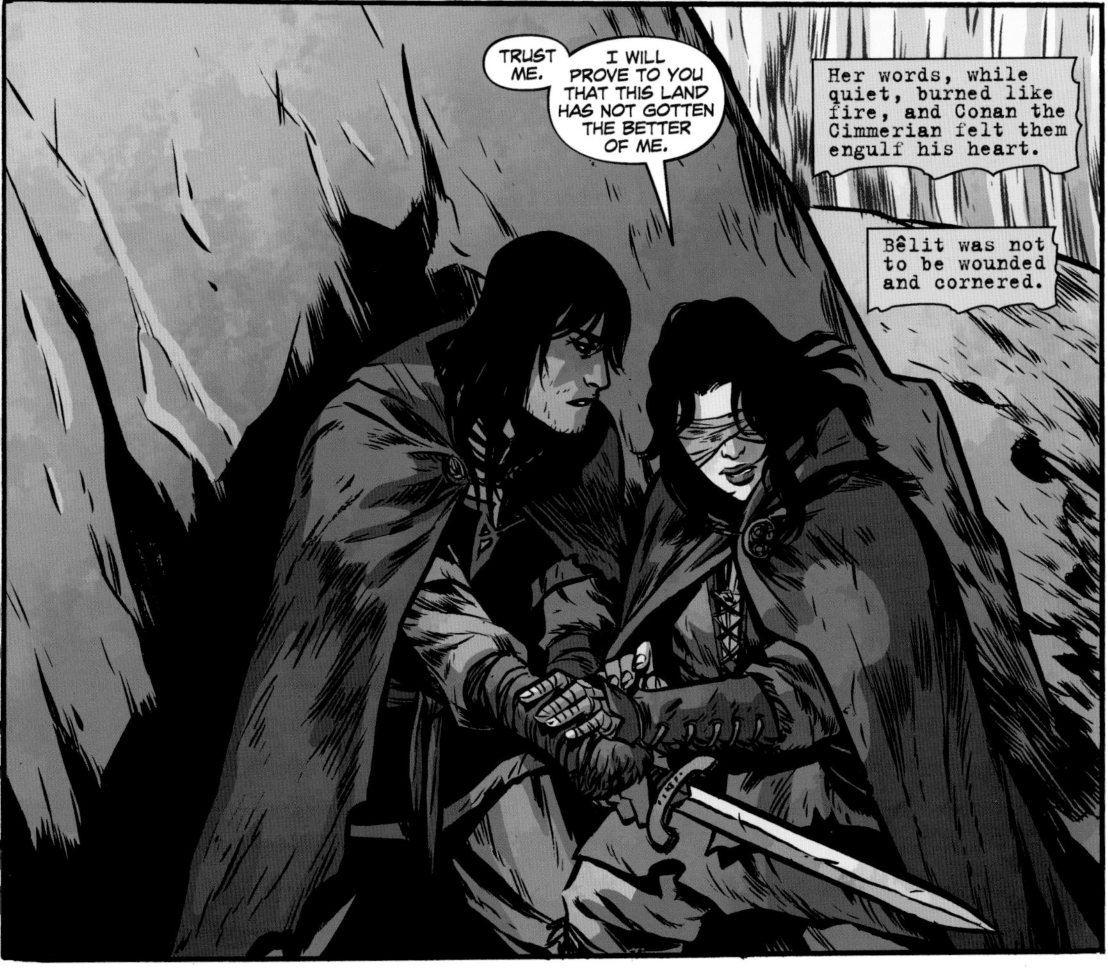

TRUST ME.
I WILL PROVE TO YOU THAT THIS LAND HAS NOT GOTTEN THE BETTER OF ME.
Her words, while quiet, burned like fire, and Conan the Cimmerian felt them engulf his heart.
Bêlit was not to be wounded and cornered.

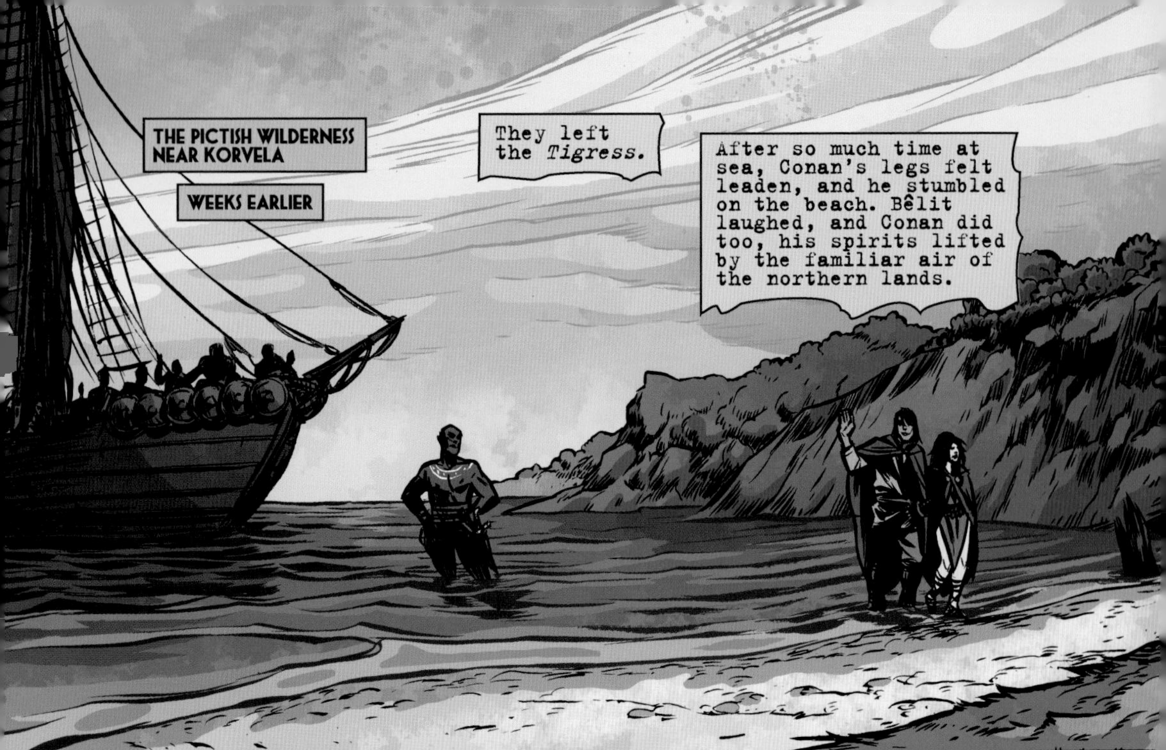
THE PICTISH WILDERNESS NEAR KORVELA
WEEKS EARLIER
They left the *Tigress.*
After so much time at sea, Conan's legs felt leaden, and he stumbled on the beach. Bêlit laughed, and Conan did too, his spirits lifted by the familiar air of the northern lands.

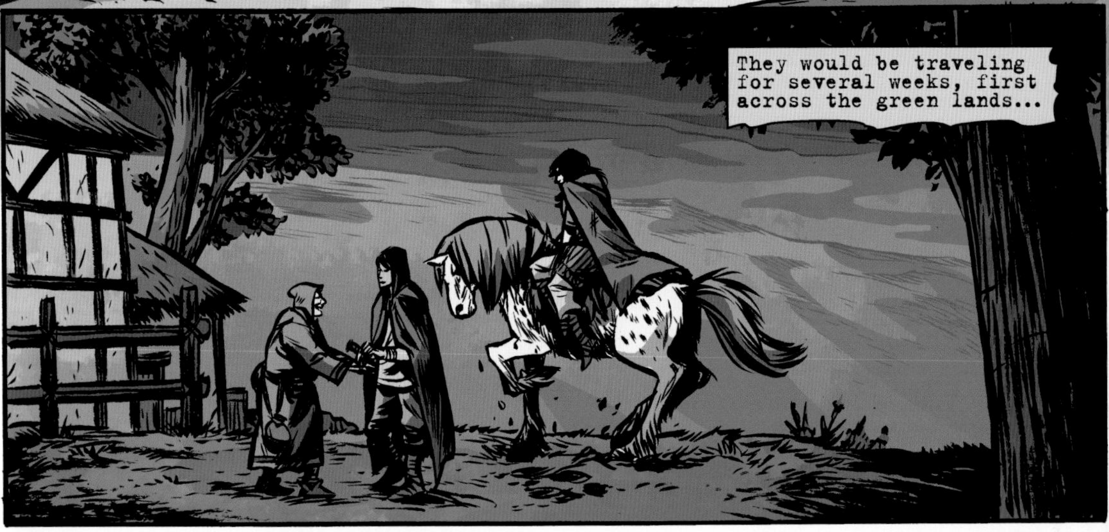
They would be traveling for several weeks, first across the green lands...

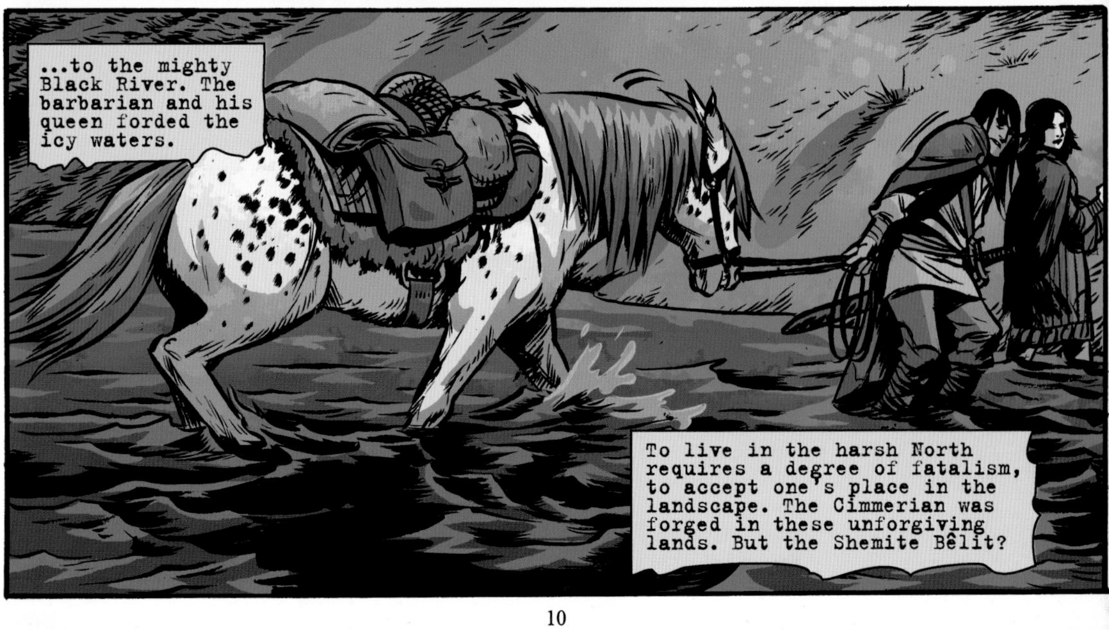
...to the mighty Black River. The barbarian and his queen forded the icy waters.
To live in the harsh North requires a degree of fatalism, to accept one's place in the landscape. The Cimmerian was forged in these unforgiving lands. But the Shemite Bêlit?

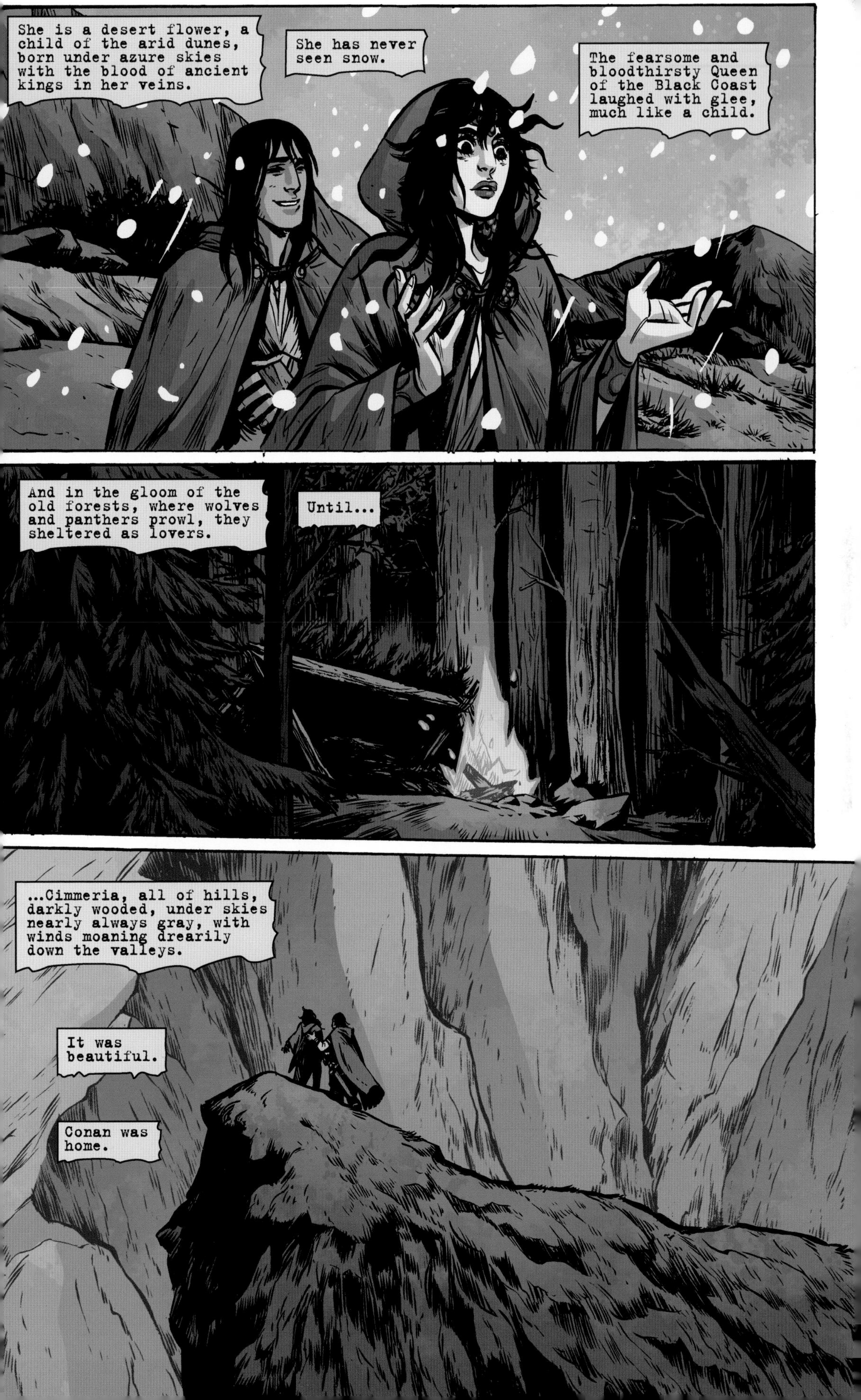
She is a desert flower, a child of the arid dunes, born under azure skies with the blood of ancient kings in her veins.
She has never seen snow.
The fearsome and bloodthirsty Queen of the Black Coast laughed with glee, much like a child.
And in the gloom of the old forests, where wolves and panthers prowl, they sheltered as lovers.
Until...
...Cimmeria, all of hills, darkly wooded, under skies nearly always gray, with winds moaning drearily down the valleys.
It was beautiful.
Conan was home.

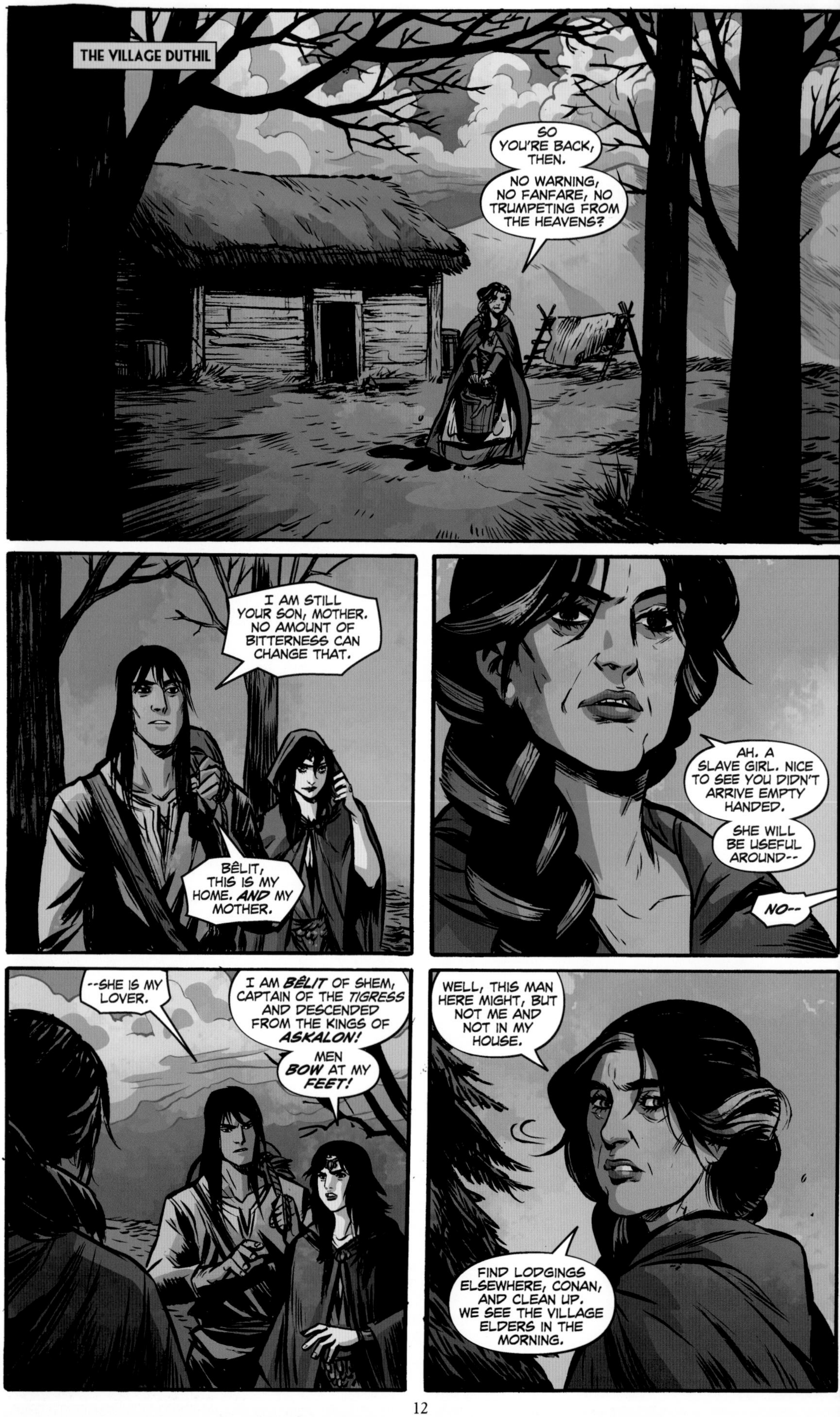
THE VILLAGE DUTHIL
SO YOU'RE BACK, THEN.
NO WARNING, NO FANFARE, NO TRUMPETING FROM THE HEAVENS?
I AM STILL YOUR SON, MOTHER. NO AMOUNT OF BITTERNESS CAN CHANGE THAT.
BÊLIT, THIS IS MY HOME. AND MY MOTHER.
AH. A SLAVE GIRL. NICE TO SEE YOU DIDN'T ARRIVE EMPTY HANDED.
SHE WILL BE USEFUL AROUND--
NO--
--SHE IS MY LOVER.
I AM BÊLIT OF SHEM, CAPTAIN OF THE TIGRESS AND DESCENDED FROM THE KINGS OF ASKALON!
MEN BOW AT MY FEET!
WELL, THIS MAN HERE MIGHT, BUT NOT ME AND NOT IN MY HOUSE.
FIND LODGINGS ELSEWHERE, CONAN, AND CLEAN UP. WE SEE THE VILLAGE ELDERS IN THE MORNING.

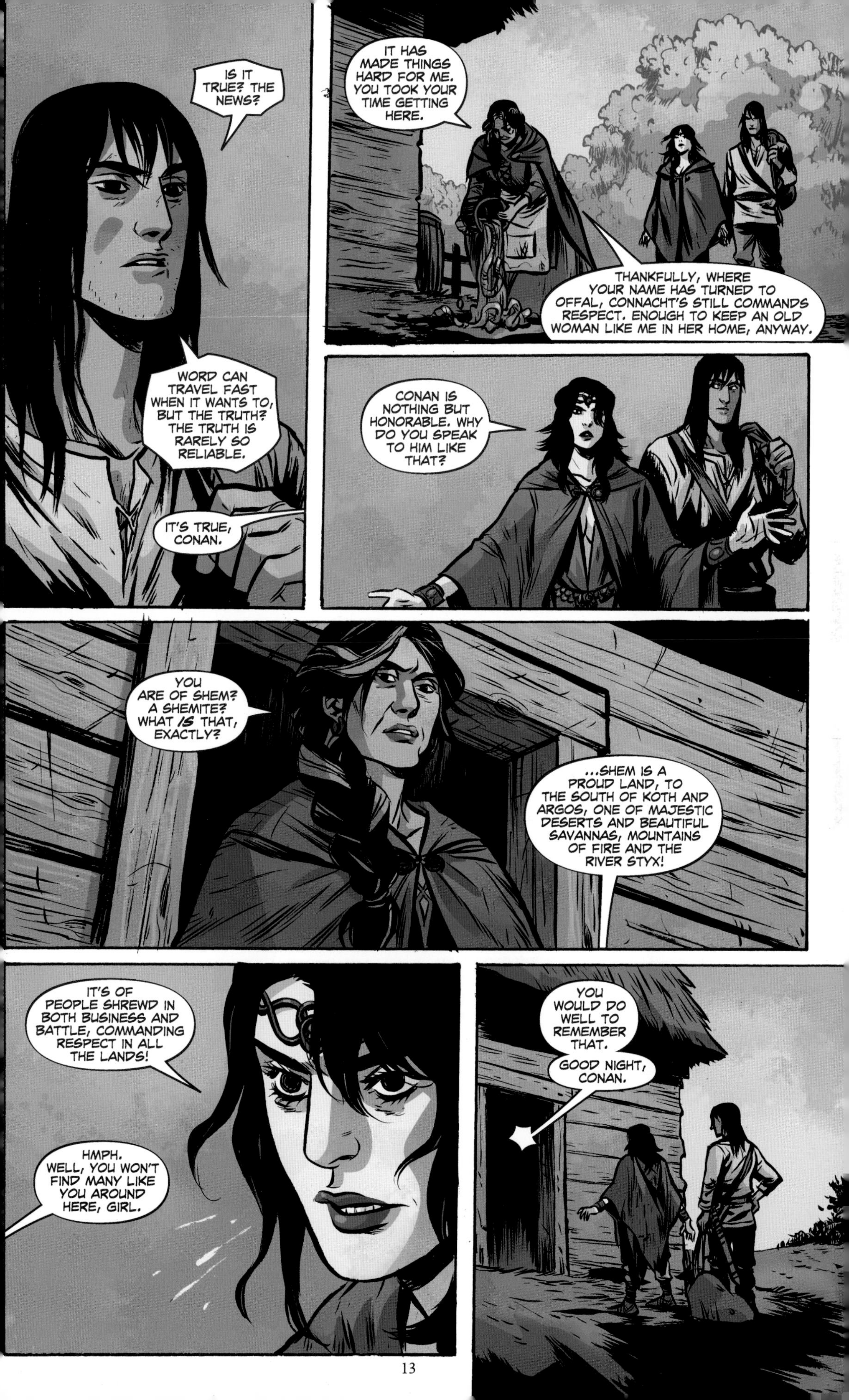
IS IT TRUE? THE NEWS?
IT HAS MADE THINGS HARD FOR ME. YOU TOOK YOUR TIME GETTING HERE.
THANKFULLY, WHERE YOUR NAME HAS TURNED TO OFFAL, CONNACHT'S STILL COMMANDS RESPECT. ENOUGH TO KEEP AN OLD WOMAN LIKE ME IN HER HOME, ANYWAY.
WORD CAN TRAVEL FAST WHEN IT WANTS TO, BUT THE TRUTH? THE TRUTH IS RARELY SO RELIABLE.
IT'S TRUE, CONAN.
CONAN IS NOTHING BUT HONORABLE. WHY DO YOU SPEAK TO HIM LIKE THAT?
YOU ARE OF SHEM? A SHEMITE? WHAT *IS* THAT, EXACTLY?
...SHEM IS A PROUD LAND, TO THE SOUTH OF KOTH AND ARGOS, ONE OF MAJESTIC DESERTS AND BEAUTIFUL SAVANNAS, MOUNTAINS OF FIRE AND THE RIVER STYX!
IT'S OF PEOPLE SHREWD IN BOTH BUSINESS AND BATTLE, COMMANDING RESPECT IN ALL THE LANDS!
HMPH. WELL, YOU WON'T FIND MANY LIKE YOU AROUND HERE, GIRL.
YOU WOULD DO WELL TO REMEMBER THAT.
GOOD NIGHT, CONAN.

It was a long night, not helped by the weather, the accommodations, or Bêlit's fury.

For even in the wilderness of Cimmeria, she was the infamous Queen of the Black Coast. Not a slave, not a mere girl to be looked down upon.

Her anger, her embarrassment, and her frustration lashed against Conan, but he could not rise to the fight. His heart was heavy...

...faced with not just the strangeness of his once-familiar home, not just the hardness and bitterness in his mother's voice and on her face, not just the troubling news that brought him here in the first place...

SPLISH

WHAP

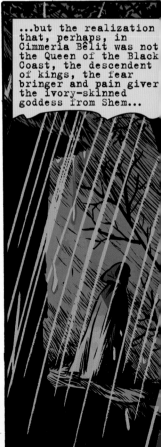

...but the realization that, perhaps, in Cimmeria Bêlit was not the Queen of the Black Coast, the descendent of kings, the fear bringer and pain giver the ivory-skinned goddess from Shem...

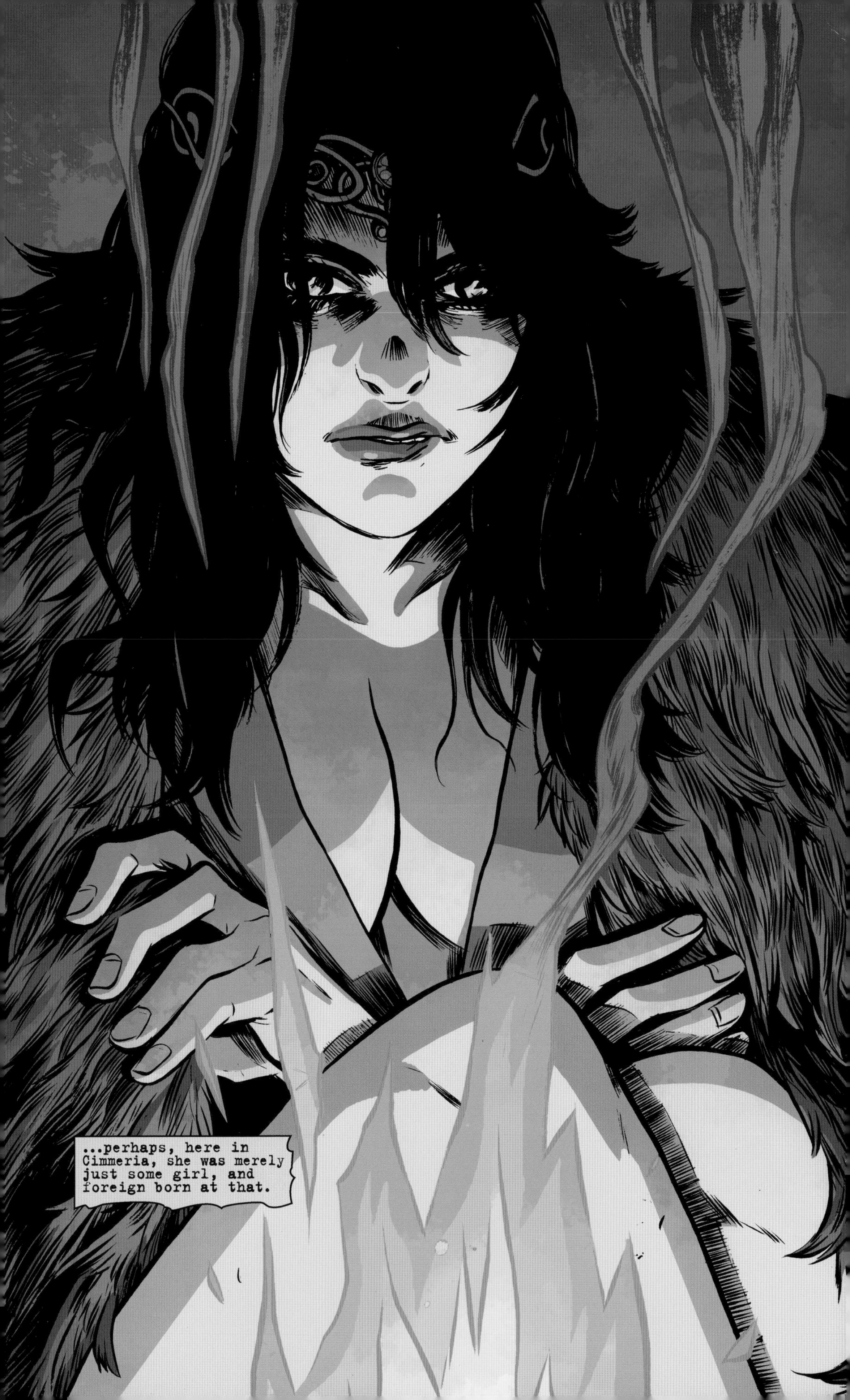
...perhaps, here in Cimmeria, she was merely just some girl, and foreign born at that.

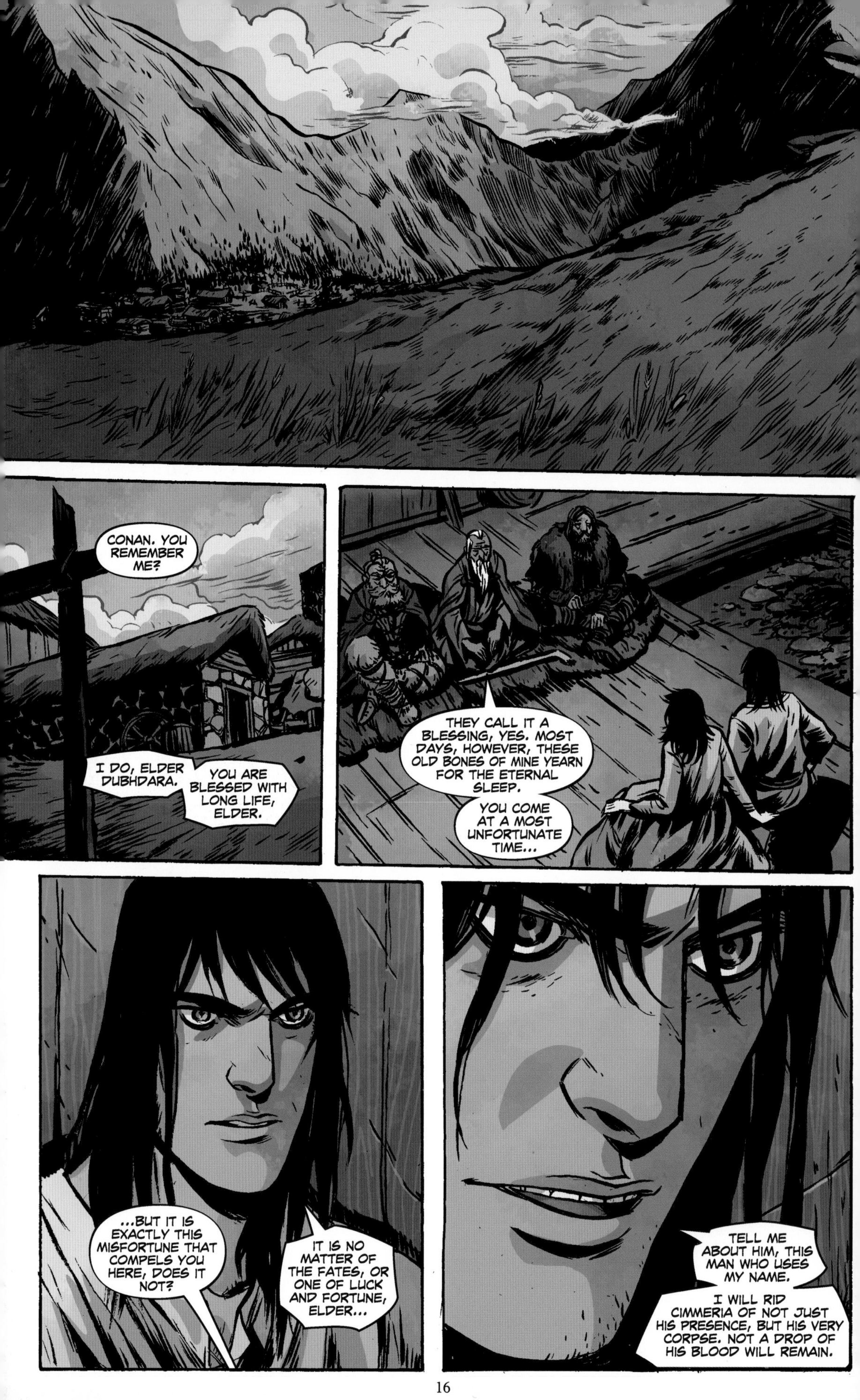

CONAN. YOU REMEMBER ME?
I DO, ELDER DUBHDARA.
YOU ARE BLESSED WITH LONG LIFE, ELDER.
THEY CALL IT A BLESSING, YES. MOST DAYS, HOWEVER, THESE OLD BONES OF MINE YEARN FOR THE ETERNAL SLEEP.
YOU COME AT A MOST UNFORTUNATE TIME...
...BUT IT IS EXACTLY THIS MISFORTUNE THAT COMPELS YOU HERE, DOES IT NOT?
IT IS NO MATTER OF THE FATES, OR ONE OF LUCK AND FORTUNE, ELDER...
TELL ME ABOUT HIM, THIS MAN WHO USES MY NAME.
I WILL RID CIMMERIA OF NOT JUST HIS PRESENCE, BUT HIS VERY CORPSE. NOT A DROP OF HIS BLOOD WILL REMAIN.

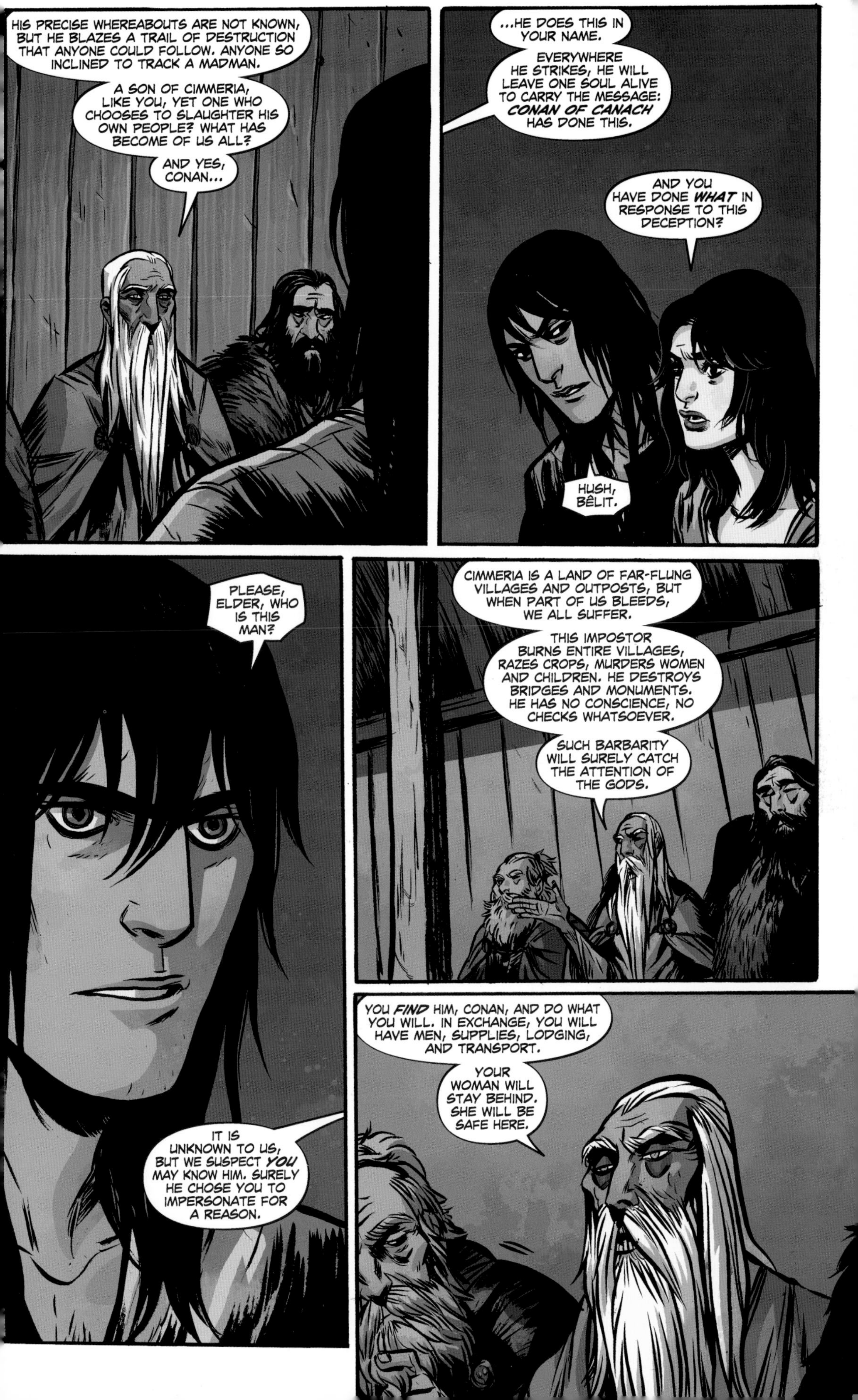

HIS PRECISE WHEREABOUTS ARE NOT KNOWN, BUT HE BLAZES A TRAIL OF DESTRUCTION THAT ANYONE COULD FOLLOW. ANYONE SO INCLINED TO TRACK A MADMAN.
A SON OF CIMMERIA, LIKE YOU, YET ONE WHO CHOOSES TO SLAUGHTER HIS OWN PEOPLE? WHAT HAS BECOME OF US ALL?
AND YES, CONAN...
...HE DOES THIS IN YOUR NAME.
EVERYWHERE HE STRIKES, HE WILL LEAVE ONE SOUL ALIVE TO CARRY THE MESSAGE: *CONAN OF CANACH* HAS DONE THIS.
AND YOU HAVE DONE *WHAT* IN RESPONSE TO THIS DECEPTION?
HUSH, BÊLIT.
PLEASE, ELDER, WHO IS THIS MAN?
IT IS UNKNOWN TO US, BUT WE SUSPECT *YOU* MAY KNOW HIM. SURELY HE CHOSE YOU TO IMPERSONATE FOR A REASON.
CIMMERIA IS A LAND OF FAR-FLUNG VILLAGES AND OUTPOSTS, BUT WHEN PART OF US BLEEDS, WE ALL SUFFER.
THIS IMPOSTOR BURNS ENTIRE VILLAGES, RAZES CROPS, MURDERS WOMEN AND CHILDREN. HE DESTROYS BRIDGES AND MONUMENTS. HE HAS NO CONSCIENCE, NO CHECKS WHATSOEVER.
SUCH BARBARITY WILL SURELY CATCH THE ATTENTION OF THE GODS.
YOU *FIND* HIM, CONAN, AND DO WHAT YOU WILL. IN EXCHANGE, YOU WILL HAVE MEN, SUPPLIES, LODGING, AND TRANSPORT.
YOUR WOMAN WILL STAY BEHIND. SHE WILL BE SAFE HERE.

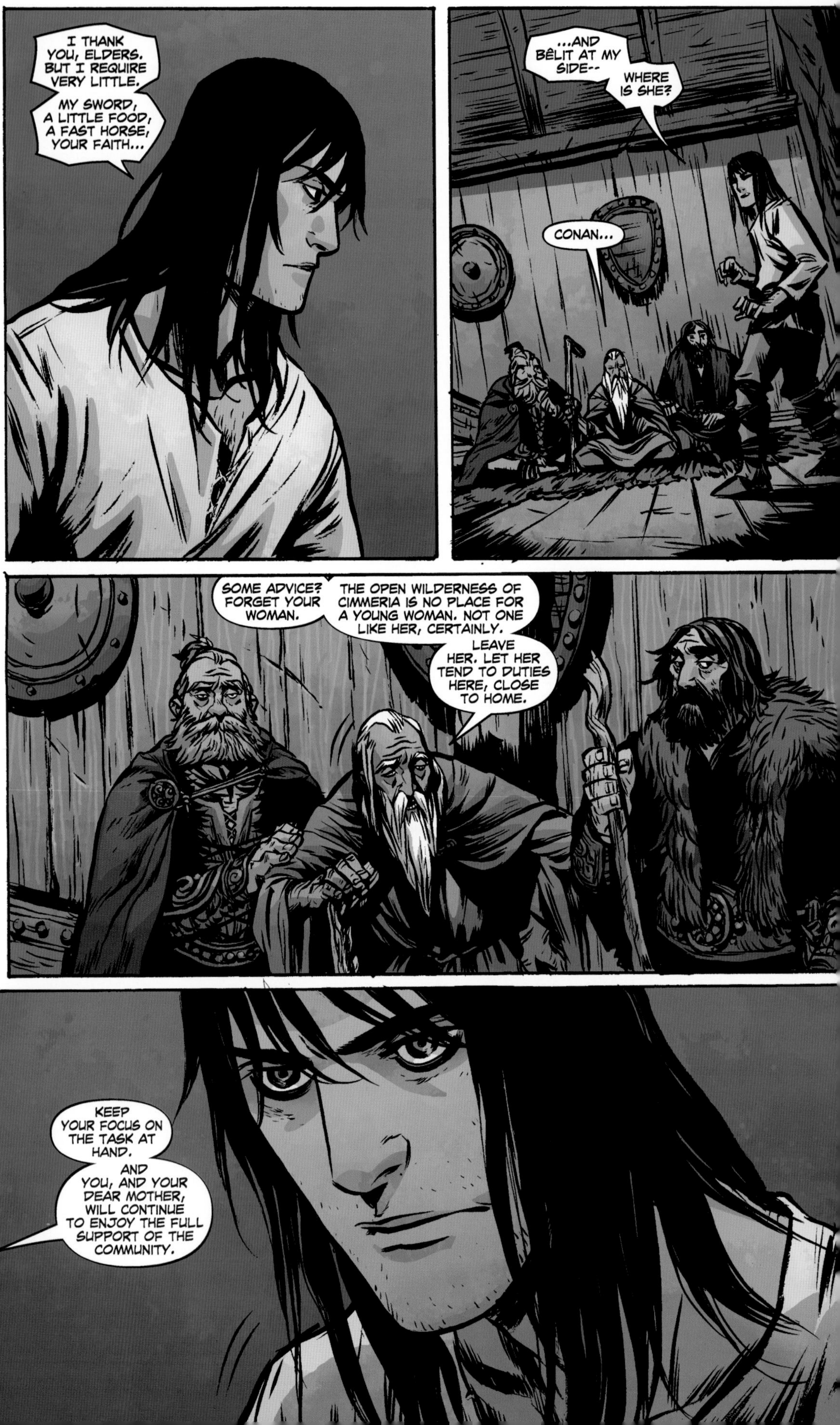

I THANK YOU, ELDERS. BUT I REQUIRE VERY LITTLE.
MY SWORD, A LITTLE FOOD, A FAST HORSE, YOUR FAITH...
...AND BÊLIT AT MY SIDE--
WHERE IS SHE?
CONAN...
SOME ADVICE? FORGET YOUR WOMAN.
THE OPEN WILDERNESS OF CIMMERIA IS NO PLACE FOR A YOUNG WOMAN. NOT ONE LIKE HER, CERTAINLY.
LEAVE HER. LET HER TEND TO DUTIES HERE, CLOSE TO HOME.
KEEP YOUR FOCUS ON THE TASK AT HAND.
AND YOU, AND YOUR DEAR MOTHER, WILL CONTINUE TO ENJOY THE FULL SUPPORT OF THE COMMUNITY.

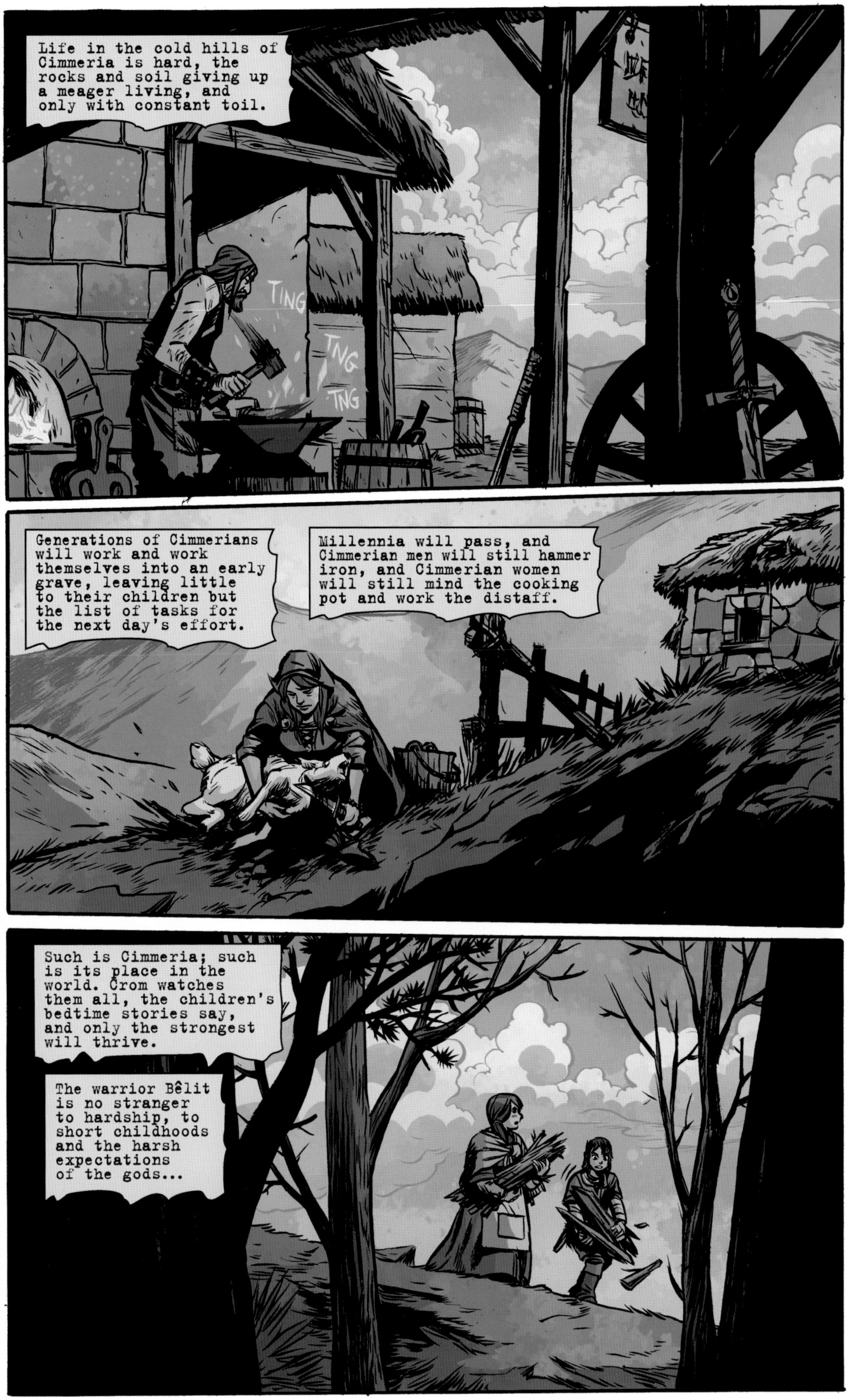
Life in the cold hills of Cimmeria is hard, the rocks and soil giving up a meager living, and only with constant toil.
TING
TNG
TNG
Generations of Cimmerians will work and work themselves into an early grave, leaving little to their children but the list of tasks for the next day's effort.
Millennia will pass, and Cimmerian men will still hammer iron, and Cimmerian women will still mind the cooking pot and work the distaff.
Such is Cimmeria; such is its place in the world. Crom watches them all, the children's bedtime stories say, and only the strongest will thrive.
The warrior Bêlit is no stranger to hardship, to short childhoods and the harsh expectations of the gods...

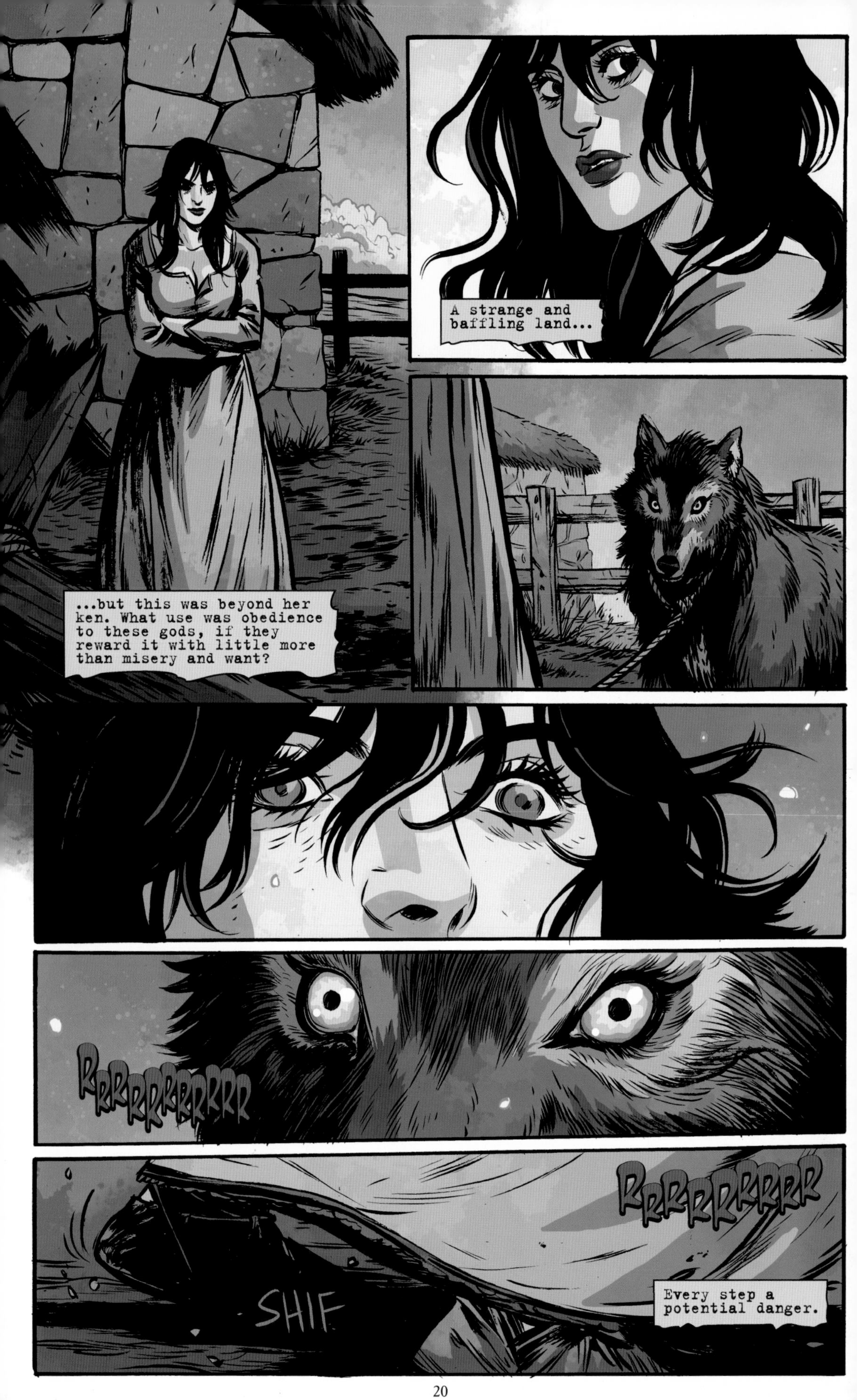
A strange and baffling land...
...but this was beyond her ken. What use was obedience to these gods, if they reward it with little more than misery and want?
RRRRRRRRRRR
RRRRRRRRR
SHIF
Every step a potential danger.

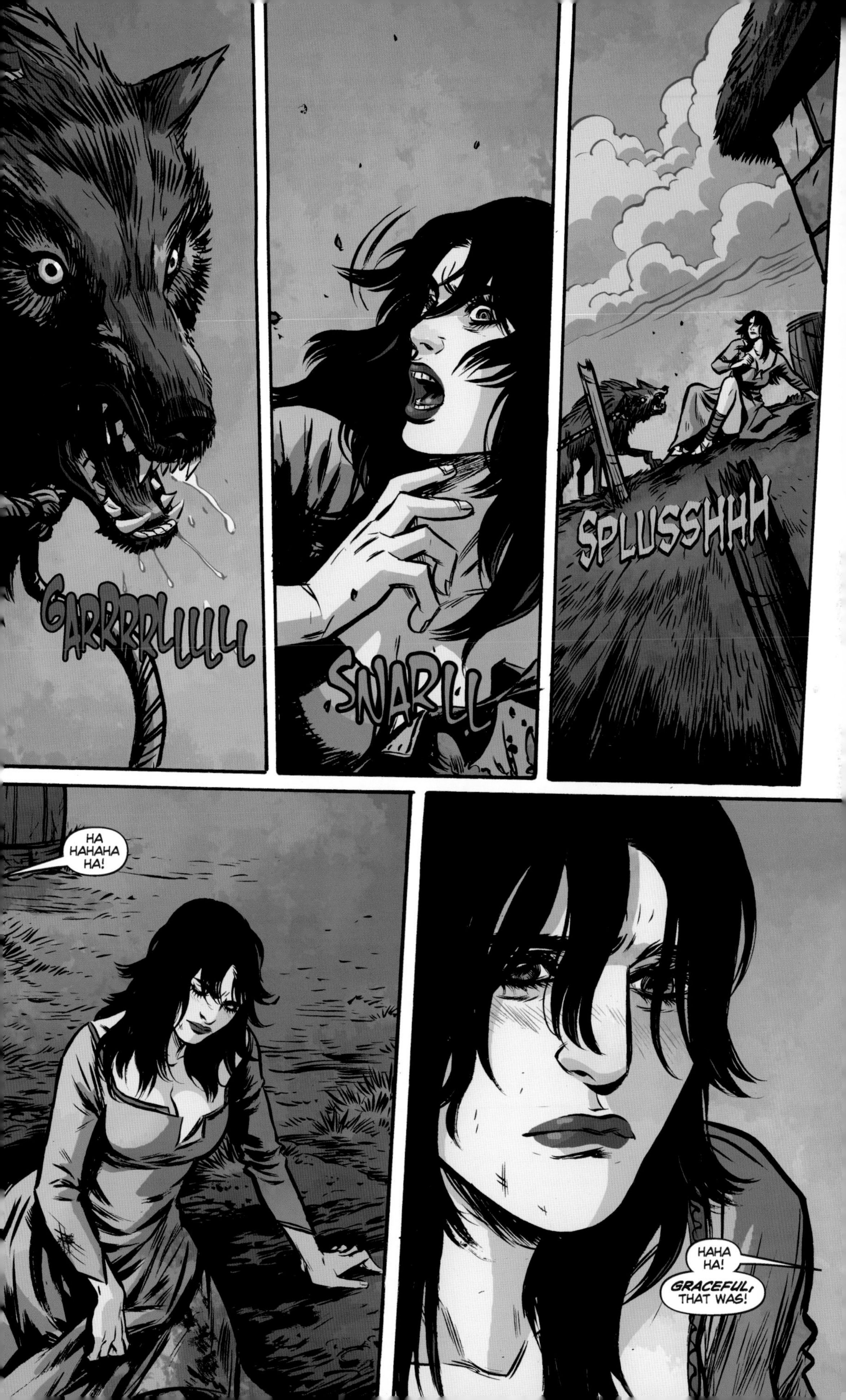
GARRRRLLLLL
SNARLL
SPLUSSHHH
HA HAHAHA HA!
HAHA HA!
GRACEFUL, THAT WAS!

DID THE BIG, BAD PUPPY DOG SCARE YOU?

HAHA!

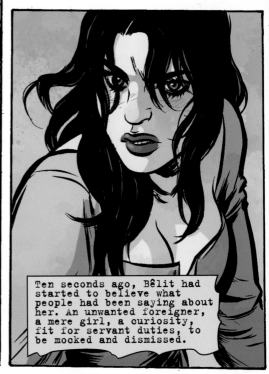

Ten seconds ago, Bêlit had started to believe what people had been saying about her. An unwanted foreigner, a mere girl, a curiosity, fit for servant duties, to be mocked and dismissed.

She was preoccupied with what the elder said to her lover Conan, and feared he would leave her behind.

That was ten seconds ago. Now, she wasn't dirty from the Cimmerian mud, not wearing heavy, ugly clothing, the mocking laughter no longer burning in her ears.

She was back on the *Tigress*, closing on the enemy, her blood up, her crew whooping, weapons drawn...

...the smell of freshly spilled blood already filling her nostrils.

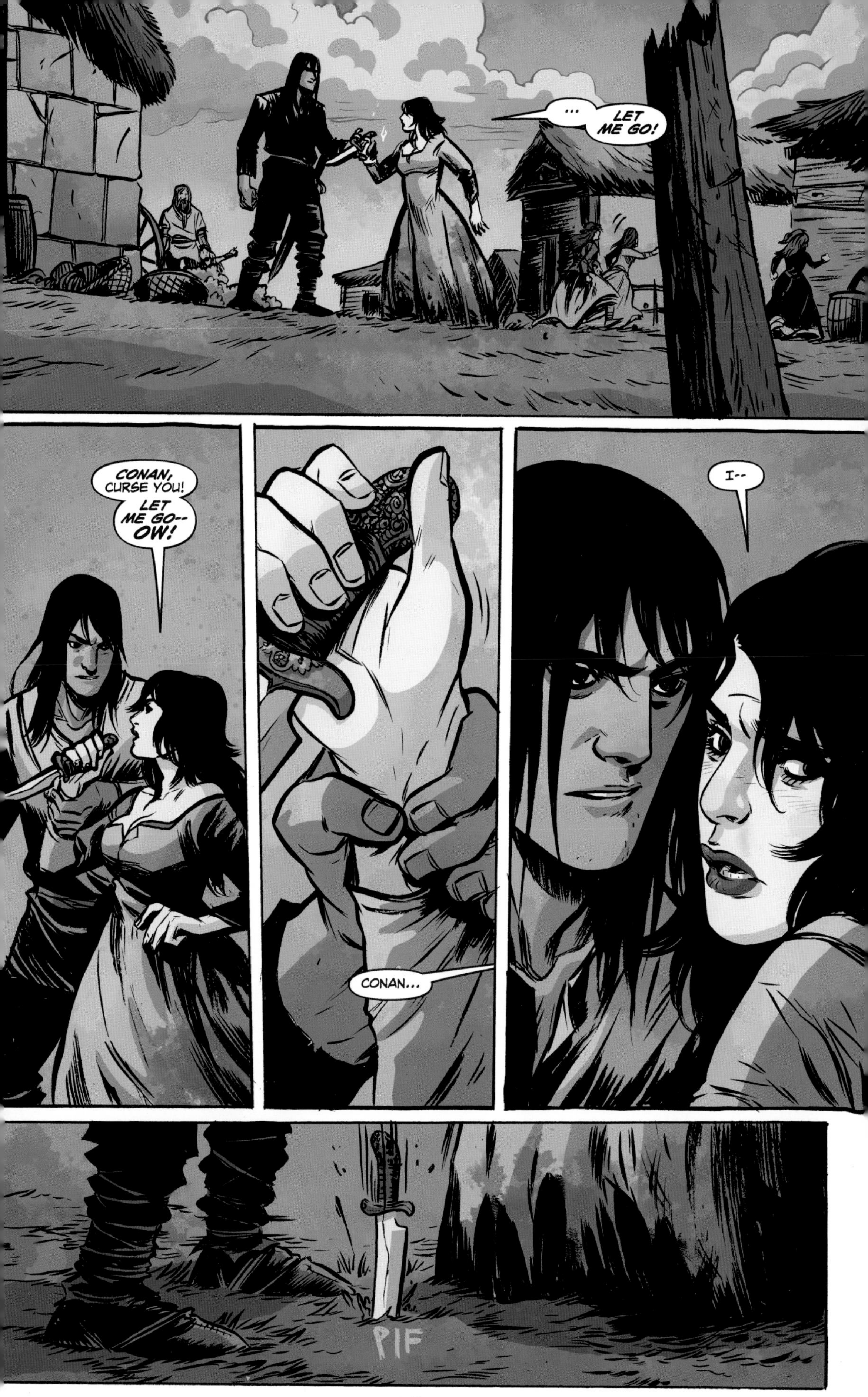
... LET ME GO!
CONAN, CURSE YOU! LET ME GO-- OW!
CONAN...
I--
PIF

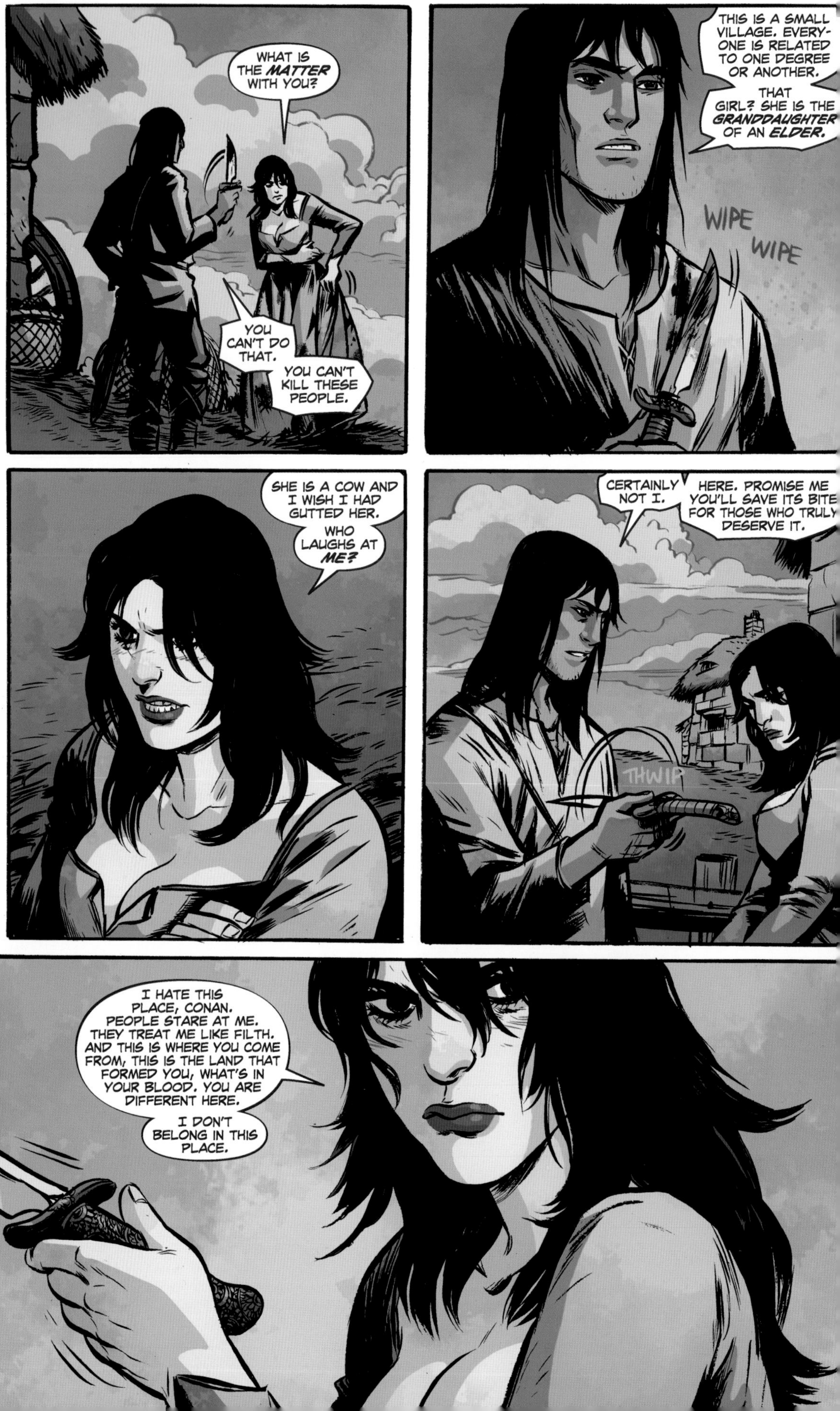
WHAT IS THE MATTER WITH YOU?
YOU CAN'T DO THAT.
YOU CAN'T KILL THESE PEOPLE.
THIS IS A SMALL VILLAGE. EVERYONE IS RELATED TO ONE DEGREE OR ANOTHER.
THAT GIRL? SHE IS THE GRANDDAUGHTER OF AN ELDER.
WIPE WIPE
SHE IS A COW AND I WISH I HAD GUTTED HER.
WHO LAUGHS AT ME?
CERTAINLY NOT I.
HERE. PROMISE ME YOU'LL SAVE ITS BITE FOR THOSE WHO TRULY DESERVE IT.
THWIP
I HATE THIS PLACE, CONAN. PEOPLE STARE AT ME. THEY TREAT ME LIKE FILTH. AND THIS IS WHERE YOU COME FROM, THIS IS THE LAND THAT FORMED YOU, WHAT'S IN YOUR BLOOD. YOU ARE DIFFERENT HERE.
I DON'T BELONG IN THIS PLACE.

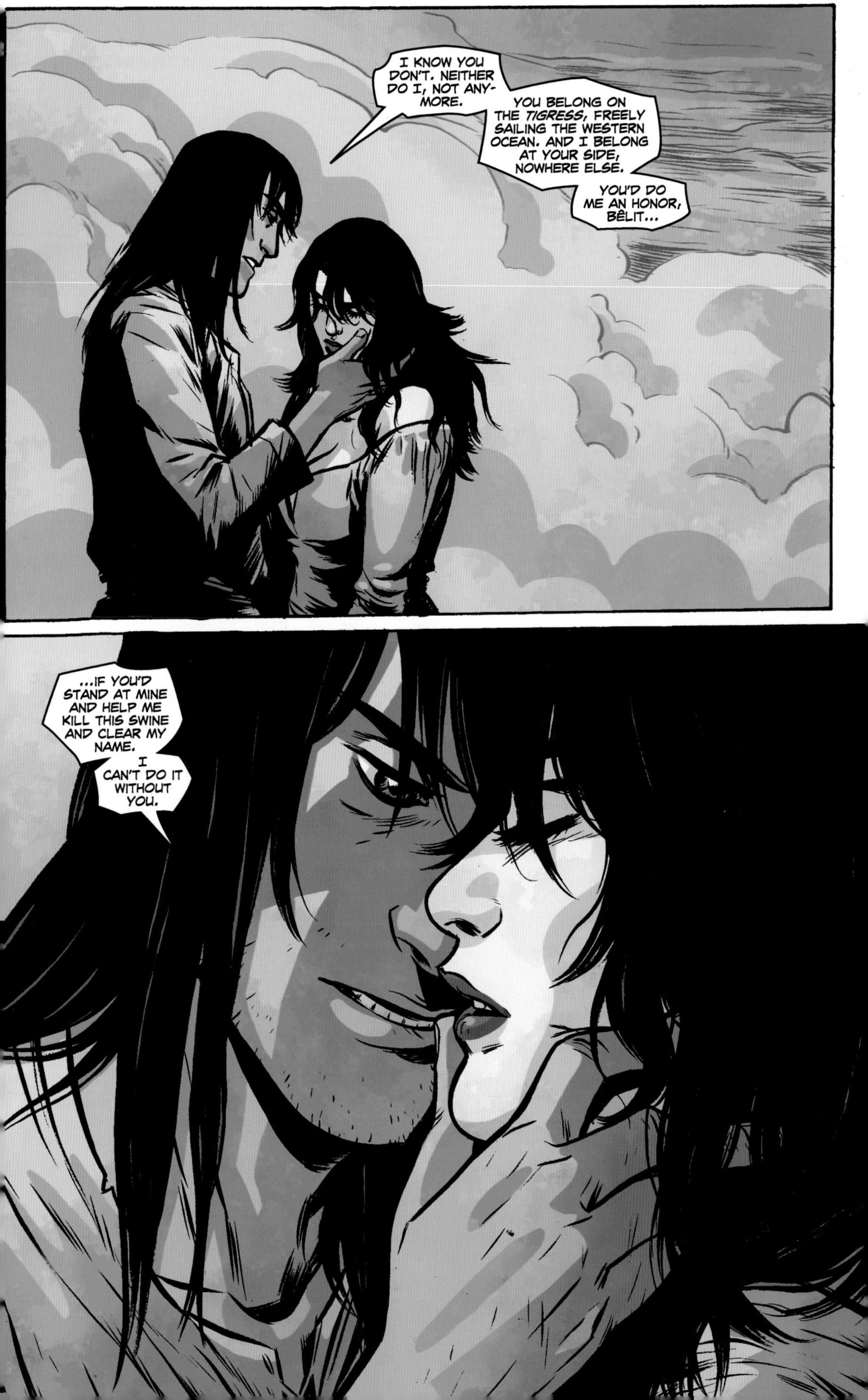
I KNOW YOU DON'T. NEITHER DO I, NOT ANY-MORE.
YOU BELONG ON THE *TIGRESS*, FREELY SAILING THE WESTERN OCEAN. AND I BELONG AT YOUR SIDE, NOWHERE ELSE.
YOU'D DO ME AN HONOR, BÊLIT...
...IF YOU'D STAND AT MINE AND HELP ME KILL THIS SWINE AND CLEAR MY NAME.
I CAN'T DO IT WITHOUT YOU.

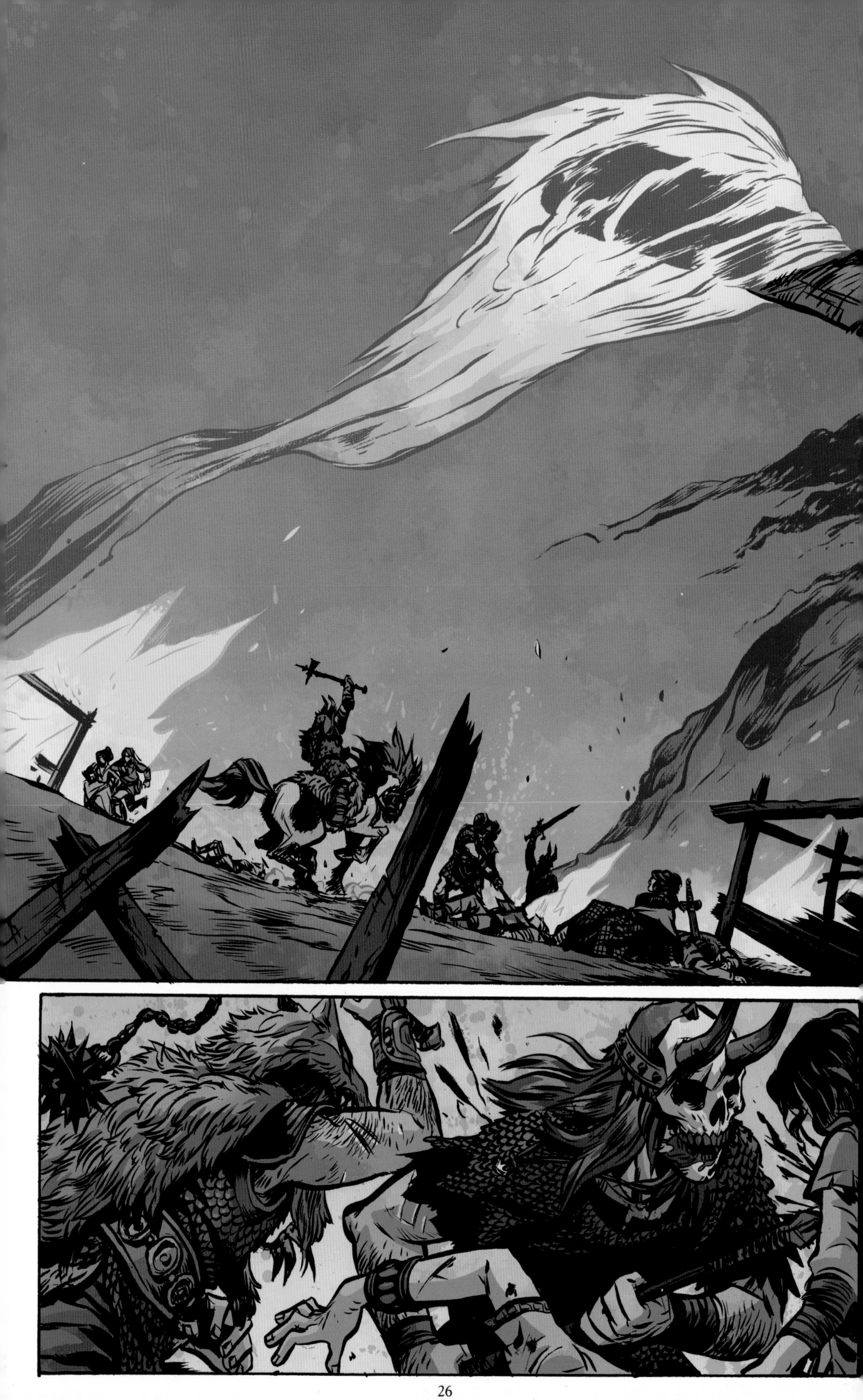

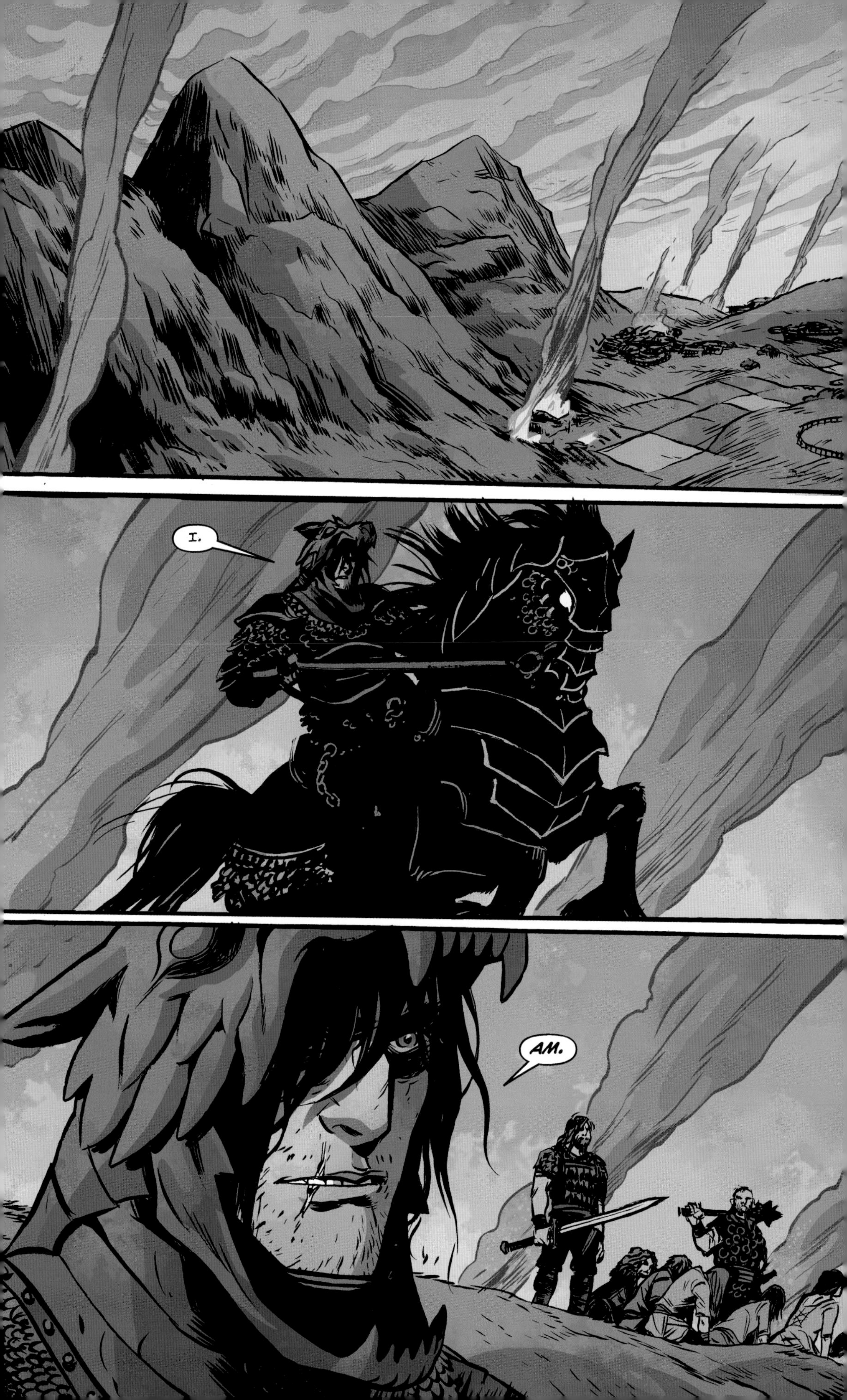
I.
AM.

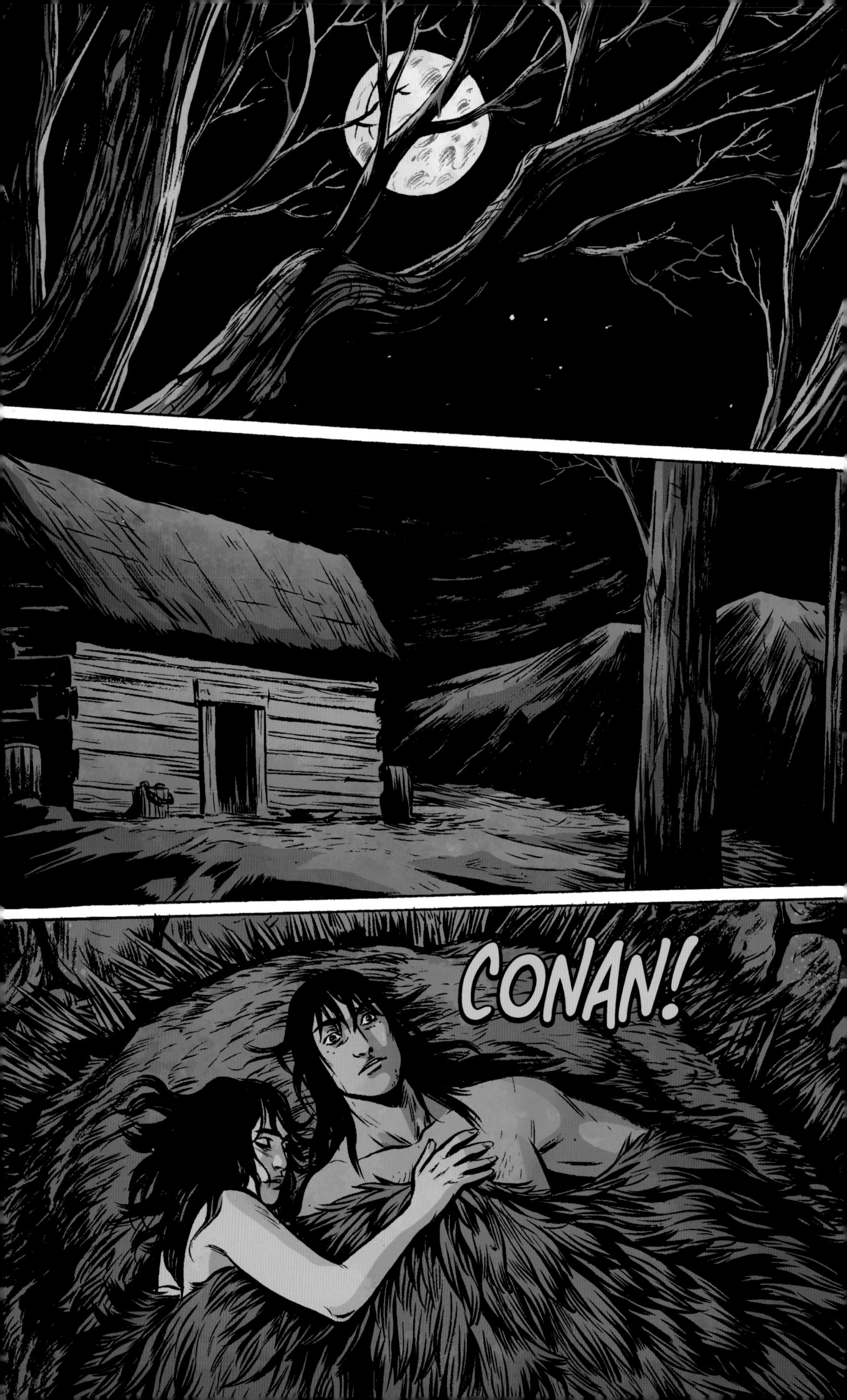
CONAN!

CHAPTER TWO

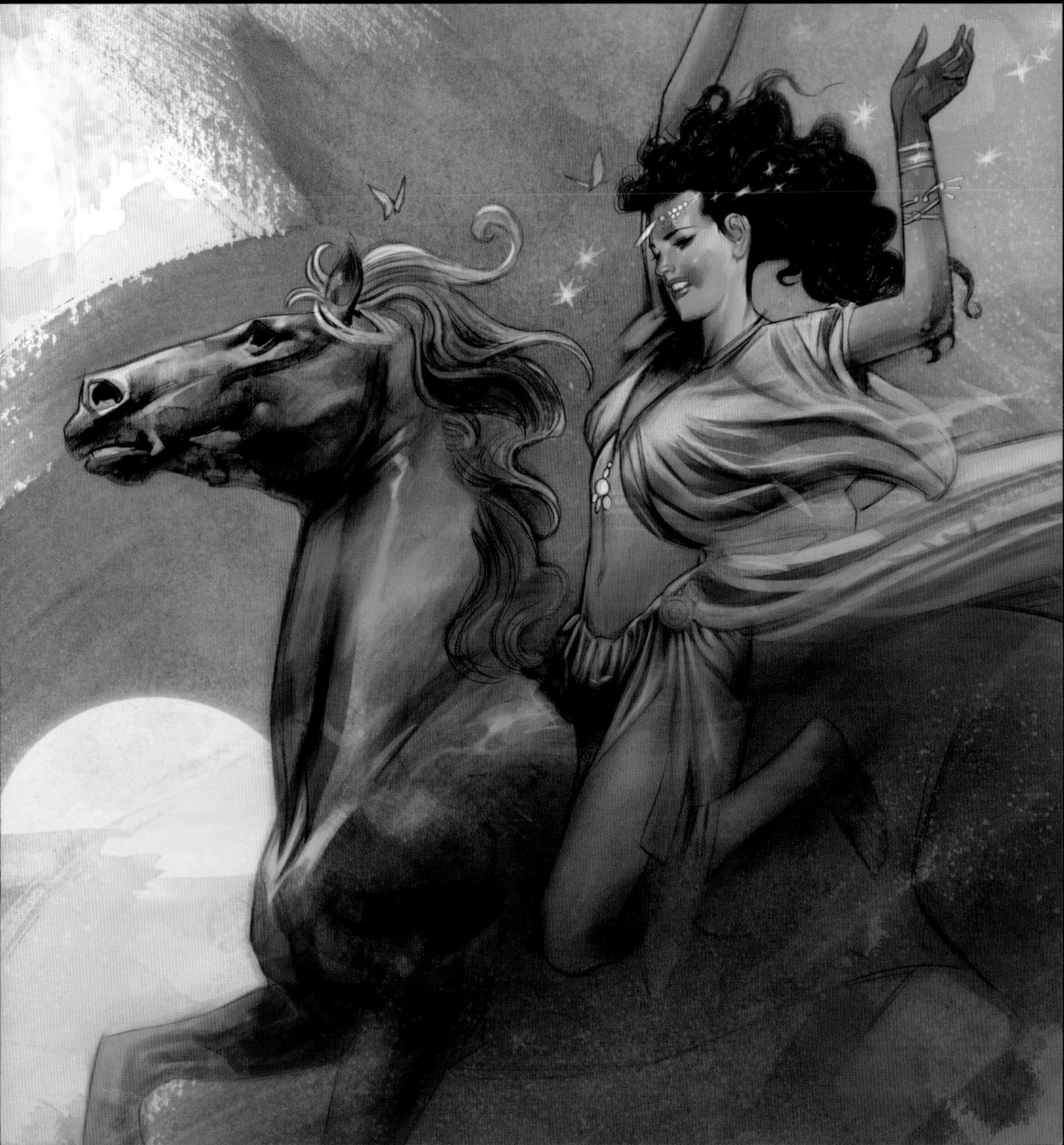

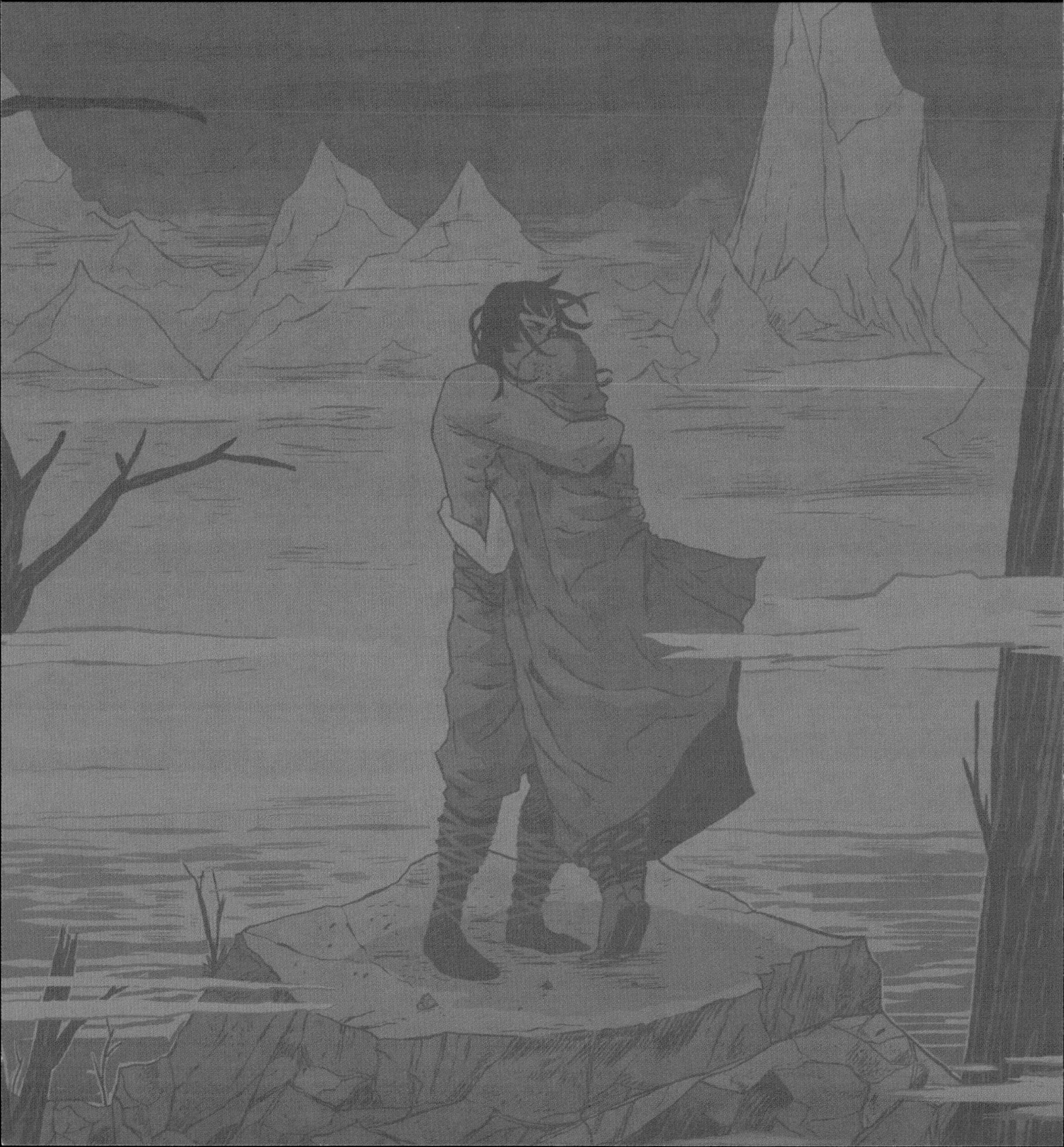

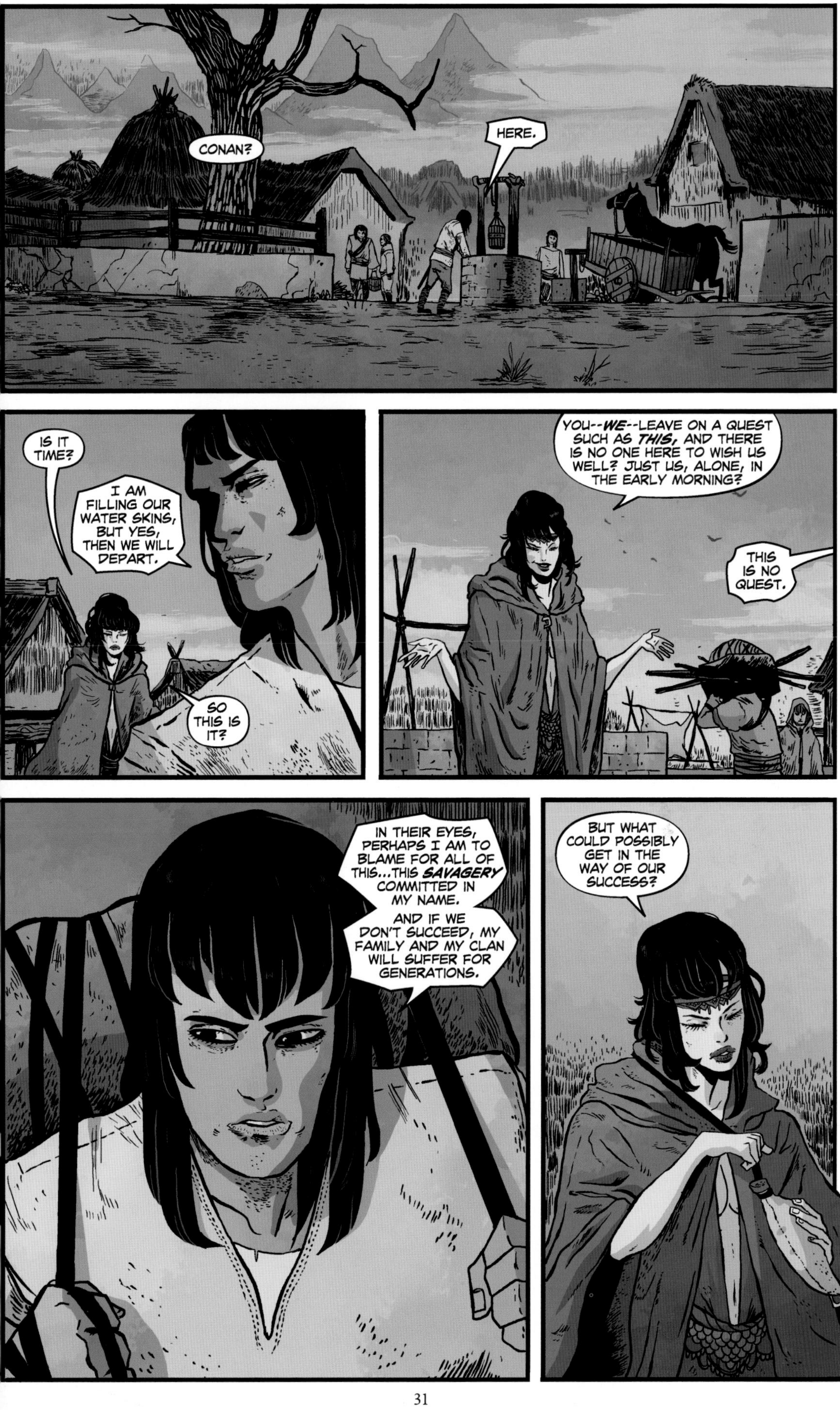

CONAN?
HERE.
IS IT TIME?
I AM FILLING OUR WATER SKINS, BUT YES, THEN WE WILL DEPART.
SO THIS IS IT?
YOU--*WE*--LEAVE ON A QUEST SUCH AS *THIS,* AND THERE IS NO ONE HERE TO WISH US WELL? JUST US, ALONE, IN THE EARLY MORNING?
THIS IS NO QUEST.
IN THEIR EYES, PERHAPS I AM TO BLAME FOR ALL OF THIS...THIS *SAVAGERY* COMMITTED IN MY NAME.
AND IF WE DON'T SUCCEED, MY FAMILY AND MY CLAN WILL SUFFER FOR GENERATIONS.
BUT WHAT COULD POSSIBLY GET IN THE WAY OF OUR SUCCESS?

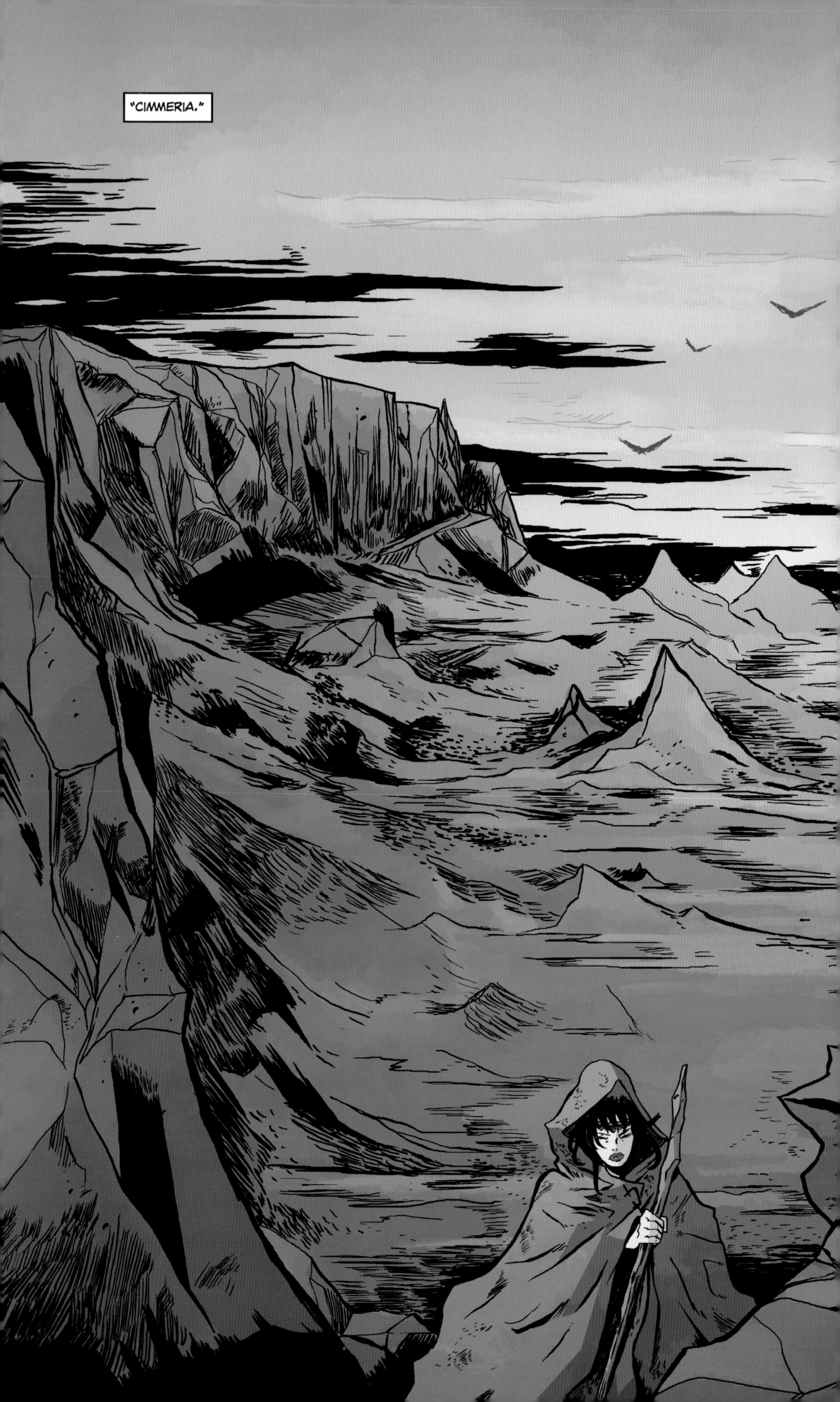
"CIMMERIA."

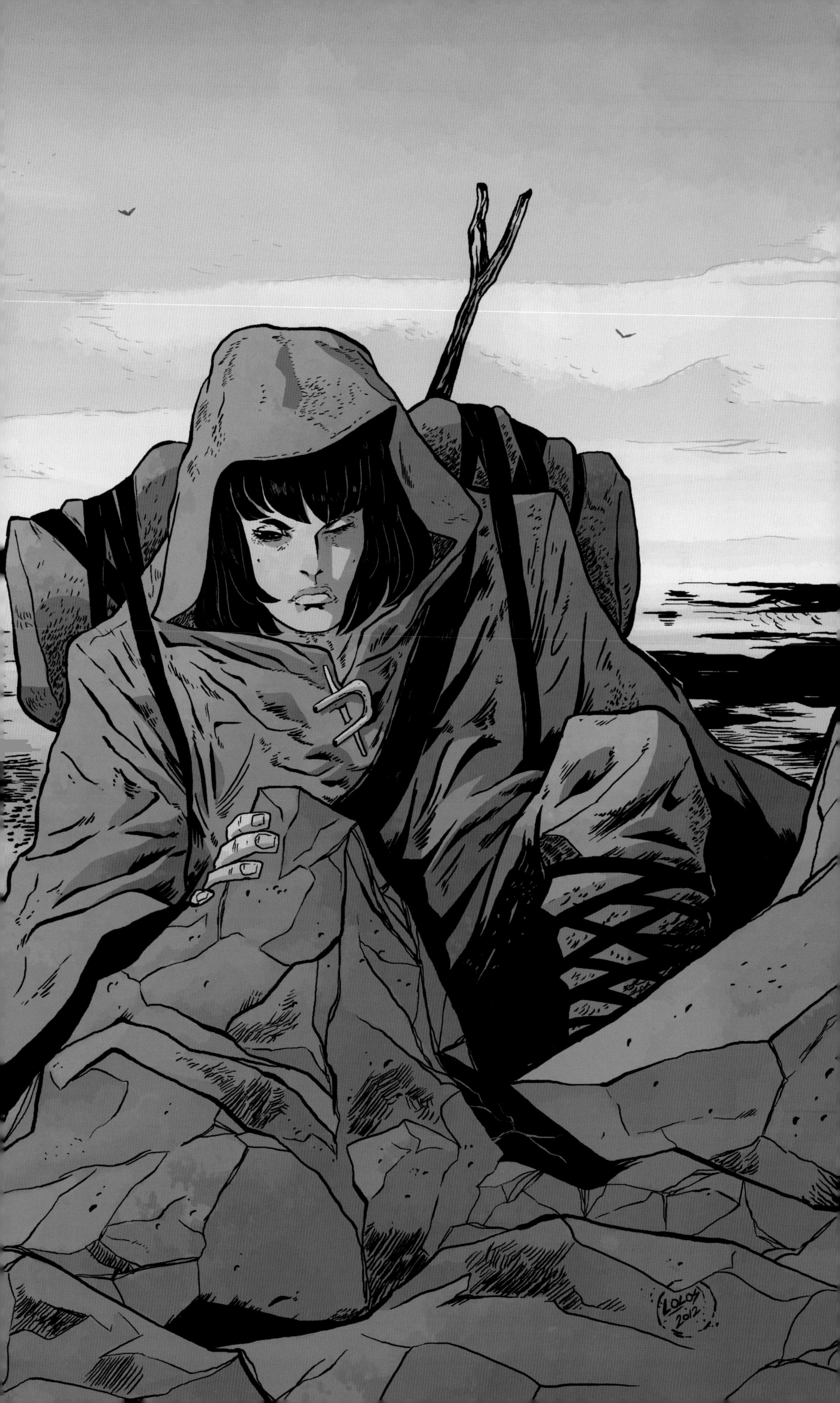

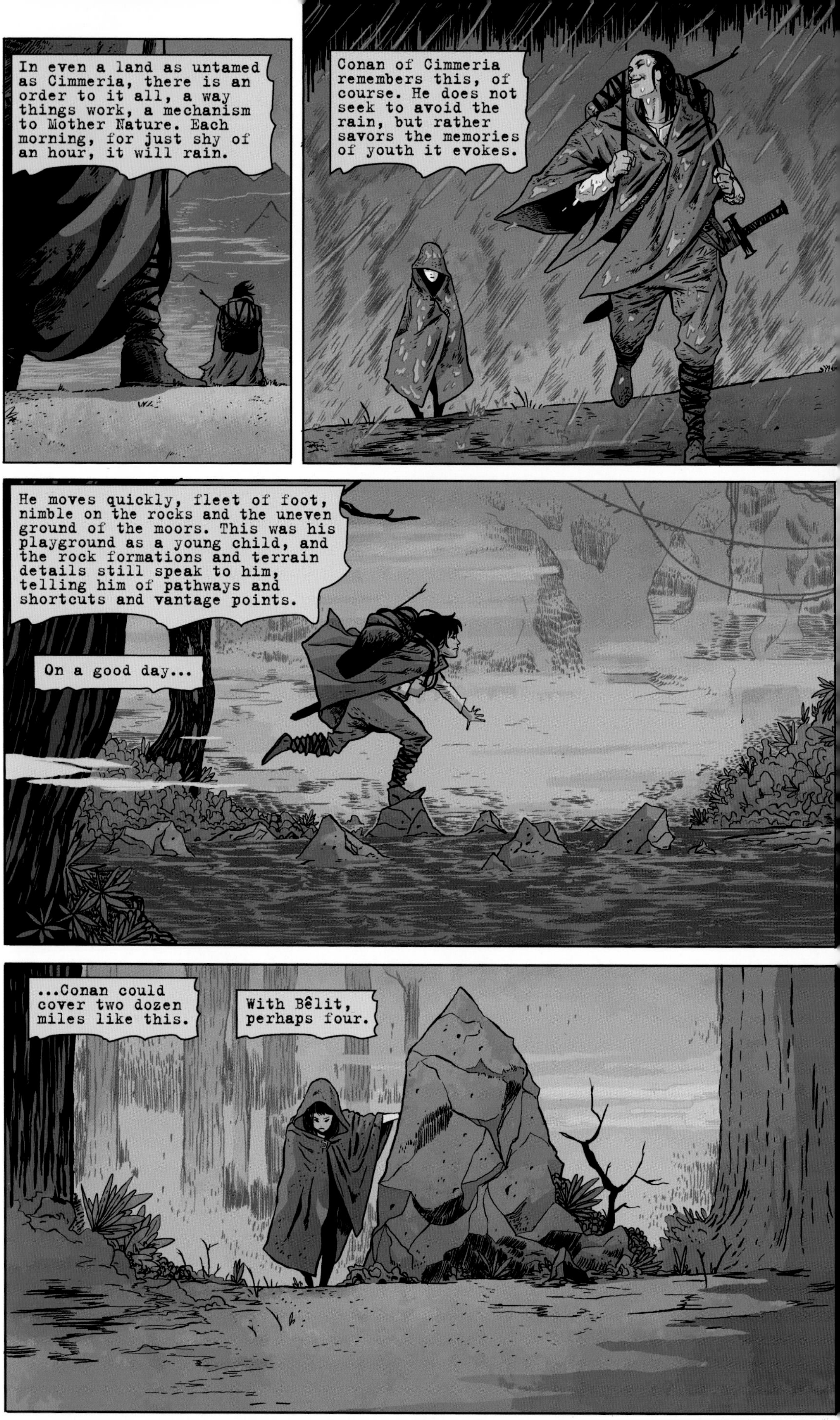
In even a land as untamed as Cimmeria, there is an order to it all, a way things work, a mechanism to Mother Nature. Each morning, for just shy of an hour, it will rain.
Conan of Cimmeria remembers this, of course. He does not seek to avoid the rain, but rather savors the memories of youth it evokes.
He moves quickly, fleet of foot, nimble on the rocks and the uneven ground of the moors. This was his playground as a young child, and the rock formations and terrain details still speak to him, telling him of pathways and shortcuts and vantage points.
On a good day...
...Conan could cover two dozen miles like this.
With Bêlit, perhaps four.

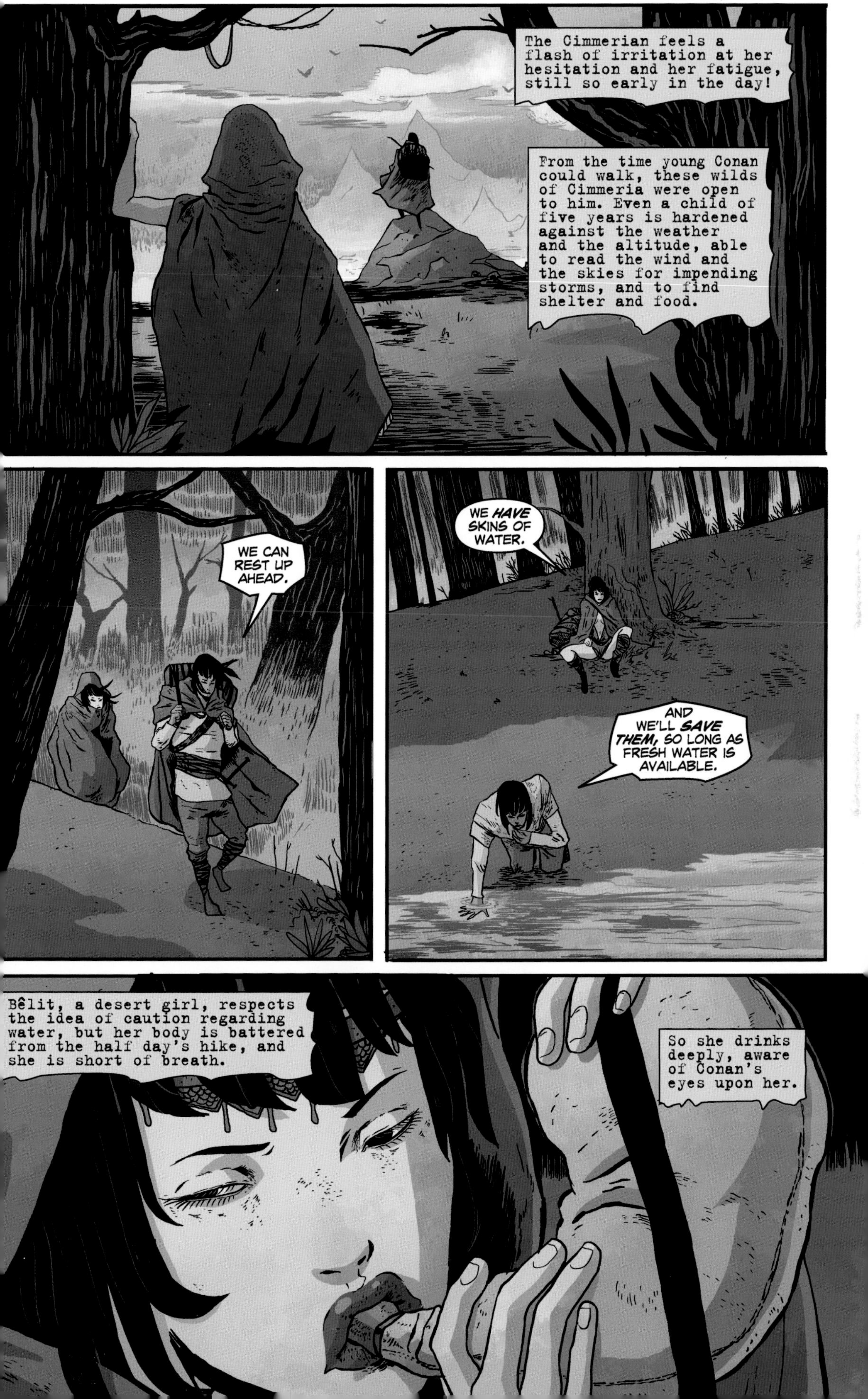

The Cimmerian feels a flash of irritation at her hesitation and her fatigue, still so early in the day!
From the time young Conan could walk, these wilds of Cimmeria were open to him. Even a child of five years is hardened against the weather and the altitude, able to read the wind and the skies for impending storms, and to find shelter and food.
WE CAN REST UP AHEAD.
WE *HAVE* SKINS OF WATER.
AND WE'LL *SAVE THEM,* SO LONG AS FRESH WATER IS AVAILABLE.
Bêlit, a desert girl, respects the idea of caution regarding water, but her body is battered from the half day's hike, and she is short of breath.
So she drinks deeply, aware of Conan's eyes upon her.

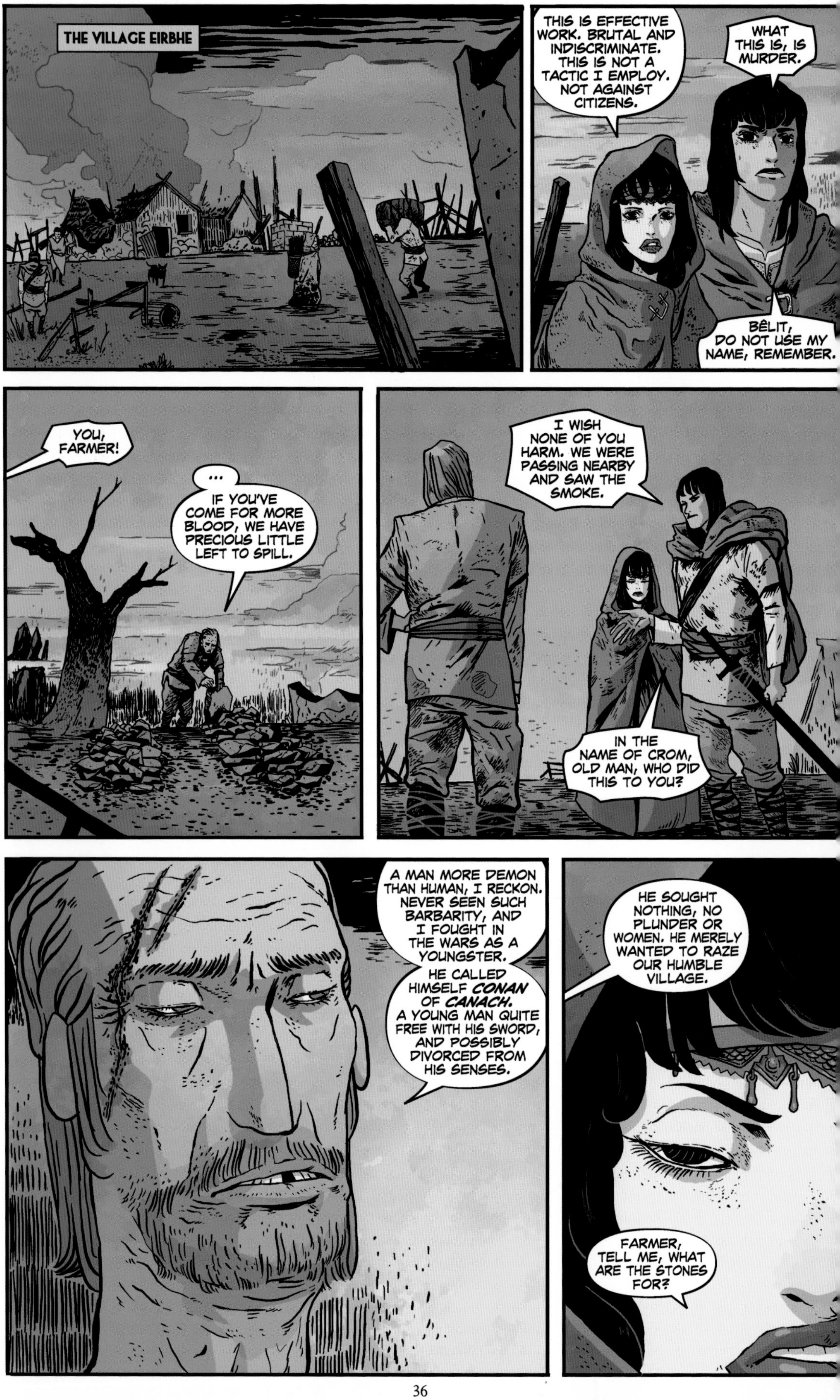
THE VILLAGE EIRBHE
THIS IS EFFECTIVE WORK. BRUTAL AND INDISCRIMINATE. THIS IS NOT A TACTIC I EMPLOY. NOT AGAINST CITIZENS.
WHAT THIS IS, IS MURDER.
BÊLIT, DO NOT USE MY NAME, REMEMBER.
YOU, FARMER!
...
IF YOU'VE COME FOR MORE BLOOD, WE HAVE PRECIOUS LITTLE LEFT TO SPILL.
I WISH NONE OF YOU HARM. WE WERE PASSING NEARBY AND SAW THE SMOKE.
IN THE NAME OF CROM, OLD MAN, WHO DID THIS TO YOU?
A MAN MORE DEMON THAN HUMAN, I RECKON. NEVER SEEN SUCH BARBARITY, AND I FOUGHT IN THE WARS AS A YOUNGSTER.
HE CALLED HIMSELF *CONAN* OF *CANACH.* A YOUNG MAN QUITE FREE WITH HIS SWORD, AND POSSIBLY DIVORCED FROM HIS SENSES.
HE SOUGHT NOTHING, NO PLUNDER OR WOMEN. HE MERELY WANTED TO RAZE OUR HUMBLE VILLAGE.
FARMER, TELL ME, WHAT ARE THE STONES FOR?

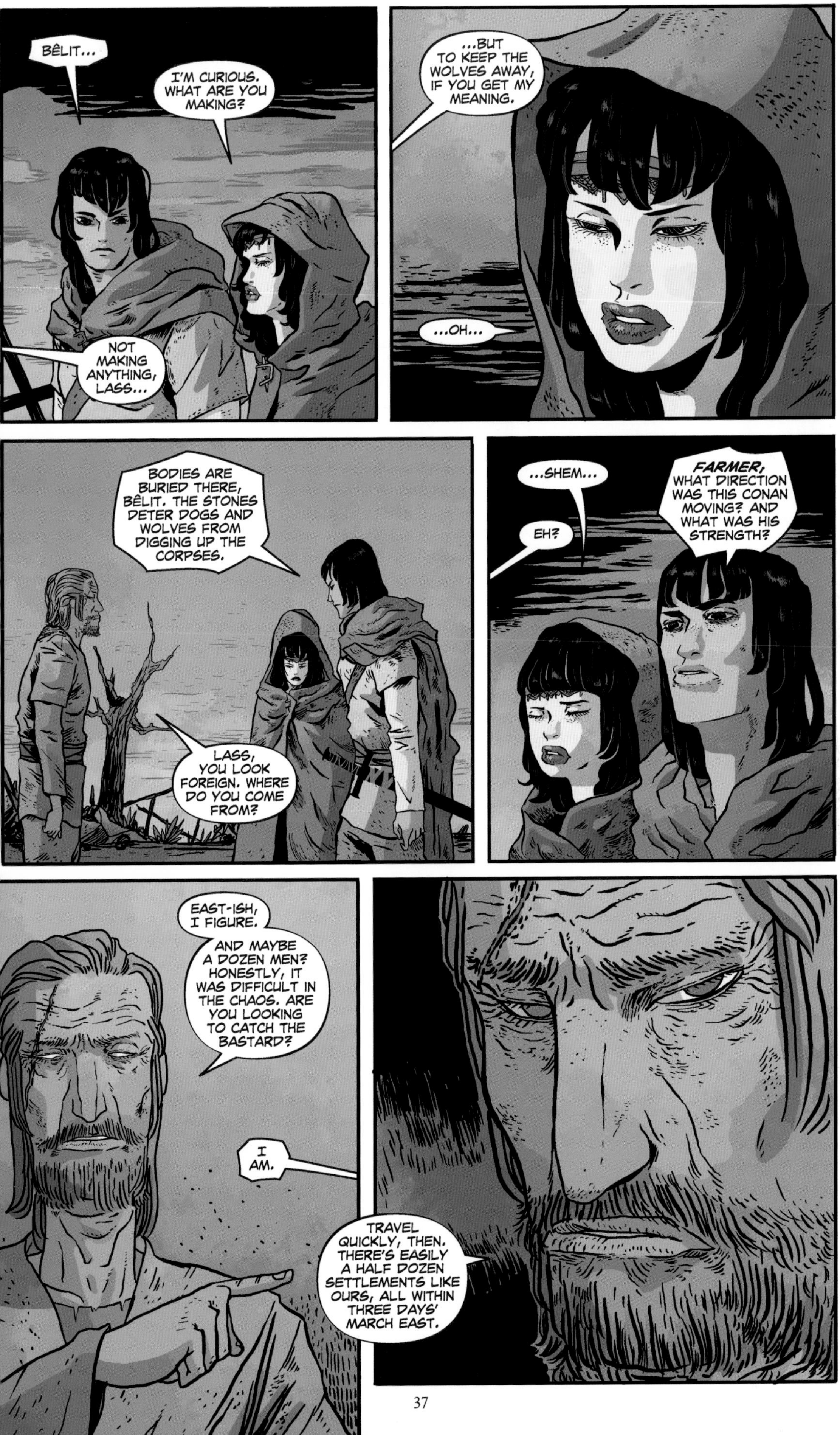
BÊLIT...
I'M CURIOUS. WHAT ARE YOU MAKING?
NOT MAKING ANYTHING, LASS...
...BUT TO KEEP THE WOLVES AWAY, IF YOU GET MY MEANING.
...OH...
BODIES ARE BURIED THERE, BÊLIT. THE STONES DETER DOGS AND WOLVES FROM DIGGING UP THE CORPSES.
LASS, YOU LOOK FOREIGN. WHERE DO YOU COME FROM?
...SHEM...
EH?
FARMER, WHAT DIRECTION WAS THIS CONAN MOVING? AND WHAT WAS HIS STRENGTH?
EAST-ISH, I FIGURE.
AND MAYBE A DOZEN MEN? HONESTLY, IT WAS DIFFICULT IN THE CHAOS. ARE YOU LOOKING TO CATCH THE BASTARD?
I AM.
TRAVEL QUICKLY, THEN. THERE'S EASILY A HALF DOZEN SETTLEMENTS LIKE OURS, ALL WITHIN THREE DAYS' MARCH EAST.

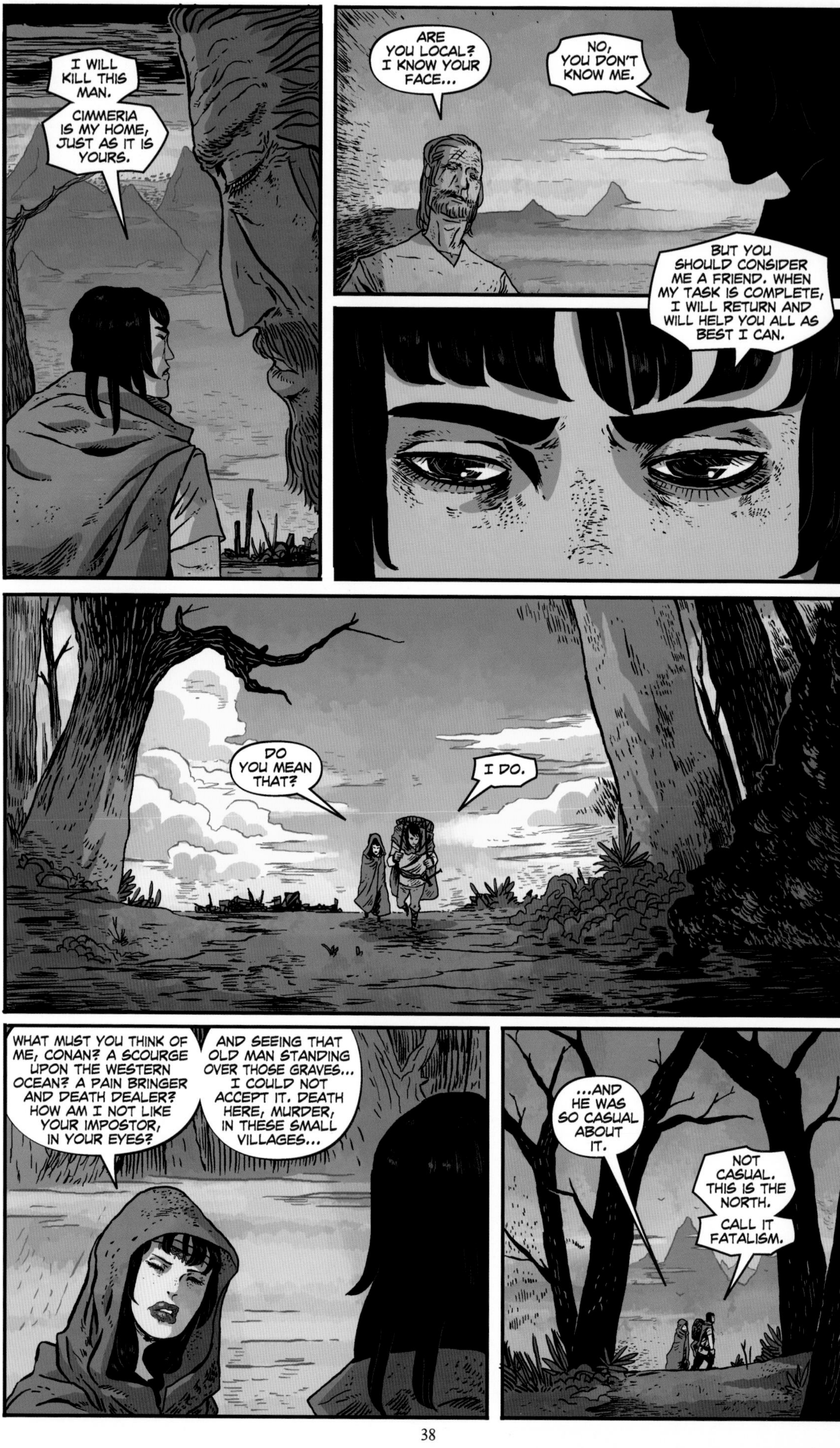
I WILL KILL THIS MAN.
CIMMERIA IS MY HOME, JUST AS IT IS YOURS.
ARE YOU LOCAL? I KNOW YOUR FACE...
NO, YOU DON'T KNOW ME.
BUT YOU SHOULD CONSIDER ME A FRIEND. WHEN MY TASK IS COMPLETE, I WILL RETURN AND WILL HELP YOU ALL AS BEST I CAN.
DO YOU MEAN THAT?
I DO.
WHAT MUST YOU THINK OF ME, CONAN? A SCOURGE UPON THE WESTERN OCEAN? A PAIN BRINGER AND DEATH DEALER? HOW AM I NOT LIKE YOUR IMPOSTOR, IN YOUR EYES?
AND SEEING THAT OLD MAN STANDING OVER THOSE GRAVES... I COULD NOT ACCEPT IT. DEATH HERE, MURDER, IN THESE SMALL VILLAGES...
...AND HE WAS SO CASUAL ABOUT IT.
NOT CASUAL. THIS IS THE NORTH.
CALL IT FATALISM.

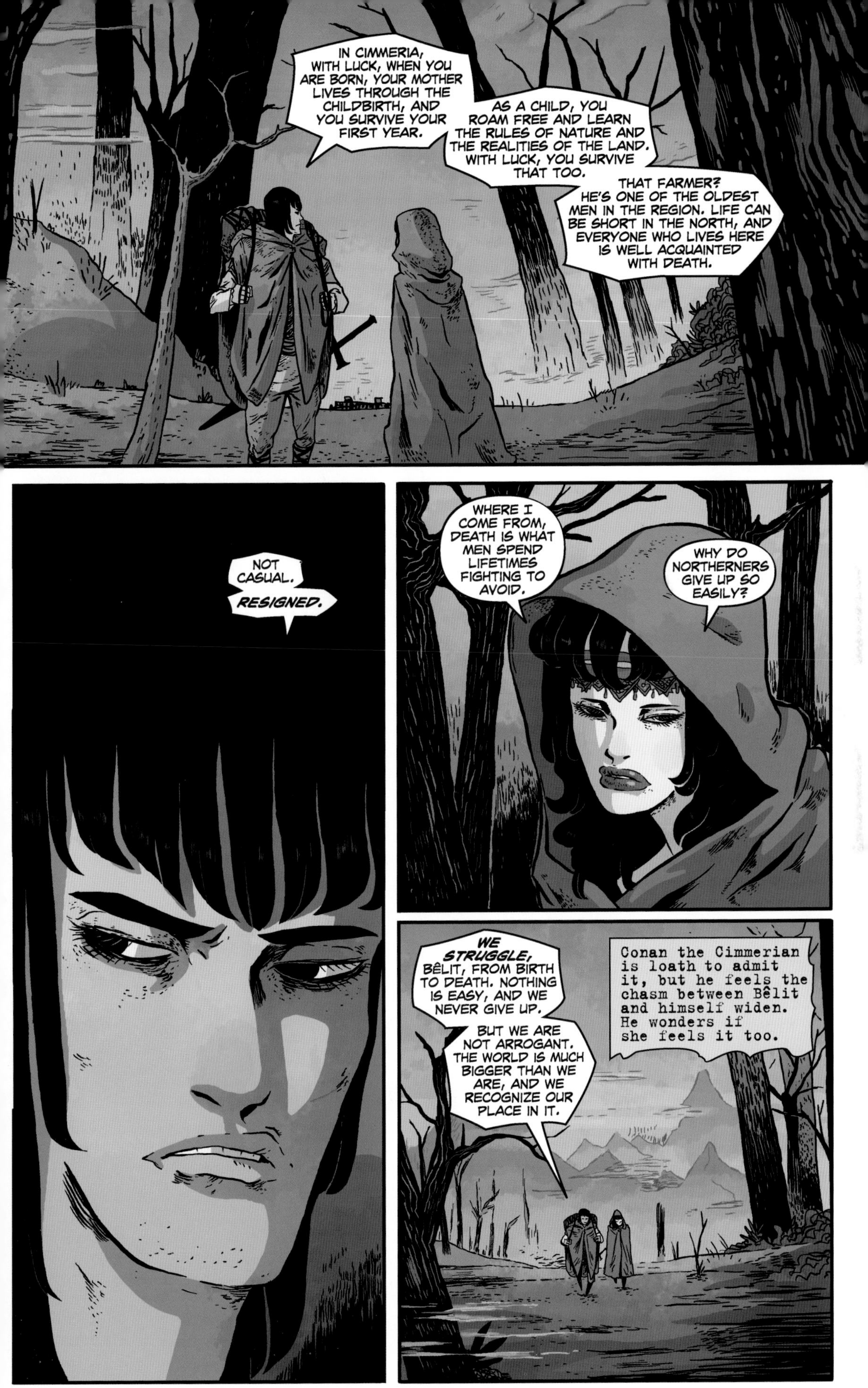

IN CIMMERIA, WITH LUCK, WHEN YOU ARE BORN, YOUR MOTHER LIVES THROUGH THE CHILDBIRTH, AND YOU SURVIVE YOUR FIRST YEAR.
AS A CHILD, YOU ROAM FREE AND LEARN THE RULES OF NATURE AND THE REALITIES OF THE LAND. WITH LUCK, YOU SURVIVE THAT TOO.
THAT FARMER? HE'S ONE OF THE OLDEST MEN IN THE REGION. LIFE CAN BE SHORT IN THE NORTH, AND EVERYONE WHO LIVES HERE IS WELL ACQUAINTED WITH DEATH.
NOT CASUAL. RESIGNED.
WHERE I COME FROM, DEATH IS WHAT MEN SPEND LIFETIMES FIGHTING TO AVOID.
WHY DO NORTHERNERS GIVE UP SO EASILY?
WE STRUGGLE, BÊLIT, FROM BIRTH TO DEATH. NOTHING IS EASY, AND WE NEVER GIVE UP.
BUT WE ARE NOT ARROGANT. THE WORLD IS MUCH BIGGER THAN WE ARE, AND WE RECOGNIZE OUR PLACE IN IT.
Conan the Cimmerian is loath to admit it, but he feels the chasm between Bêlit and himself widen. He wonders if she feels it too.

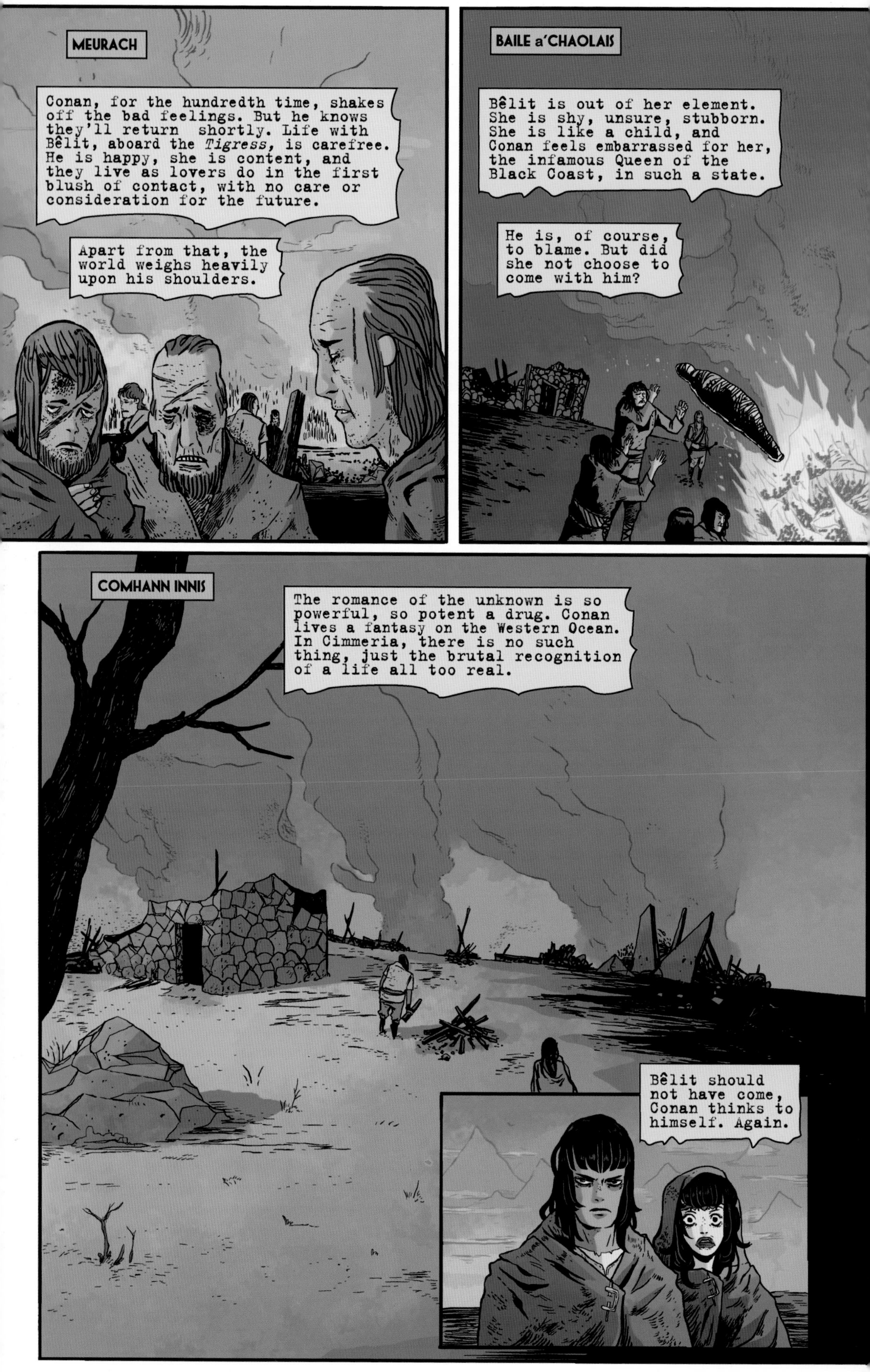
MEURACH
Conan, for the hundredth time, shakes off the bad feelings. But he knows they'll return shortly. Life with Bêlit, aboard the *Tigress,* is carefree. He is happy, she is content, and they live as lovers do in the first blush of contact, with no care or consideration for the future.
Apart from that, the world weighs heavily upon his shoulders.
BAILE a'CHAOLAIS
Bêlit is out of her element. She is shy, unsure, stubborn. She is like a child, and Conan feels embarrassed for her, the infamous Queen of the Black Coast, in such a state.
He is, of course, to blame. But did she not choose to come with him?
COMHANN INNIS
The romance of the unknown is so powerful, so potent a drug. Conan lives a fantasy on the Western Ocean. In Cimmeria, there is no such thing, just the brutal recognition of a life all too real.
Bêlit should not have come, Conan thinks to himself. Again.

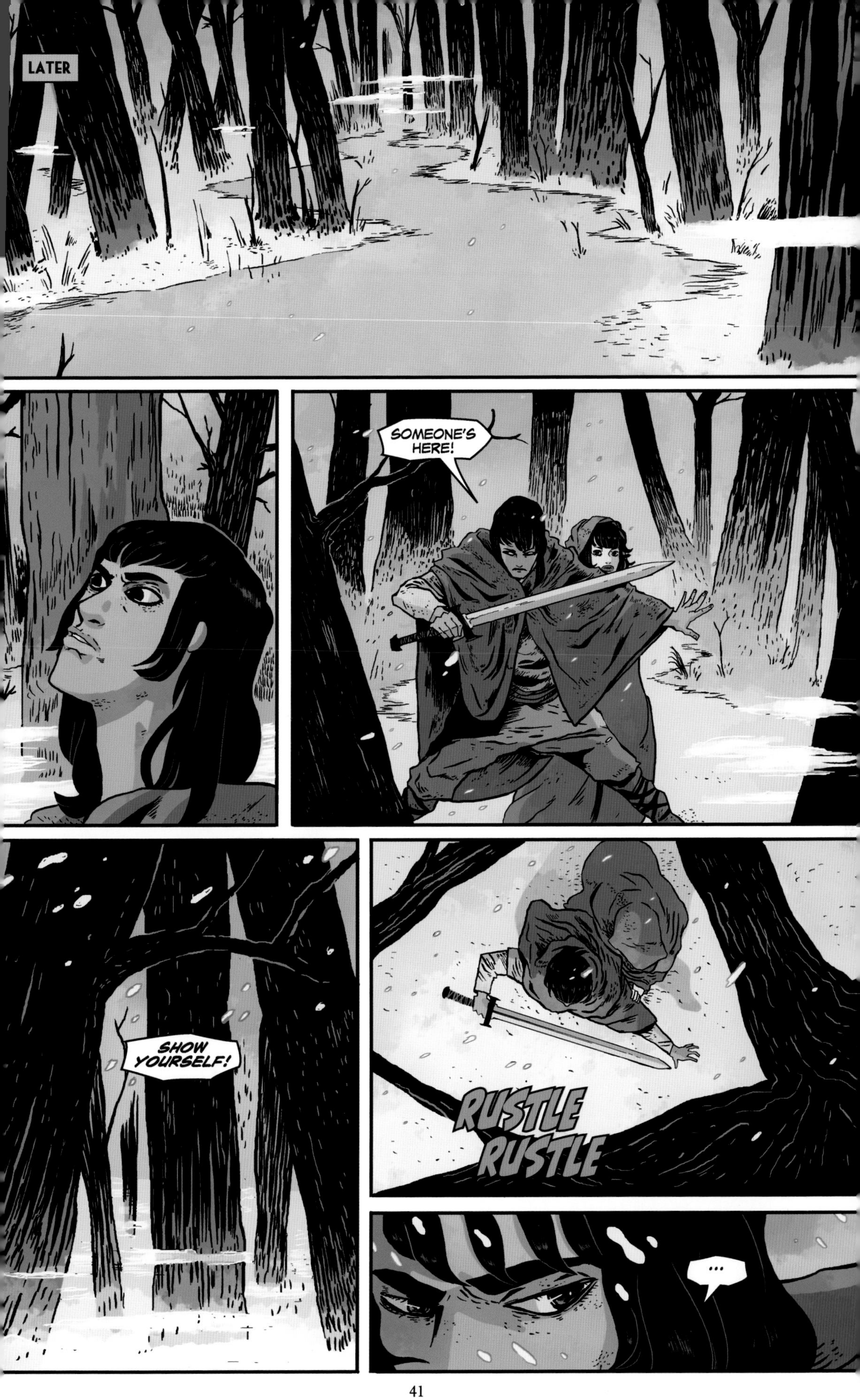
LATER
SOMEONE'S HERE!
SHOW YOURSELF!
RUSTLE RUSTLE
...

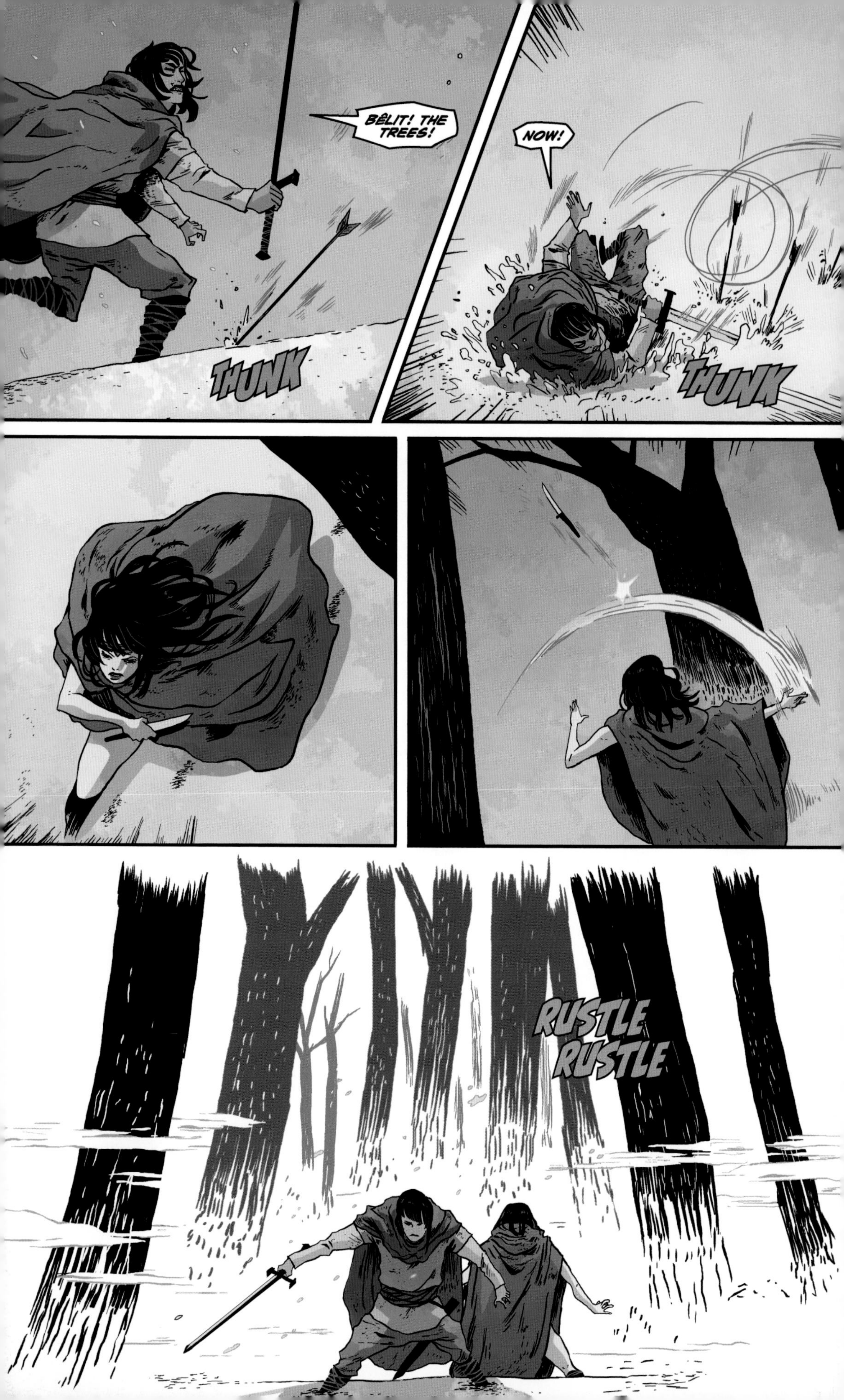
BÊLIT! THE TREES!
THUNK
NOW!
THUNK
RUSTLE RUSTLE

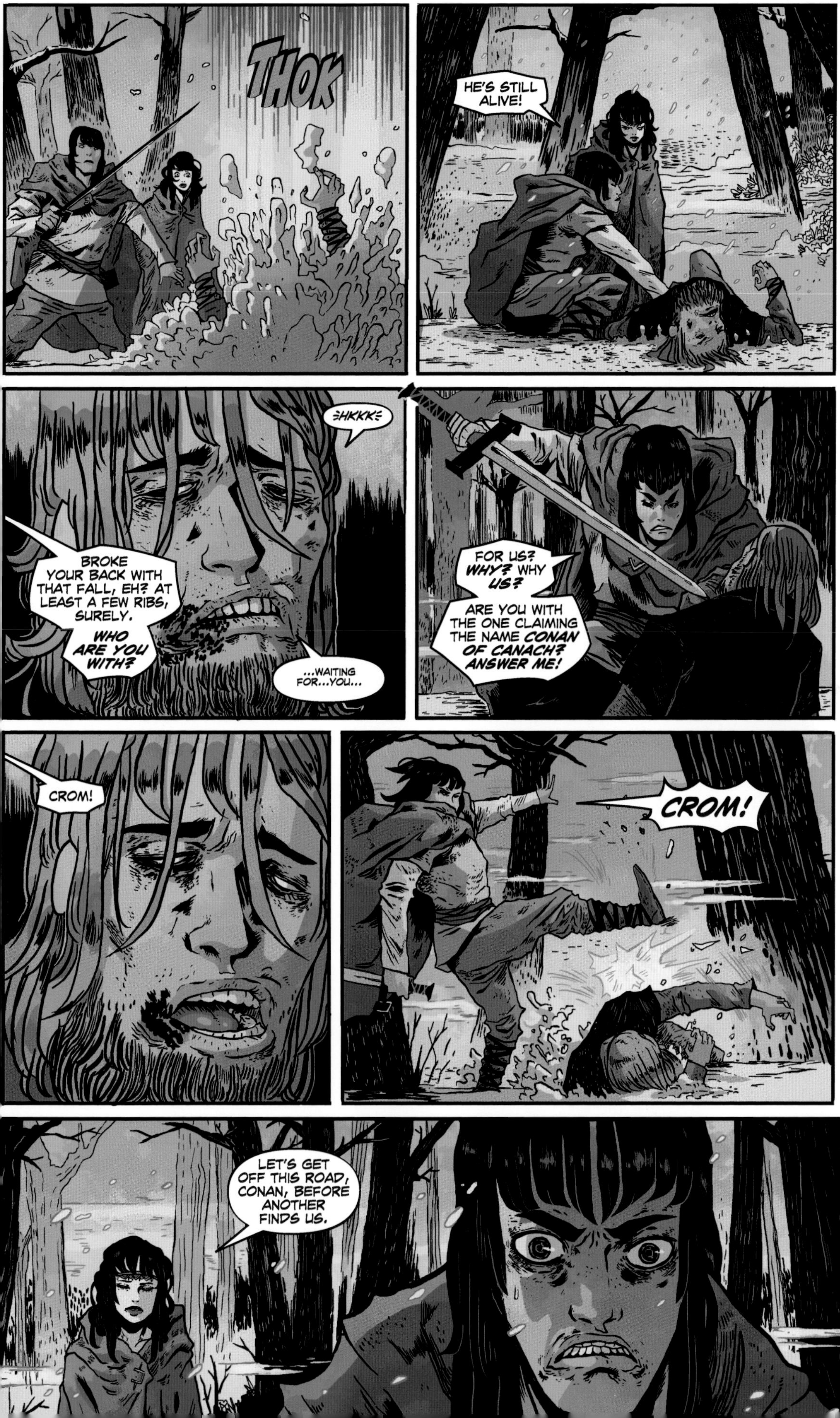
THOK
HE'S STILL ALIVE!
=HKKK=
BROKE YOUR BACK WITH THAT FALL, EH? AT LEAST A FEW RIBS, SURELY.
WHO ARE YOU WITH?
...WAITING FOR...YOU...
FOR US? WHY? WHY US?
ARE YOU WITH THE ONE CLAIMING THE NAME CONAN OF CANACH? ANSWER ME!
CROM!
CROM!
LET'S GET OFF THIS ROAD, CONAN, BEFORE ANOTHER FINDS US.

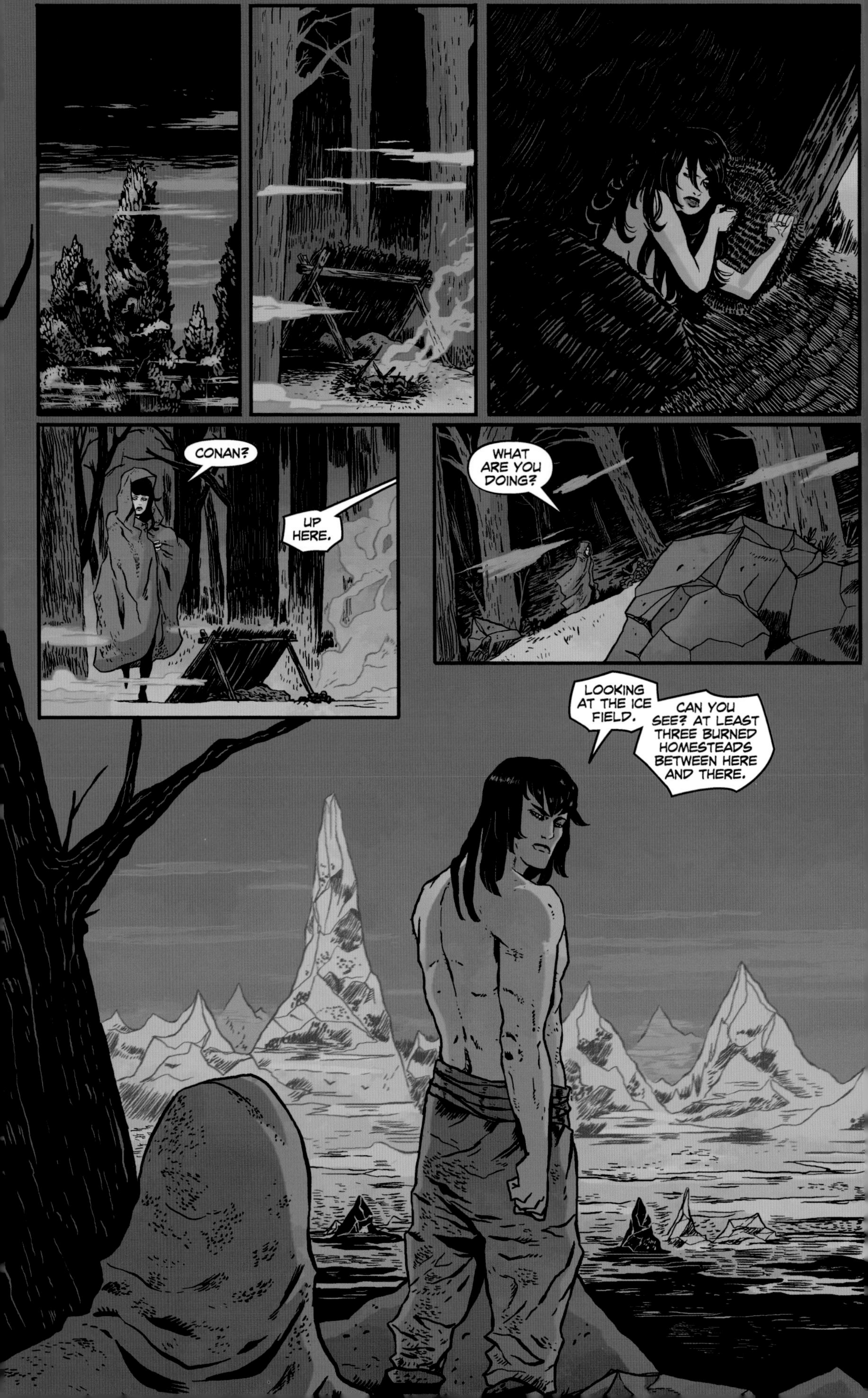
CONAN?
UP HERE.
WHAT ARE YOU DOING?
LOOKING AT THE ICE FIELD.
CAN YOU SEE? AT LEAST THREE BURNED HOMESTEADS BETWEEN HERE AND THERE.

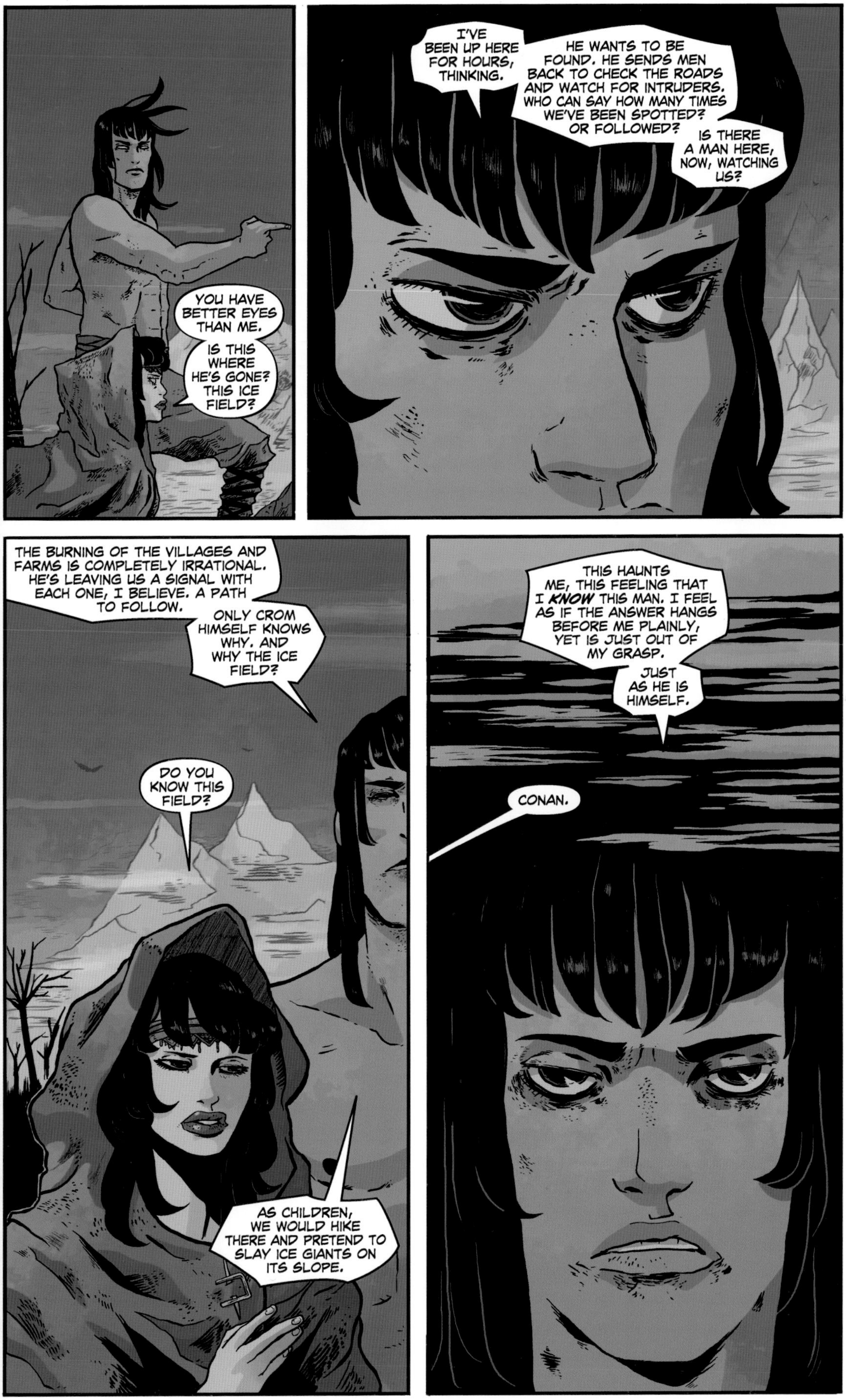
YOU HAVE BETTER EYES THAN ME.
IS THIS WHERE HE'S GONE? THIS ICE FIELD?
I'VE BEEN UP HERE FOR HOURS, THINKING.
HE WANTS TO BE FOUND. HE SENDS MEN BACK TO CHECK THE ROADS AND WATCH FOR INTRUDERS. WHO CAN SAY HOW MANY TIMES WE'VE BEEN SPOTTED? OR FOLLOWED?
IS THERE A MAN HERE, NOW, WATCHING US?
THE BURNING OF THE VILLAGES AND FARMS IS COMPLETELY IRRATIONAL. HE'S LEAVING US A SIGNAL WITH EACH ONE, I BELIEVE. A PATH TO FOLLOW.
ONLY CROM HIMSELF KNOWS WHY. AND WHY THE ICE FIELD?
DO YOU KNOW THIS FIELD?
AS CHILDREN, WE WOULD HIKE THERE AND PRETEND TO SLAY ICE GIANTS ON ITS SLOPE.
THIS HAUNTS ME, THIS FEELING THAT I *KNOW* THIS MAN. I FEEL AS IF THE ANSWER HANGS BEFORE ME PLAINLY, YET IS JUST OUT OF MY GRASP.
JUST AS HE IS HIMSELF.
CONAN.

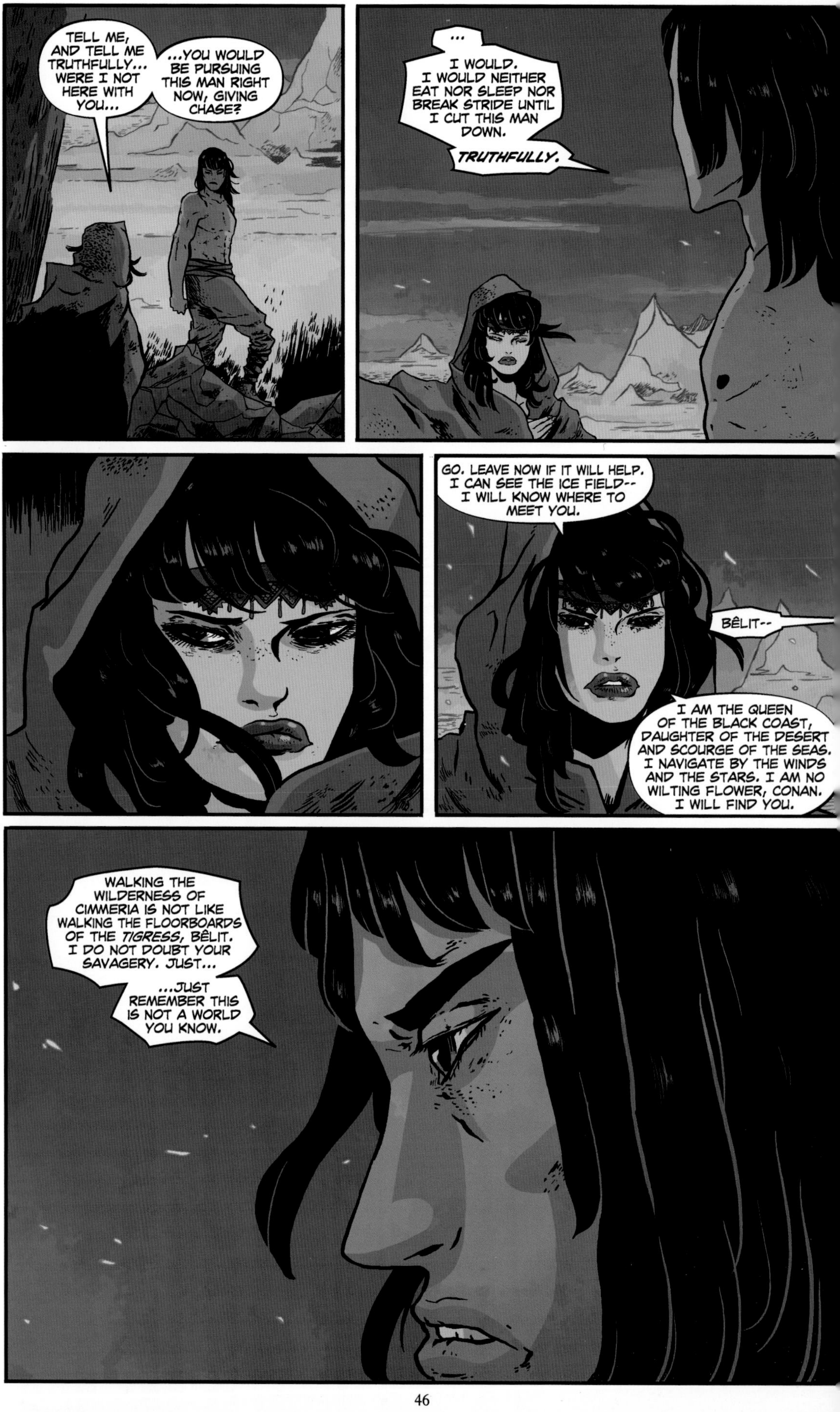
TELL ME, AND TELL ME TRUTHFULLY... WERE I NOT HERE WITH YOU...
...YOU WOULD BE PURSUING THIS MAN RIGHT NOW, GIVING CHASE?
...
I WOULD. I WOULD NEITHER EAT NOR SLEEP NOR BREAK STRIDE UNTIL I CUT THIS MAN DOWN.
TRUTHFULLY.
GO. LEAVE NOW IF IT WILL HELP. I CAN SEE THE ICE FIELD-- I WILL KNOW WHERE TO MEET YOU.
BÊLIT--
I AM THE QUEEN OF THE BLACK COAST, DAUGHTER OF THE DESERT AND SCOURGE OF THE SEAS. I NAVIGATE BY THE WINDS AND THE STARS. I AM NO WILTING FLOWER, CONAN. I WILL FIND YOU.
WALKING THE WILDERNESS OF CIMMERIA IS NOT LIKE WALKING THE FLOORBOARDS OF THE TIGRESS, BÊLIT. I DO NOT DOUBT YOUR SAVAGERY. JUST...
...JUST REMEMBER THIS IS NOT A WORLD YOU KNOW.

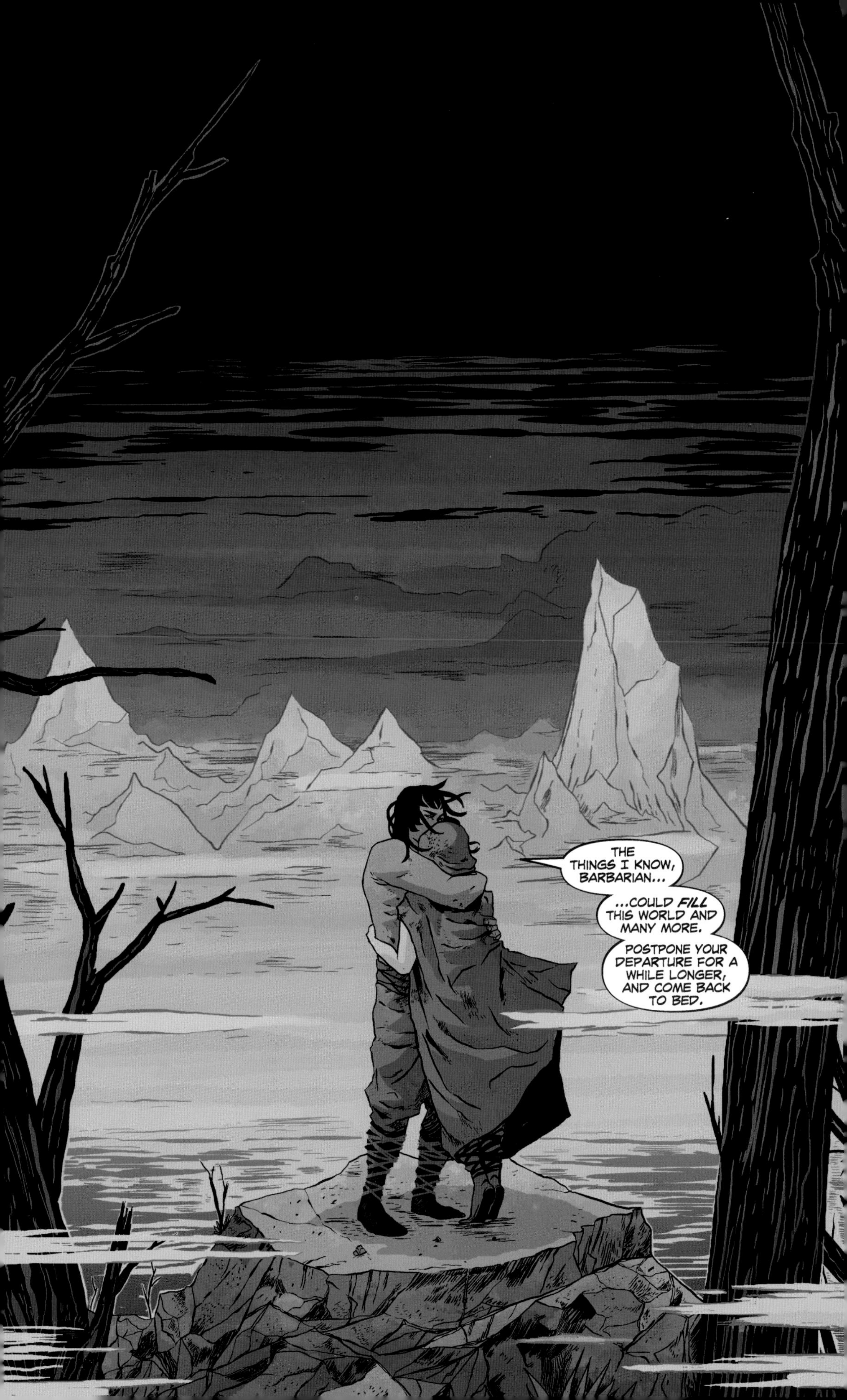
THE THINGS I KNOW, BARBARIAN...
...COULD FILL THIS WORLD AND MANY MORE.
POSTPONE YOUR DEPARTURE FOR A WHILE LONGER, AND COME BACK TO BED.

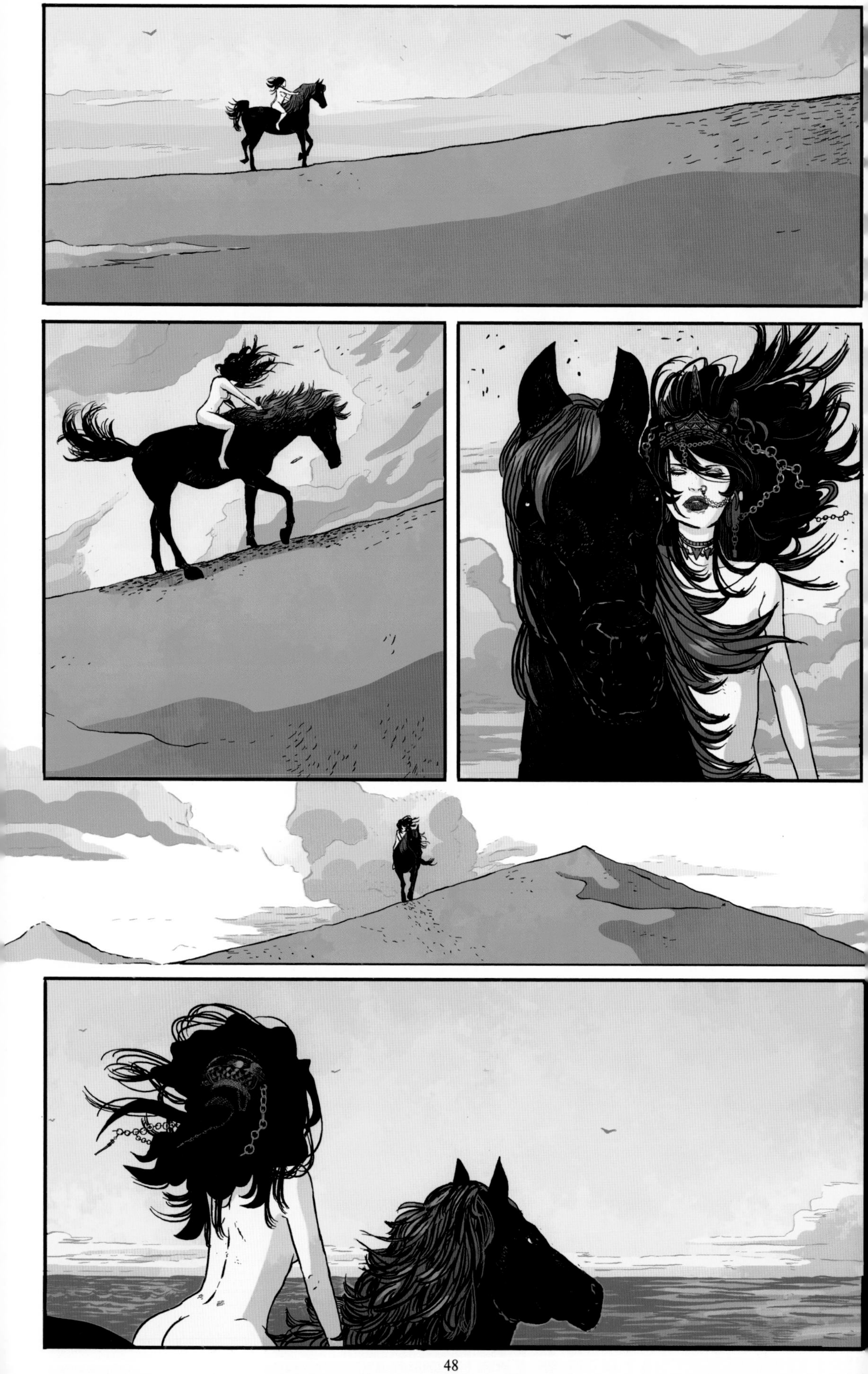

Bêlit woke, chilled to her bones. The fire had long since gone out, and Conan the Cimmerian had left her hours ago.

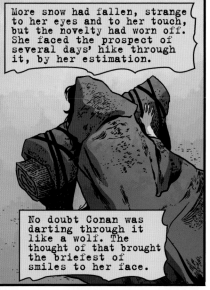

More snow had fallen, strange to her eyes and to her touch, but the novelty had worn off. She faced the prospect of several days' hike through it, by her estimation.

No doubt Conan was darting through it like a wolf. The thought of that brought the briefest of smiles to her face.

The rising sun, brilliant against the white of the snow, gave her some hope. A warmer hike, surely, and perhaps by midday, the snow will have started to melt.

And so Bêlit, feeling the weight of the silence of the forest, sets off to put it behind her, thinking of her lover Conan...

...and the gift of freedom she had given him.

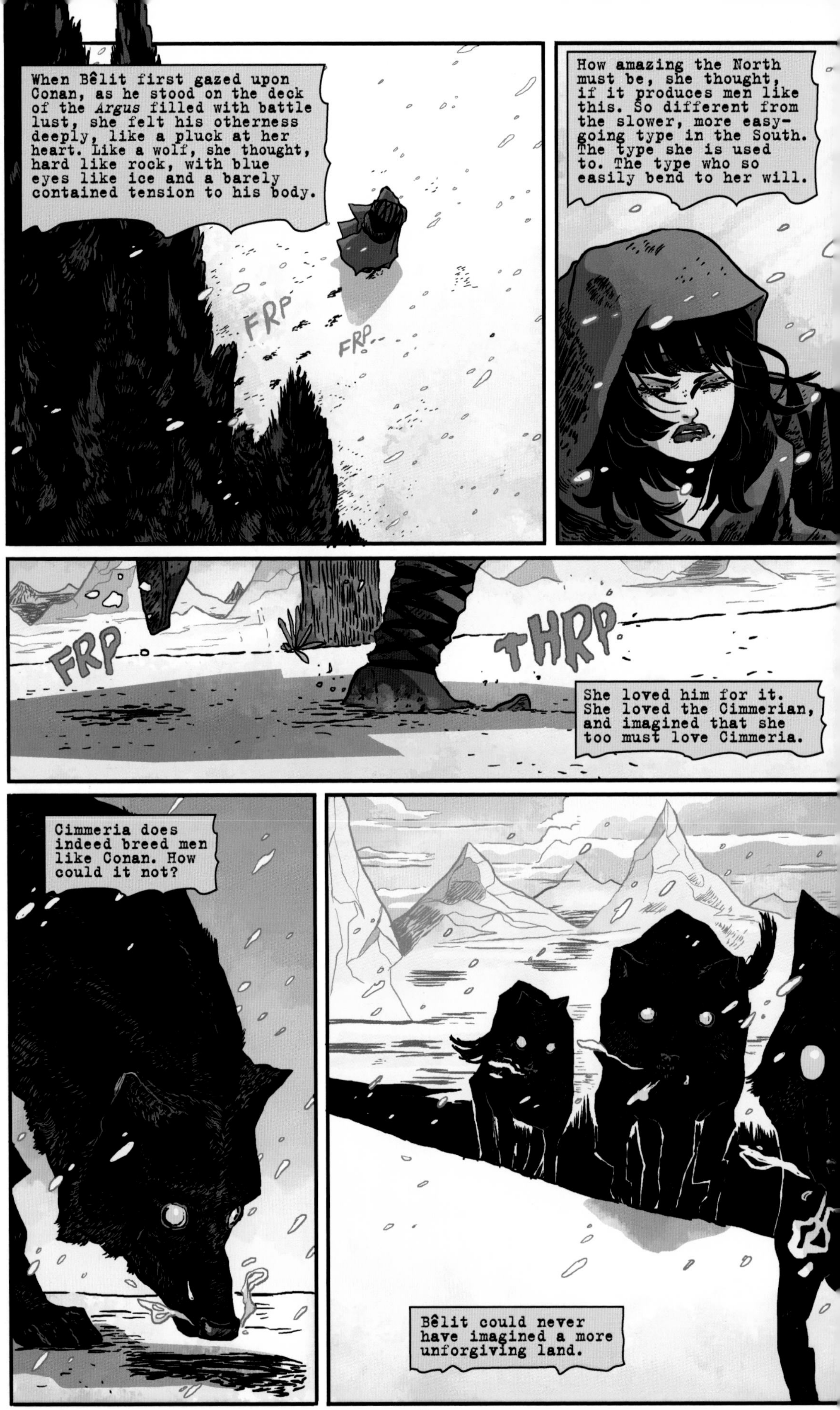
When Bêlit first gazed upon Conan, as he stood on the deck of the *Argus* filled with battle lust, she felt his otherness deeply, like a pluck at her heart. Like a wolf, she thought, hard like rock, with blue eyes like ice and a barely contained tension to his body.
FRP
FRP
How amazing the North must be, she thought, if it produces men like this. So different from the slower, more easy-going type in the South. The type she is used to. The type who so easily bend to her will.
FRP
THRP
She loved him for it. She loved the Cimmerian, and imagined that she too must love Cimmeria.
Cimmeria does indeed breed men like Conan. How could it not?
Bêlit could never have imagined a more unforgiving land.

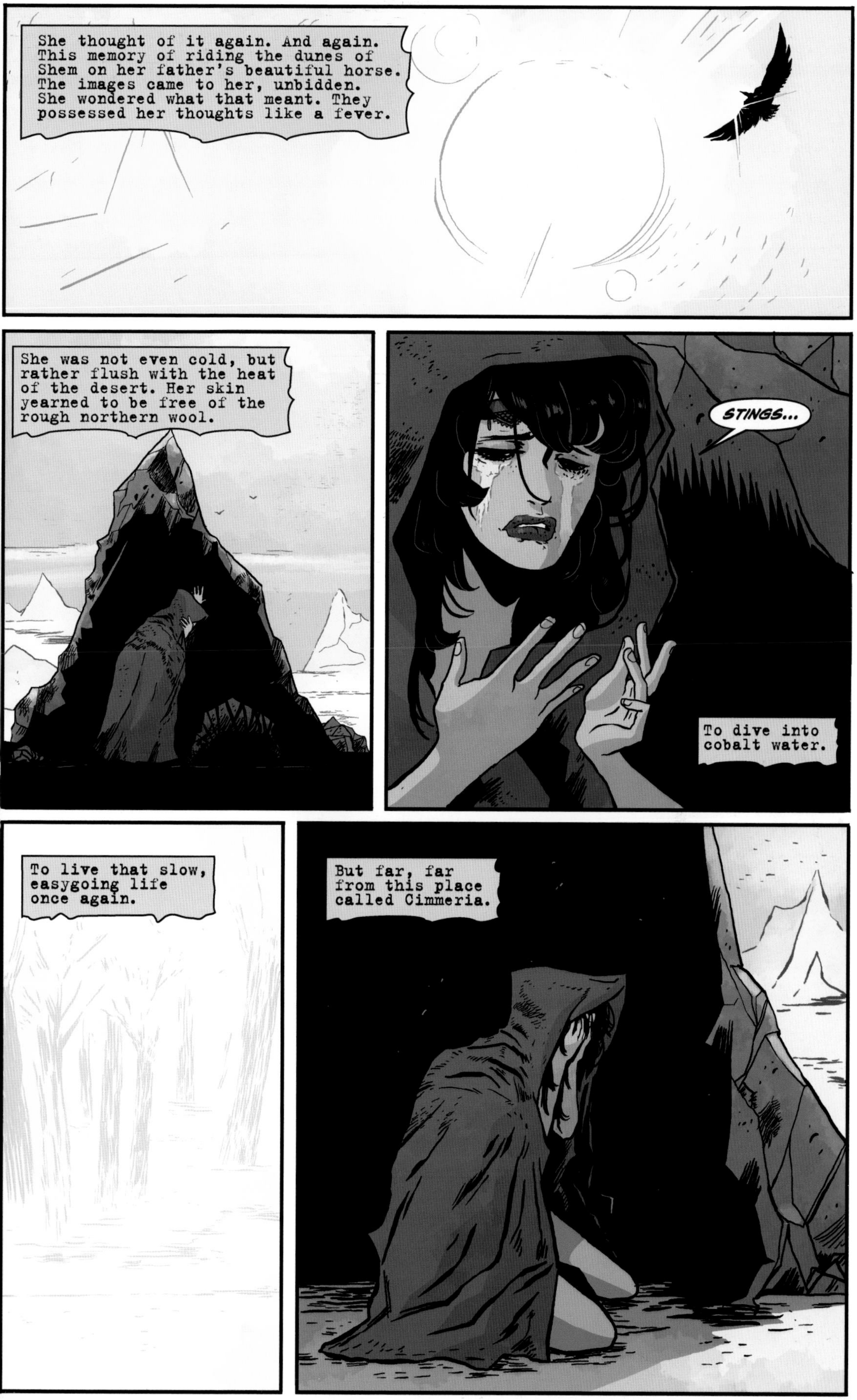
She thought of it again. And again. This memory of riding the dunes of Shem on her father's beautiful horse. The images came to her, unbidden. She wondered what that meant. They possessed her thoughts like a fever.
She was not even cold, but rather flush with the heat of the desert. Her skin yearned to be free of the rough northern wool.
STINGS...
To dive into cobalt water.
To live that slow, easygoing life once again.
But far, far from this place called Cimmeria.

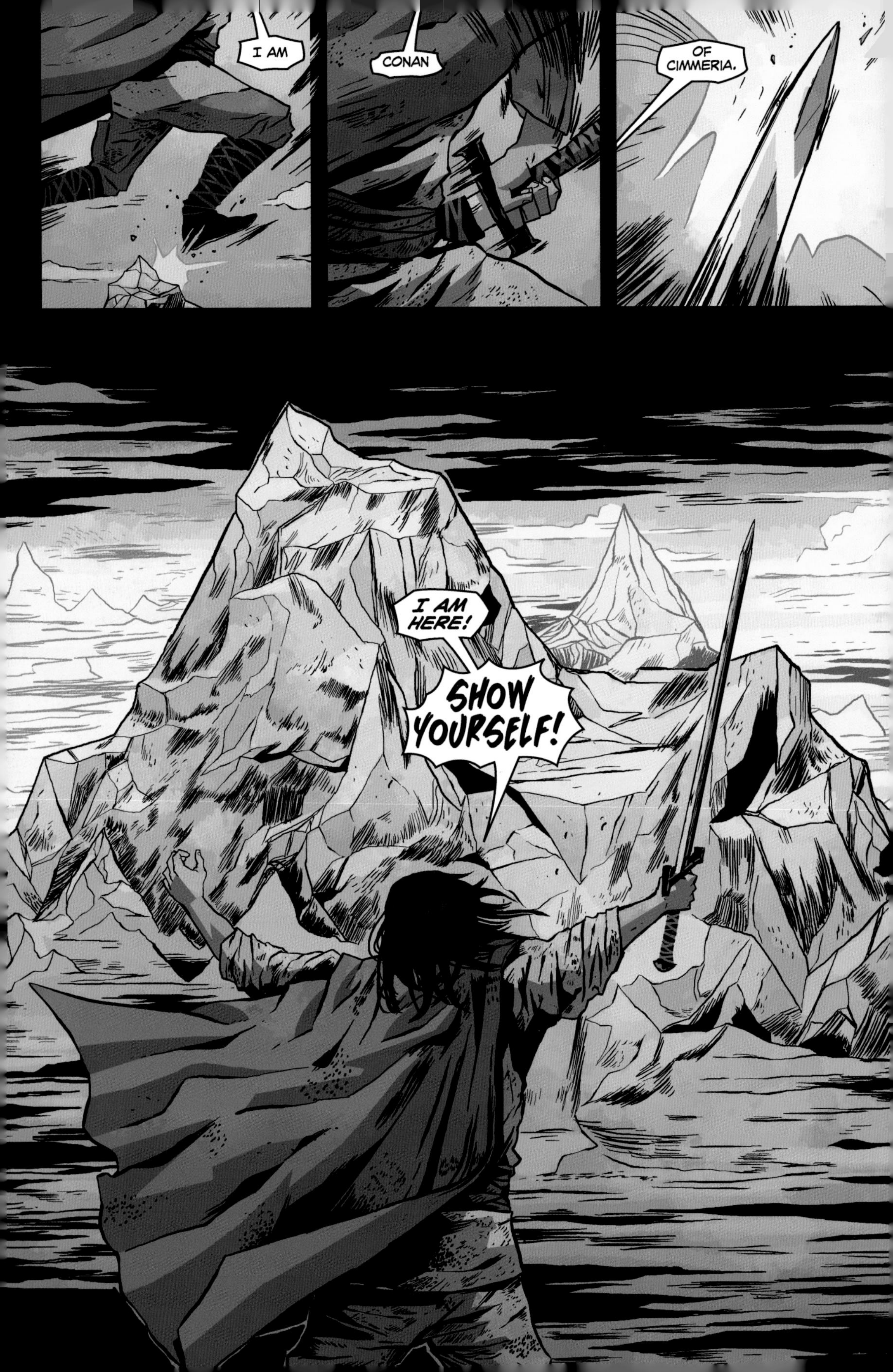
I AM
CONAN
OF CIMMERIA.
I AM HERE!
SHOW YOURSELF!

CHAPTER THREE

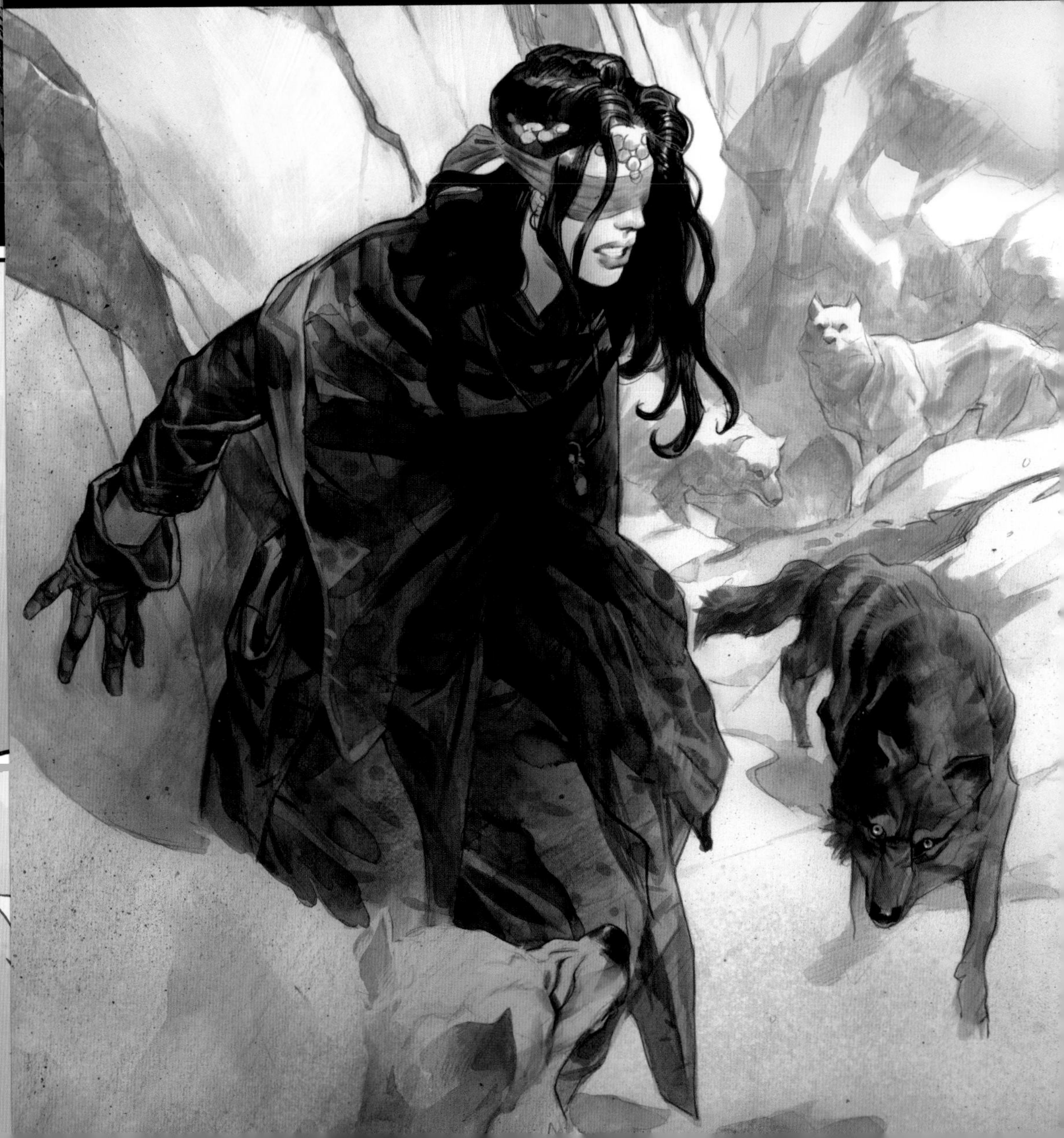

They seemed to be seeking her out, testing her in both strength and resolve...

RRRRRRRRRRRRRR

RRRRRRRRR

..and perhaps...

CHOP

YIPE

...testing her worth as Conan's companion?

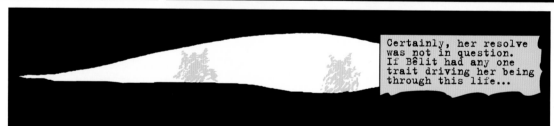

Certainly, her resolve was not in question. If Bêlit had any one trait driving her being through this life...

RRRRRRRRRRRRRRR

UMF!

...it was a powerful sense of self. She dared the cosmos itself to take that away from her.

This was not the *Tigress*. Men did not quake at the mere mention of her name in these lands. This was not the Western Ocean, a body she knew intimately, like that of a lover.

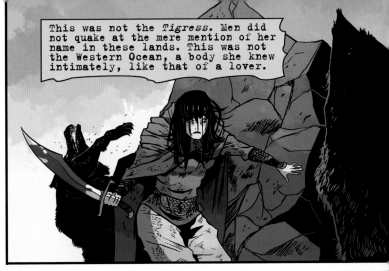

Here, Bêlit was to be underestimated, mocked, and marginalized.

SWOOSH!

Cimmeria, a rugged land of iron ore and rock, was not accustomed to polished stones such as she. But unlike a crown jewel of the realm, or a prized diamond on the neck of a nobleman's wife...

...Bêlit kept her razor-sharp edges. And if not handled carefully...

...she cut.

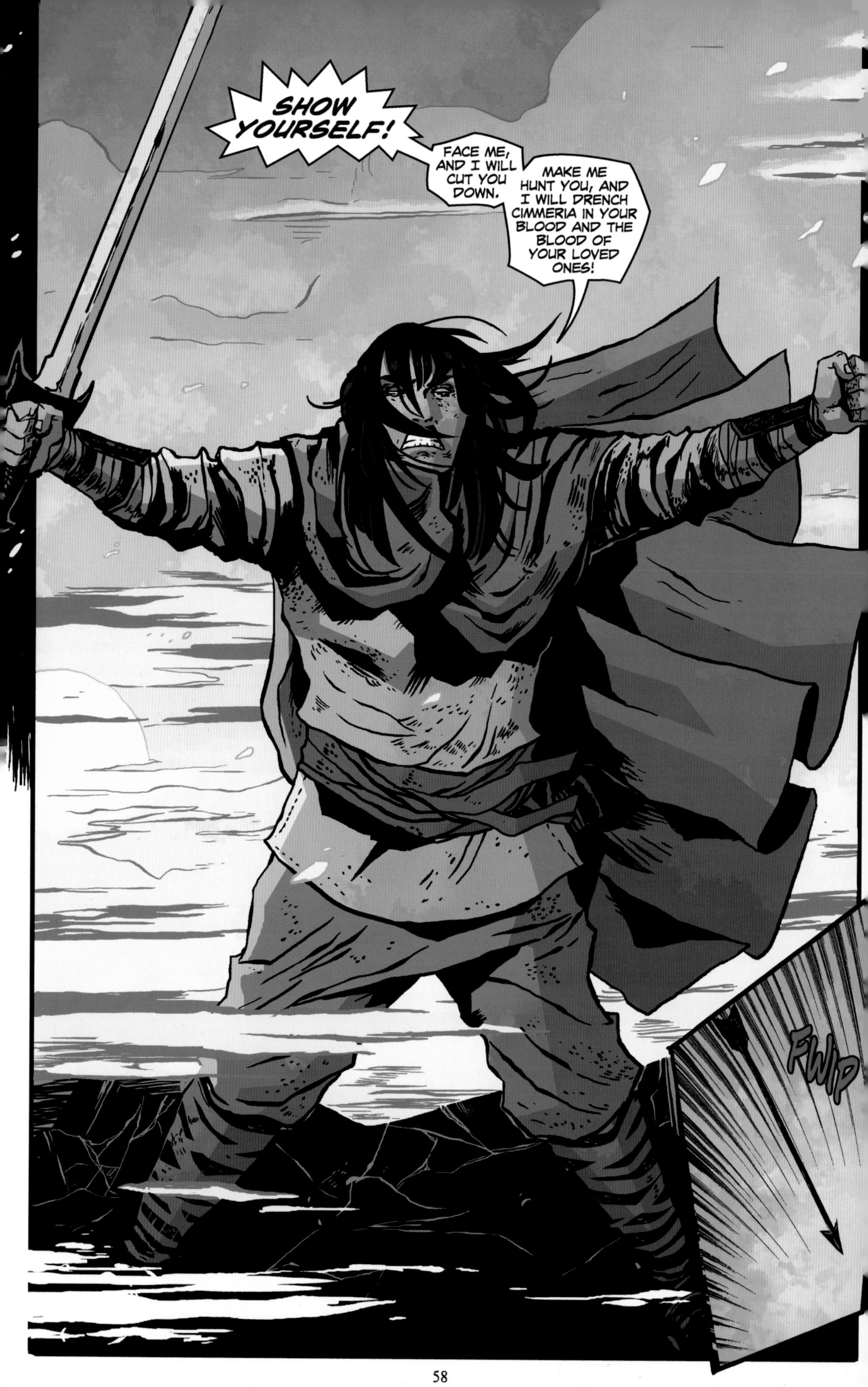
SHOW YOURSELF!
FACE ME, AND I WILL CUT YOU DOWN.
MAKE ME HUNT YOU, AND I WILL DRENCH CIMMERIA IN YOUR BLOOD AND THE BLOOD OF YOUR LOVED ONES!
FWIP

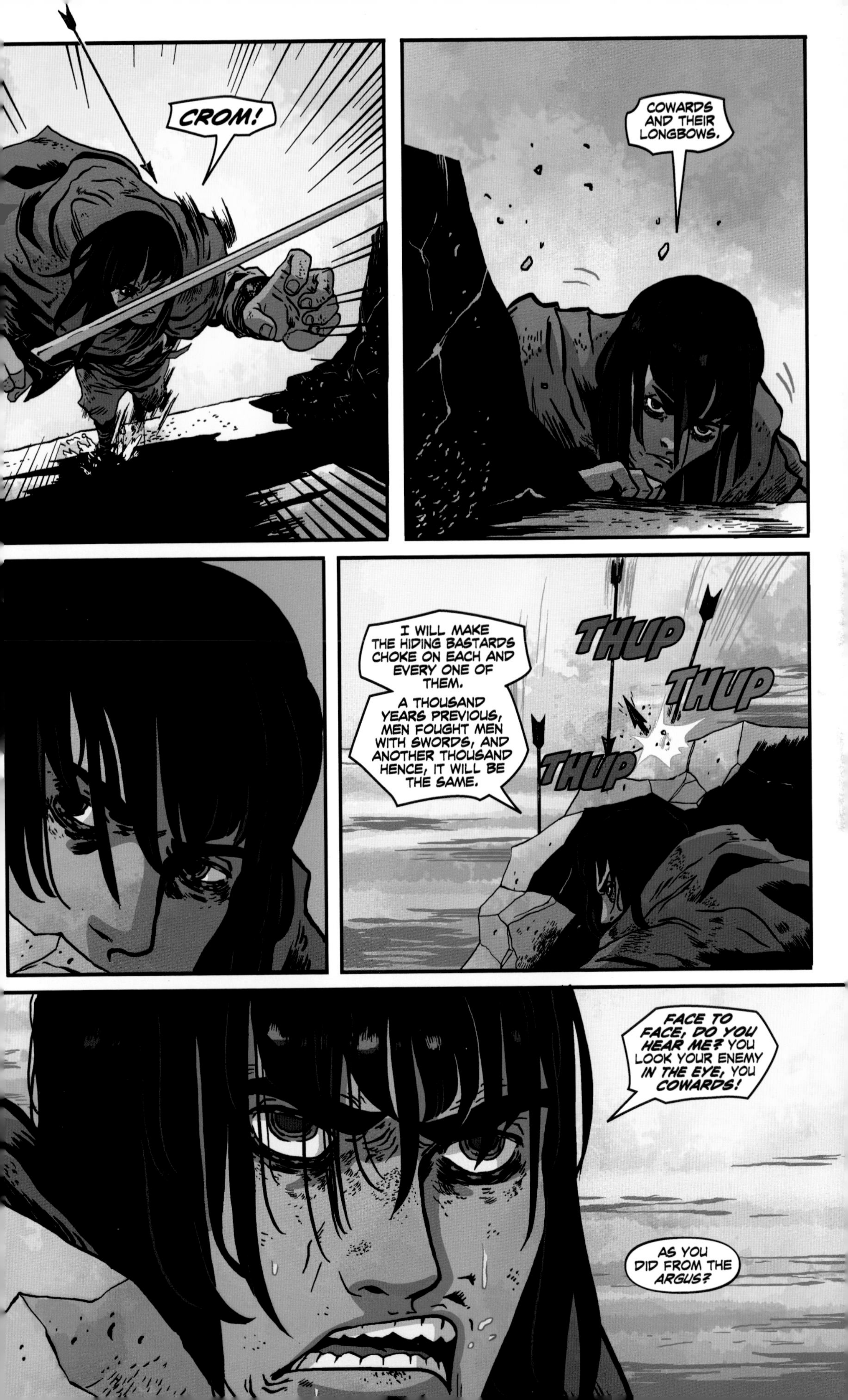
CROM!
COWARDS AND THEIR LONGBOWS.
I WILL MAKE THE HIDING BASTARDS CHOKE ON EACH AND EVERY ONE OF THEM.
A THOUSAND YEARS PREVIOUS, MEN FOUGHT MEN WITH SWORDS, AND ANOTHER THOUSAND HENCE, IT WILL BE THE SAME.
THUP
THUP
THUP
FACE TO FACE, DO YOU HEAR ME? YOU LOOK YOUR ENEMY IN THE EYE, YOU COWARDS!
AS YOU DID FROM THE ARGUS?

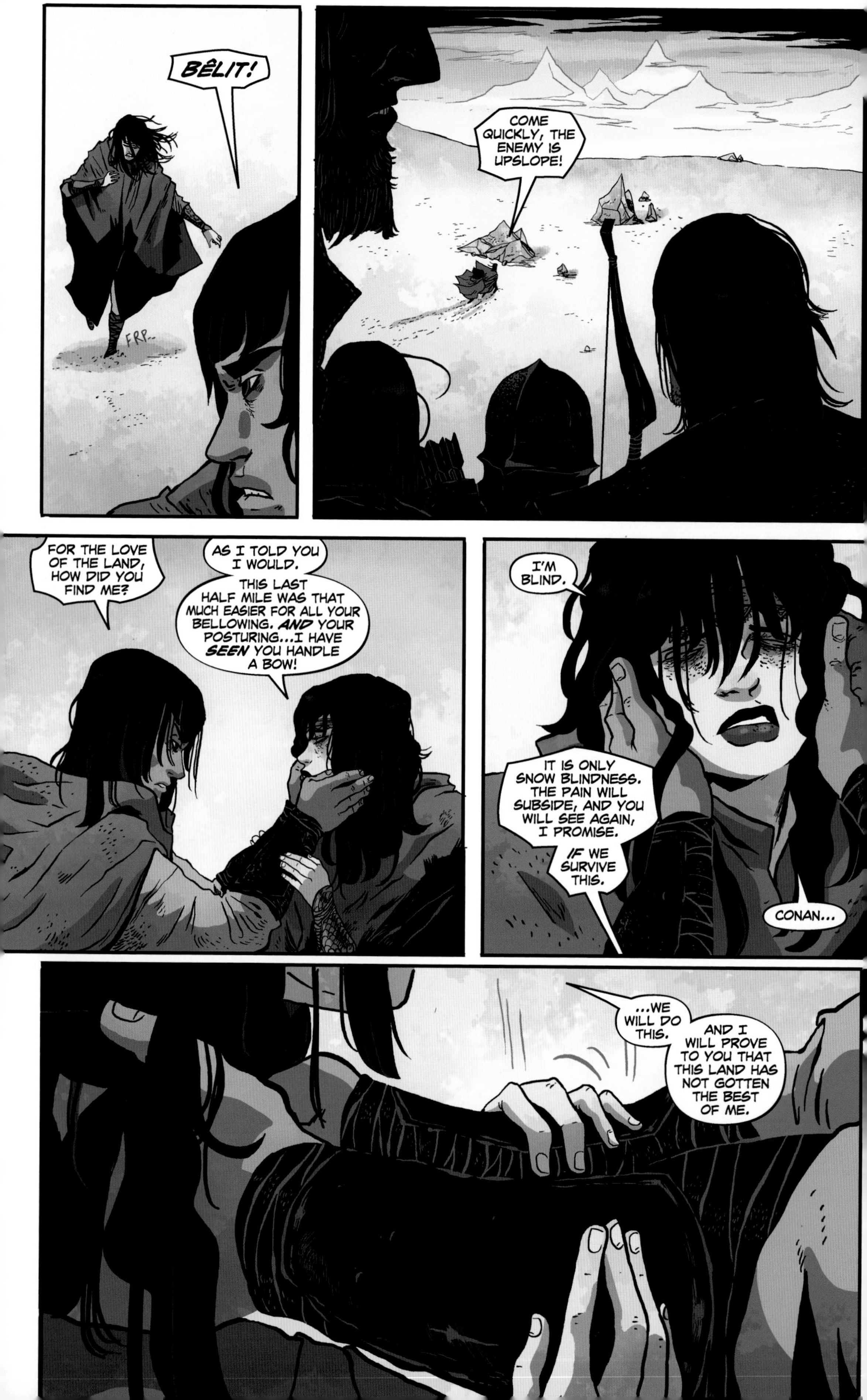
BÊLIT!
FRP
COME QUICKLY, THE ENEMY IS UPSLOPE!
FOR THE LOVE OF THE LAND, HOW DID YOU FIND ME?
AS I TOLD YOU I WOULD.
THIS LAST HALF MILE WAS THAT MUCH EASIER FOR ALL YOUR BELLOWING. AND YOUR POSTURING...I HAVE SEEN YOU HANDLE A BOW!
I'M BLIND.
IT IS ONLY SNOW BLINDNESS. THE PAIN WILL SUBSIDE, AND YOU WILL SEE AGAIN, I PROMISE.
IF WE SURVIVE THIS.
CONAN...
...WE WILL DO THIS.
AND I WILL PROVE TO YOU THAT THIS LAND HAS NOT GOTTEN THE BEST OF ME.

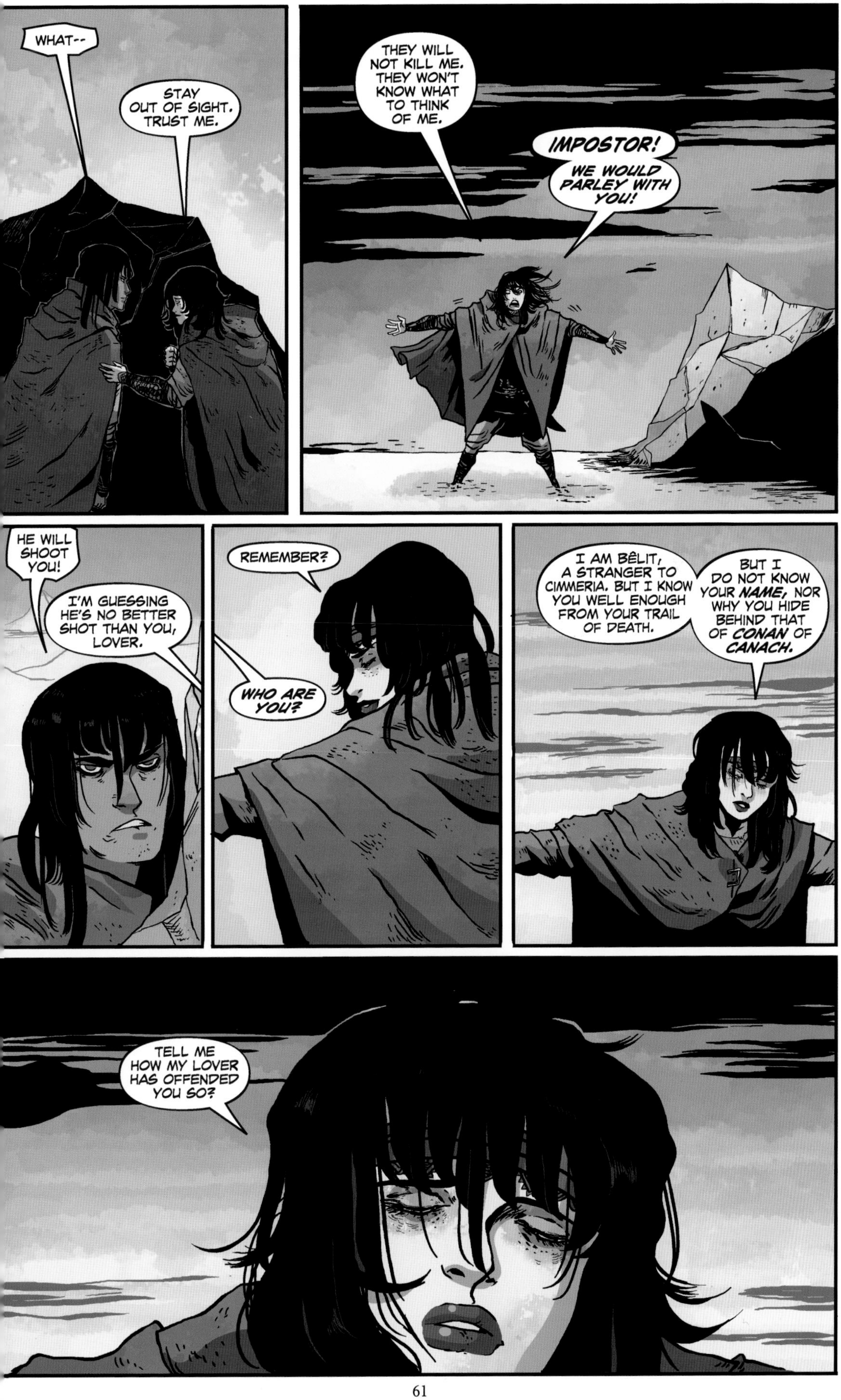
WHAT--
STAY OUT OF SIGHT. TRUST ME.
THEY WILL NOT KILL ME. THEY WON'T KNOW WHAT TO THINK OF ME.
IMPOSTOR!
WE WOULD PARLEY WITH YOU!
HE WILL SHOOT YOU!
I'M GUESSING HE'S NO BETTER SHOT THAN YOU, LOVER.
REMEMBER?
WHO ARE YOU?
I AM BÊLIT, A STRANGER TO CIMMERIA. BUT I KNOW YOU WELL ENOUGH FROM YOUR TRAIL OF DEATH.
BUT I DO NOT KNOW YOUR NAME, NOR WHY YOU HIDE BEHIND THAT OF CONAN OF CANACH.
TELL ME HOW MY LOVER HAS OFFENDED YOU SO?

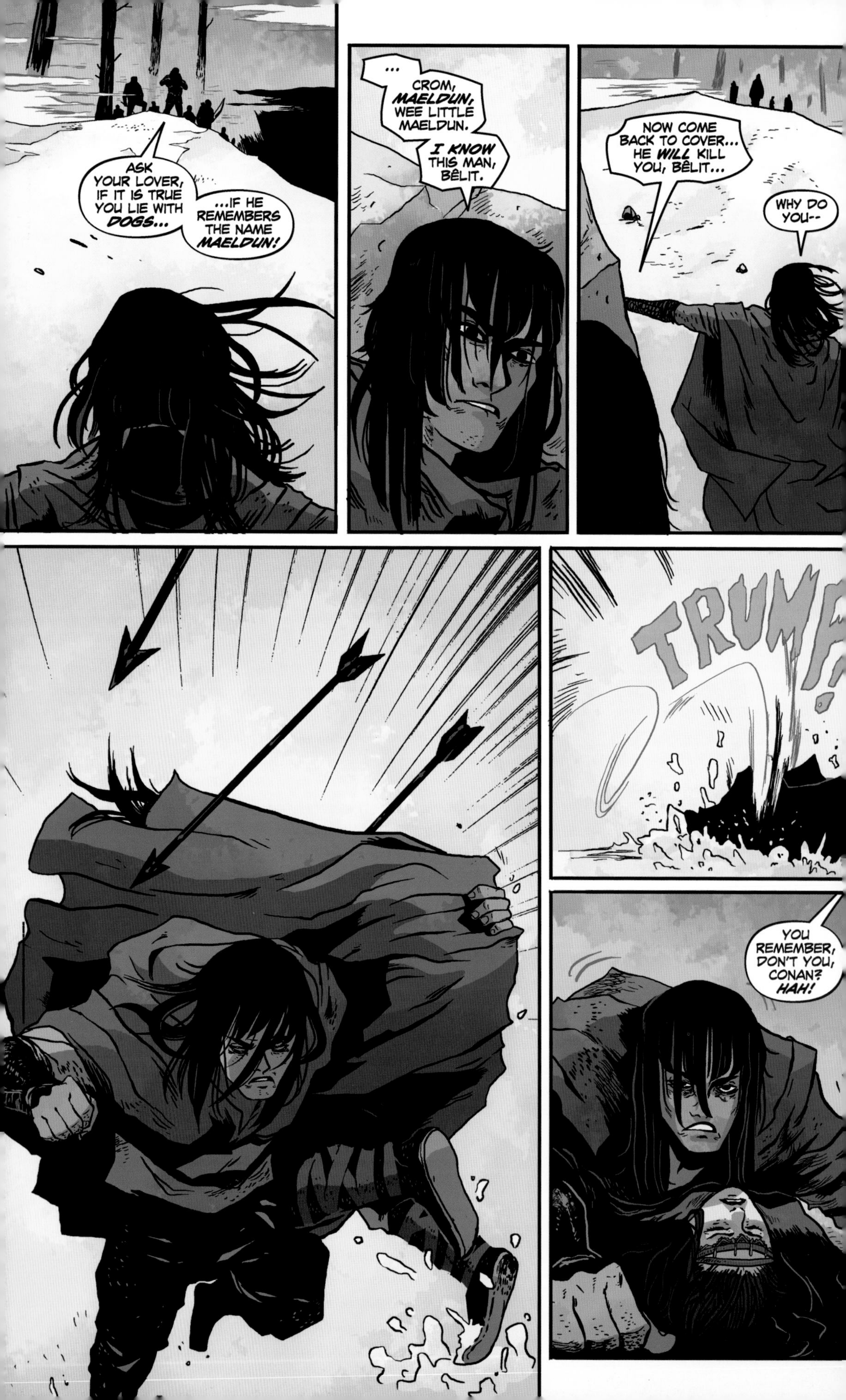

ASK YOUR LOVER, IF IT IS TRUE YOU LIE WITH DOGS...
...IF HE REMEMBERS THE NAME MAELDUN!
...
CROM, MAELDUN, WEE LITTLE MAELDUN.
I KNOW THIS MAN, BÊLIT.
NOW COME BACK TO COVER... HE WILL KILL YOU, BÊLIT...
WHY DO YOU--
TRUMP
YOU REMEMBER, DON'T YOU, CONAN? HAH!

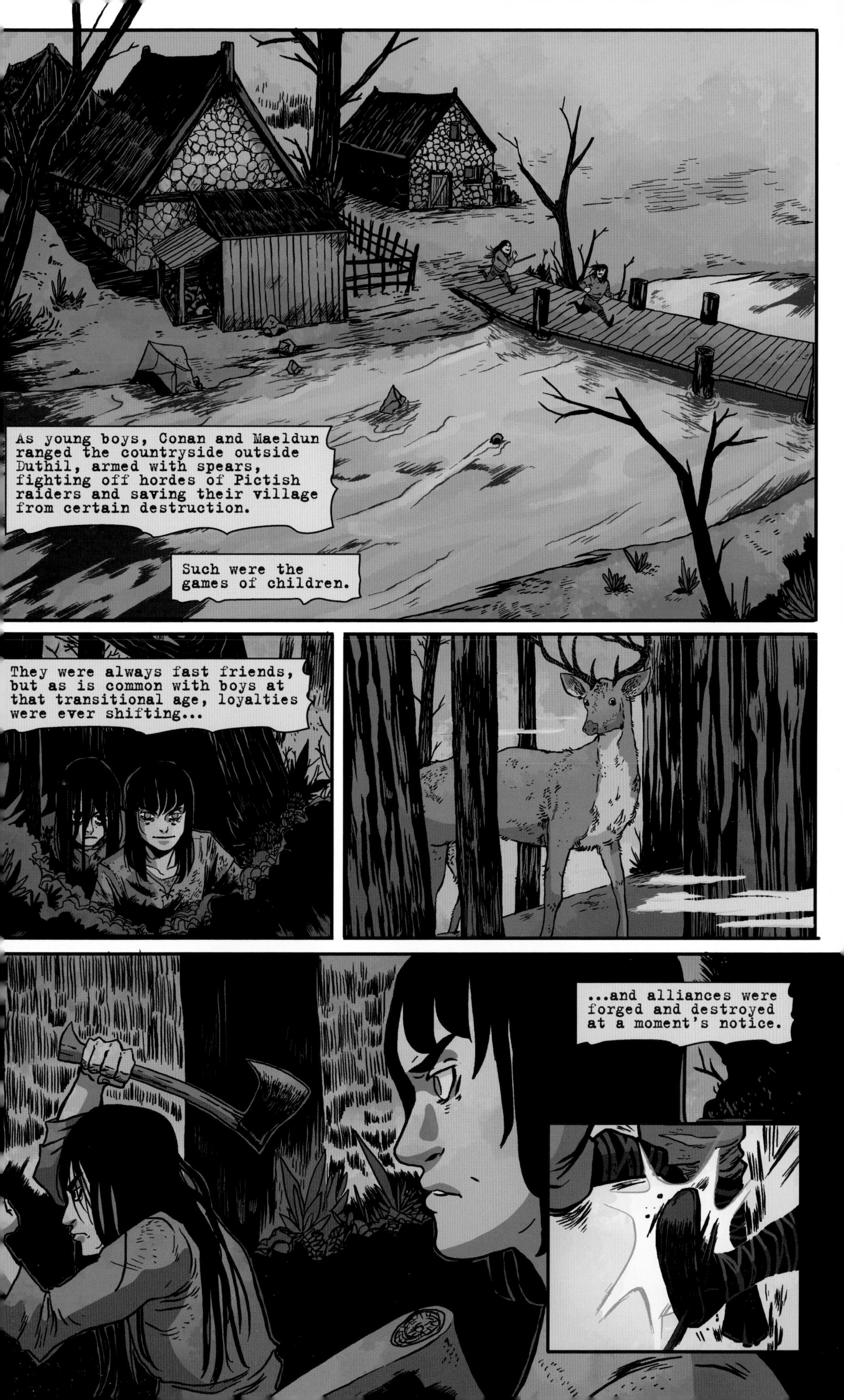
As young boys, Conan and Maeldun ranged the countryside outside Duthil, armed with spears, fighting off hordes of Pictish raiders and saving their village from certain destruction.
Such were the games of children.
They were always fast friends, but as is common with boys at that transitional age, loyalties were ever shifting...
...and alliances were forged and destroyed at a moment's notice.

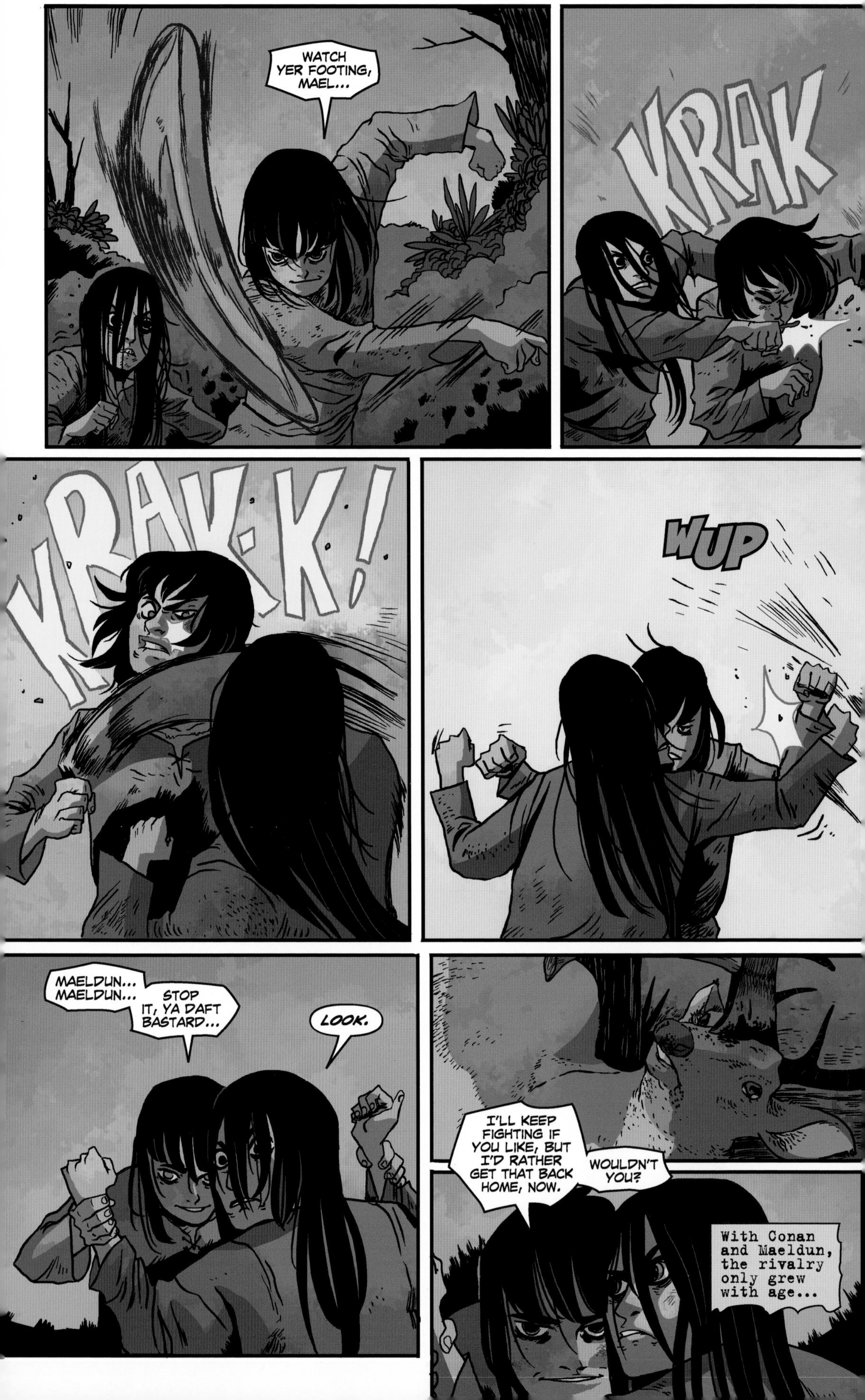
WATCH YER FOOTING, MAEL...
KRAK
KRAK-K!
WUP
MAELDUN... MAELDUN...
STOP IT, YA DAFT BASTARD...
LOOK.
I'LL KEEP FIGHTING IF YOU LIKE, BUT I'D RATHER GET THAT BACK HOME, NOW.
WOULDN'T YOU?
With Conan and Maeldun, the rivalry only grew with age...

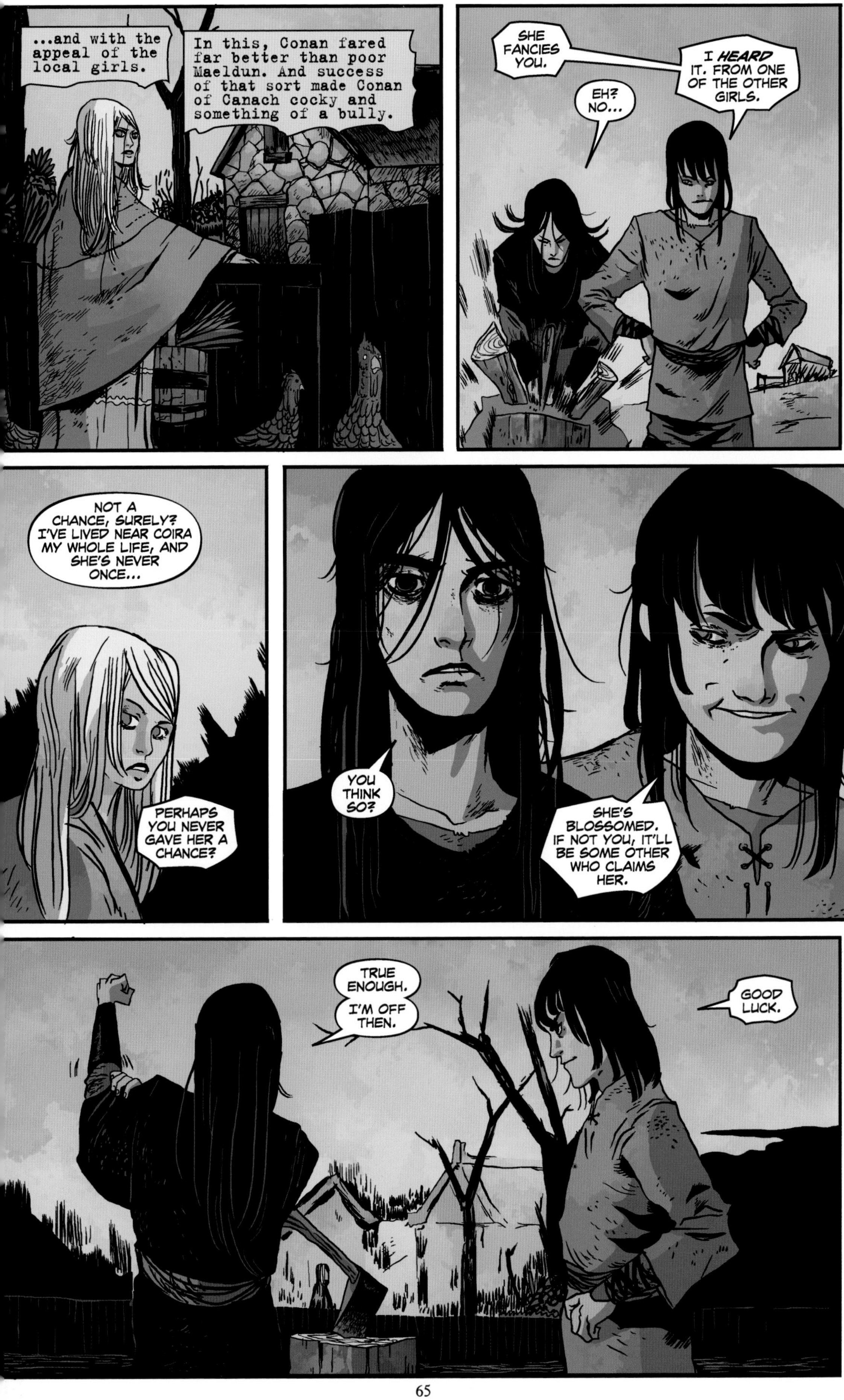
...and with the appeal of the local girls.
In this, Conan fared far better than poor Maeldun. And success of that sort made Conan of Canach cocky and something of a bully.
SHE FANCIES YOU.
EH? NO...
I HEARD IT. FROM ONE OF THE OTHER GIRLS.
NOT A CHANCE, SURELY? I'VE LIVED NEAR COIRA MY WHOLE LIFE, AND SHE'S NEVER ONCE...
PERHAPS YOU NEVER GAVE HER A CHANCE?
YOU THINK SO?
SHE'S BLOSSOMED. IF NOT YOU, IT'LL BE SOME OTHER WHO CLAIMS HER.
TRUE ENOUGH.
I'M OFF THEN.
GOOD LUCK.

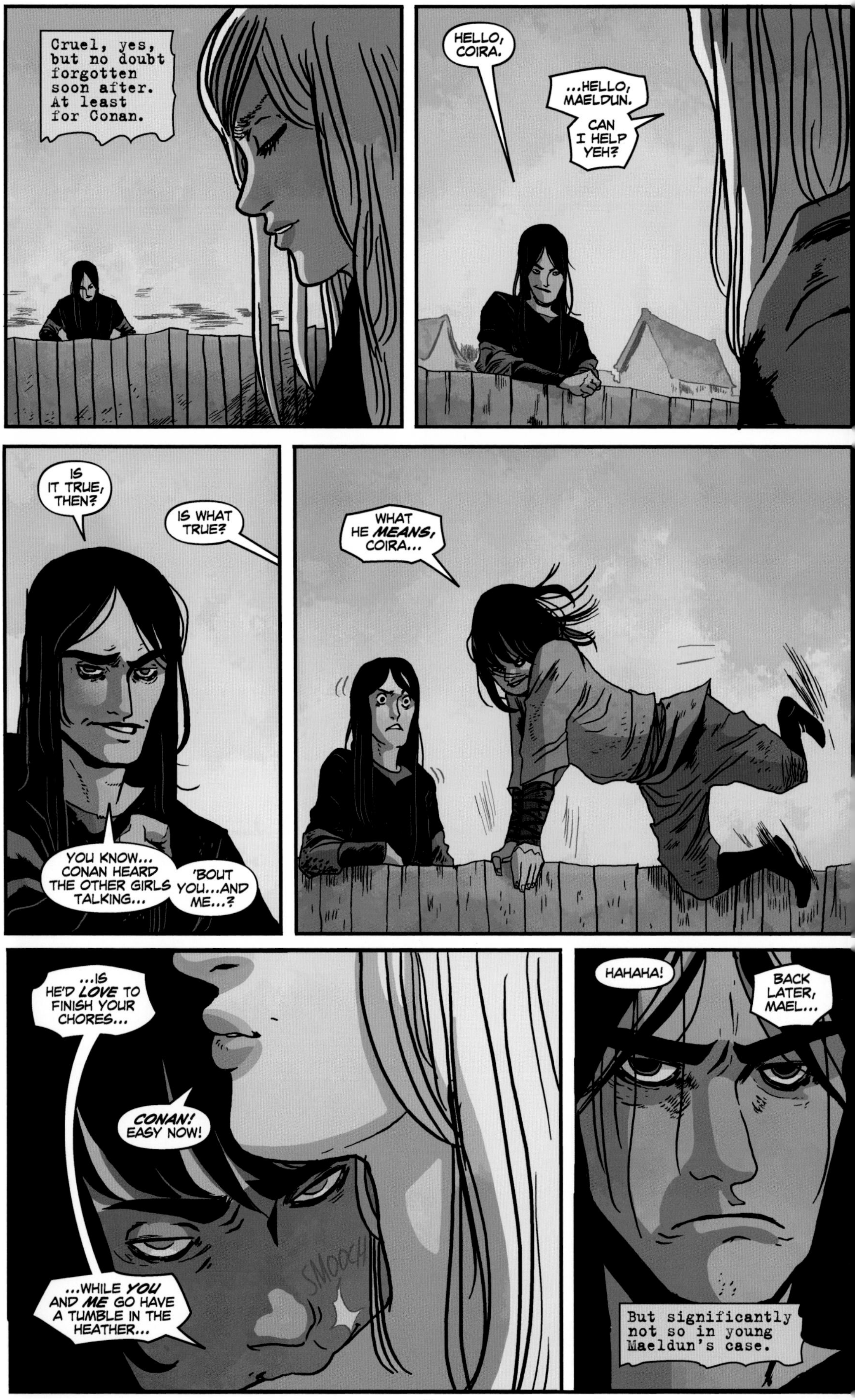
Cruel, yes, but no doubt forgotten soon after. At least for Conan.
HELLO, COIRA.
...HELLO, MAELDUN.
CAN I HELP YEH?
IS IT TRUE, THEN?
IS WHAT TRUE?
YOU KNOW... CONAN HEARD THE OTHER GIRLS TALKING...
'BOUT YOU...AND ME...?
WHAT HE MEANS, COIRA...
...IS HE'D LOVE TO FINISH YOUR CHORES...
CONAN! EASY NOW!
...WHILE YOU AND ME GO HAVE A TUMBLE IN THE HEATHER...
SMOOCH!
HAHAHA!
BACK LATER, MAEL...
But significantly not so in young Maeldun's case.

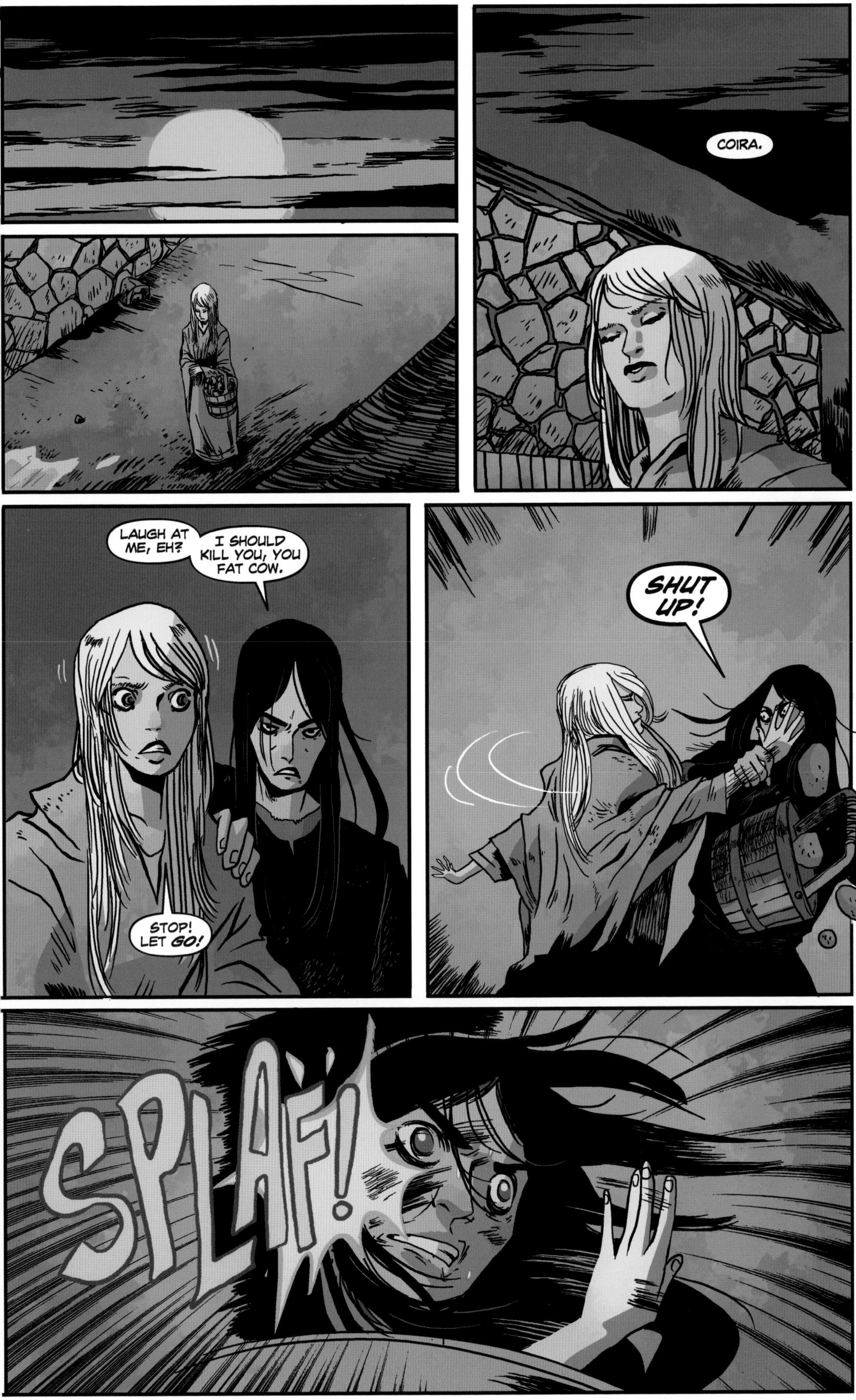
COIRA.
LAUGH AT ME, EH?
I SHOULD KILL YOU, YOU FAT COW.
STOP! LET GO!
SHUT UP!
SPLAF!

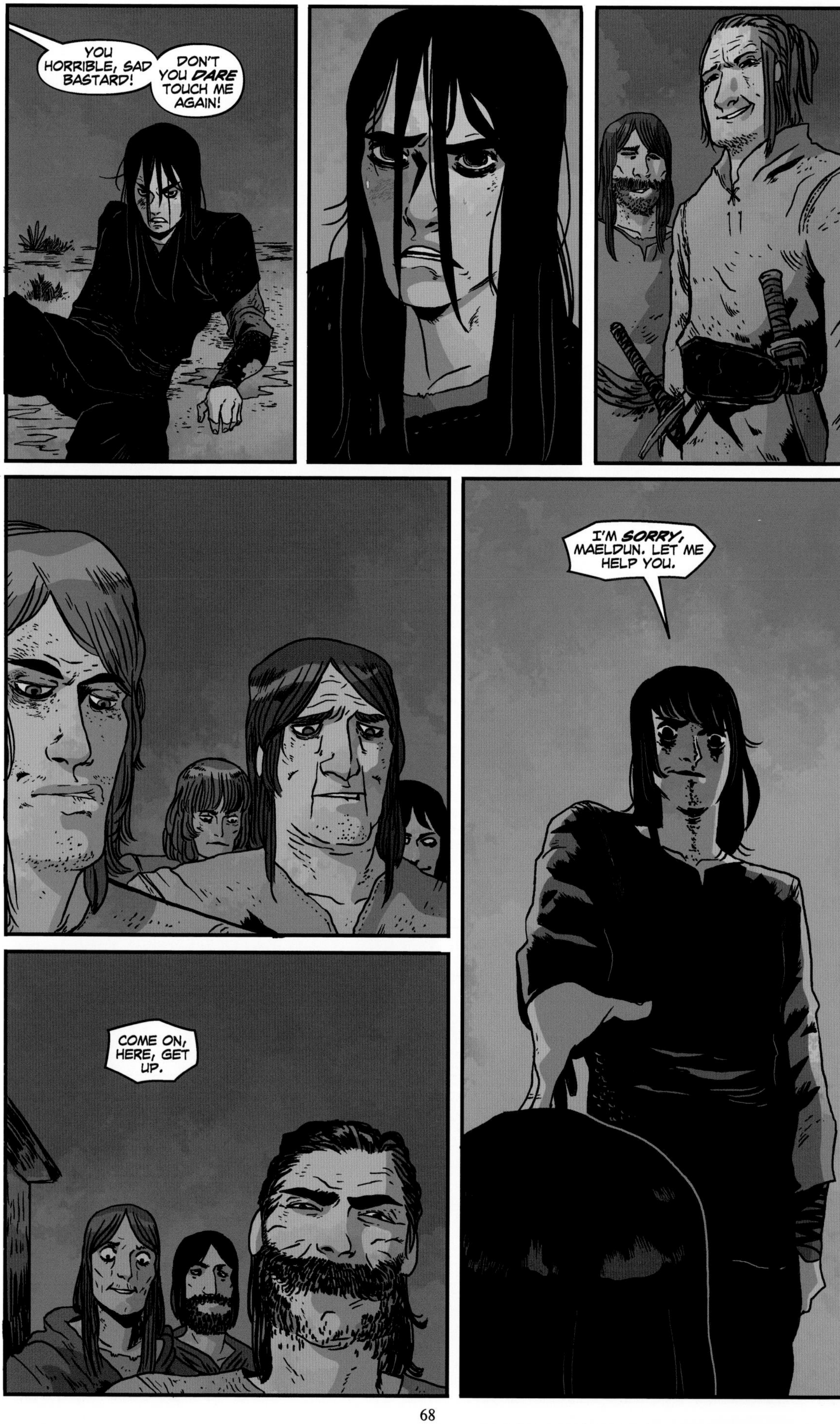
YOU HORRIBLE, SAD BASTARD!
DON'T YOU DARE TOUCH ME AGAIN!
I'M SORRY, MAELDUN. LET ME HELP YOU.
COME ON, HERE, GET UP.

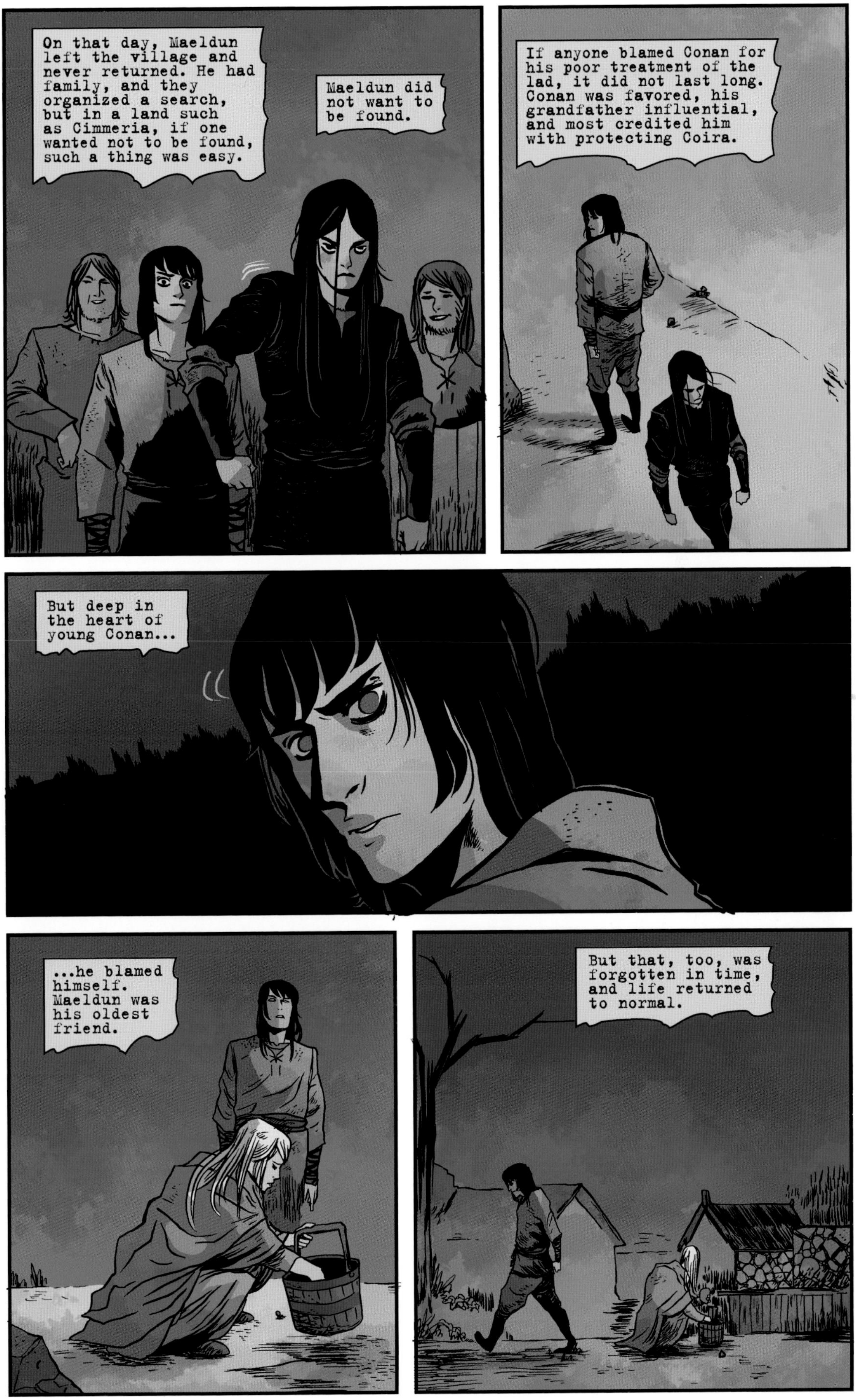
On that day, Maeldun left the village and never returned. He had family, and they organized a search, but in a land such as Cimmeria, if one wanted not to be found, such a thing was easy.
Maeldun did not want to be found.
If anyone blamed Conan for his poor treatment of the lad, it did not last long. Conan was favored, his grandfather influential, and most credited him with protecting Coira.
But deep in the heart of young Conan...
...he blamed himself. Maeldun was his oldest friend.
But that, too, was forgotten in time, and life returned to normal.

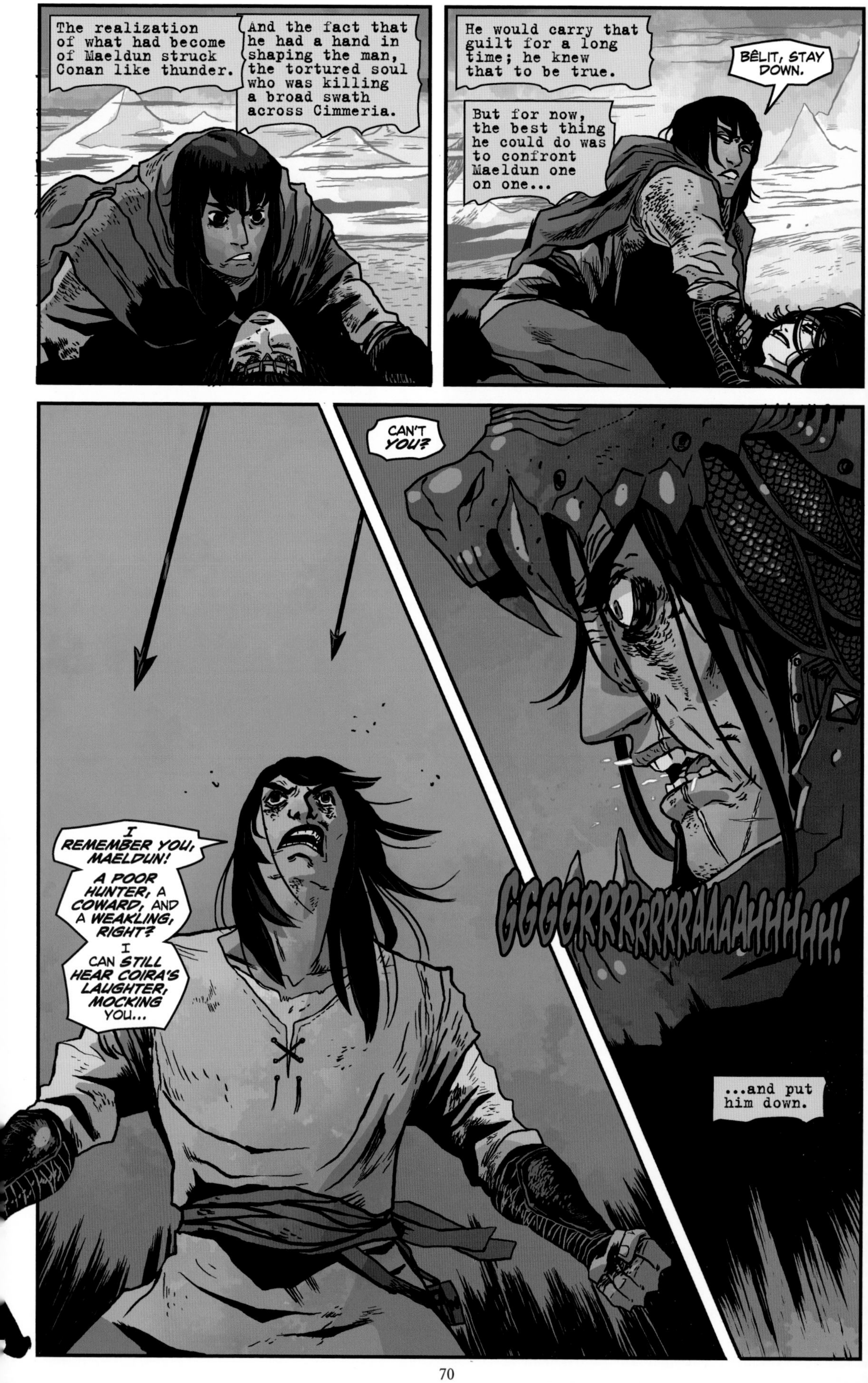
The realization of what had become of Maeldun struck Conan like thunder.
And the fact that he had a hand in shaping the man, the tortured soul who was killing a broad swath across Cimmeria.
He would carry that guilt for a long time; he knew that to be true.
But for now, the best thing he could do was to confront Maeldun one on one...
BÊLIT, STAY DOWN.
CAN'T YOU?
I REMEMBER YOU, MAELDUN!
A POOR HUNTER, A COWARD, AND A WEAKLING, RIGHT?
I CAN STILL HEAR COIRA'S LAUGHTER, MOCKING YOU...
GGGGRRRRRRRAAAAAHHHHH!
...and put him down.

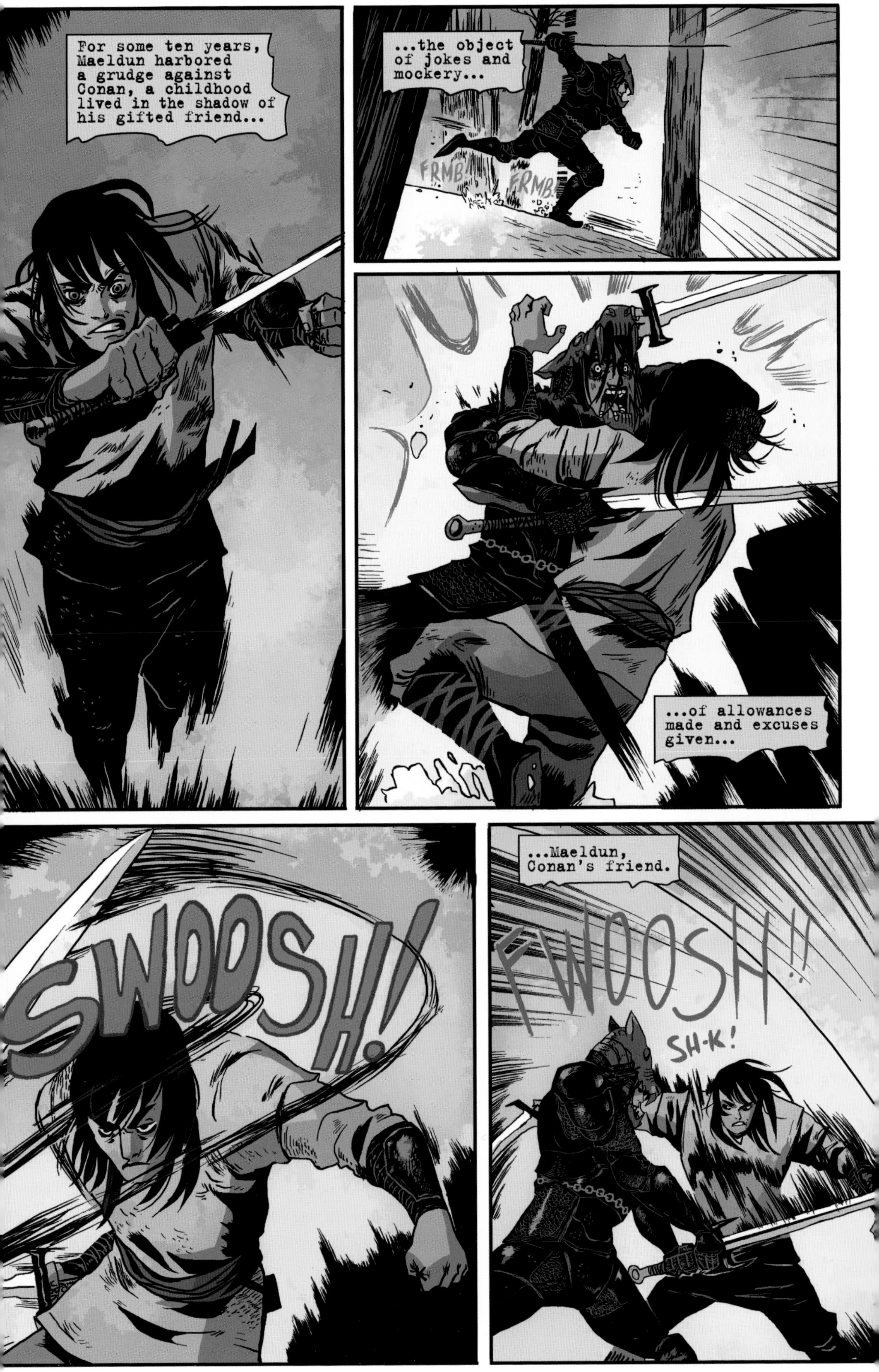
For some ten years, Maeldun harbored a grudge against Conan, a childhood lived in the shadow of his gifted friend...
...the object of jokes and mockery...
FRMB!
FRMB!
...of allowances made and excuses given...
SWOOSH!!
...Maeldun, Conan's friend.
FWOOSH!!
SH-K!

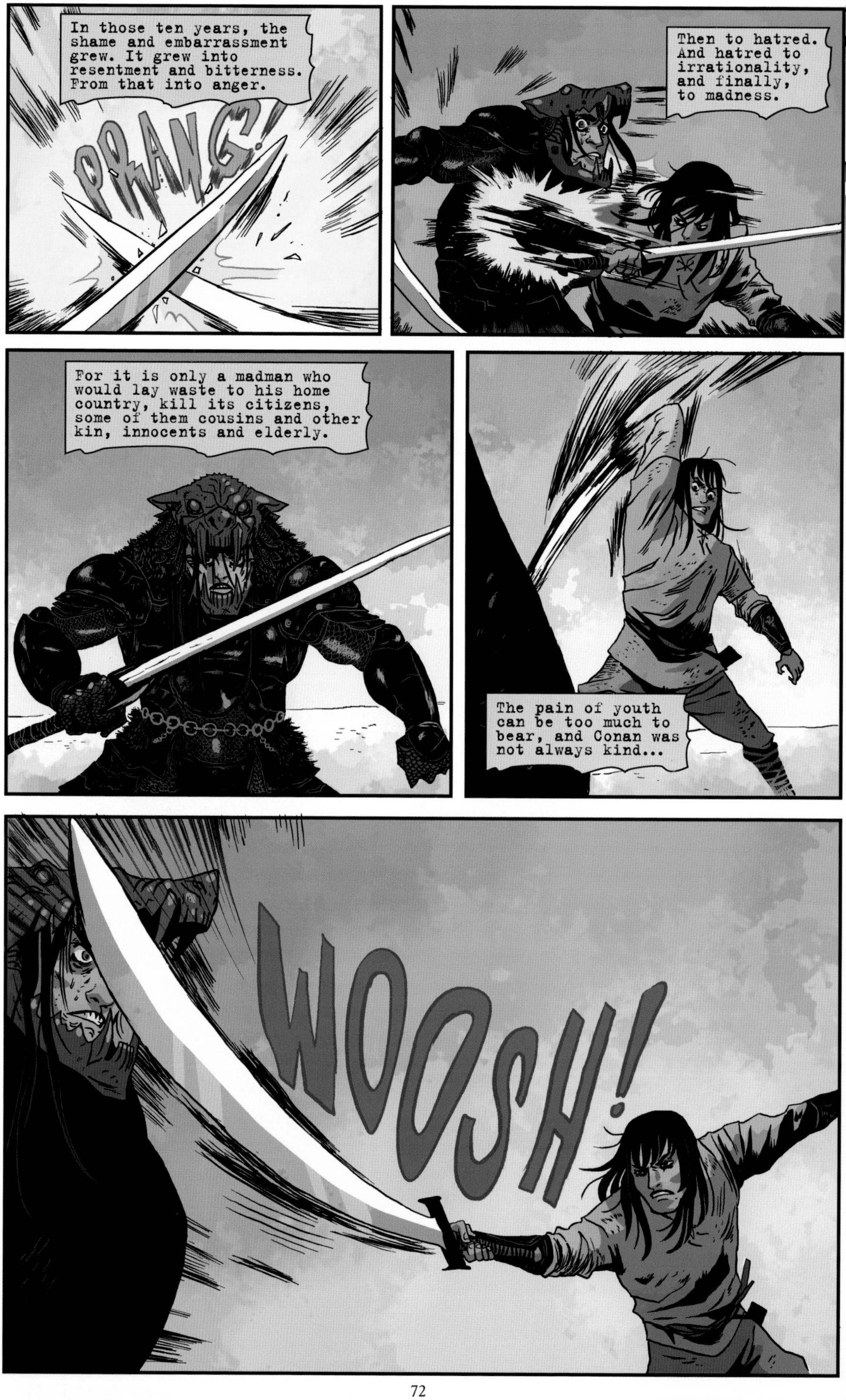
In those ten years, the shame and embarrassment grew. It grew into resentment and bitterness. From that into anger.
PRANG!
Then to hatred. And hatred to irrationality, and finally, to madness.
For it is only a madman who would lay waste to his home country, kill its citizens, some of them cousins and other kin, innocents and elderly.
The pain of youth can be too much to bear, and Conan was not always kind...
WOOSH!

...and so he pays the price, facing off against this madman in mortal combat.

But Conan feels no fear, no threat to his life.

Cimmeria is tainted not just by the violence, but also by his actions, so long ago, and that brought them both here.

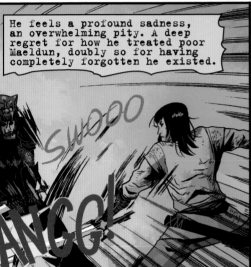

He feels a profound sadness, an overwhelming pity. A deep regret for how he treated poor Maeldun, doubly so for having completely forgotten he existed.

SWOOO

RANGG!

And Conan will carry that shame with him always.

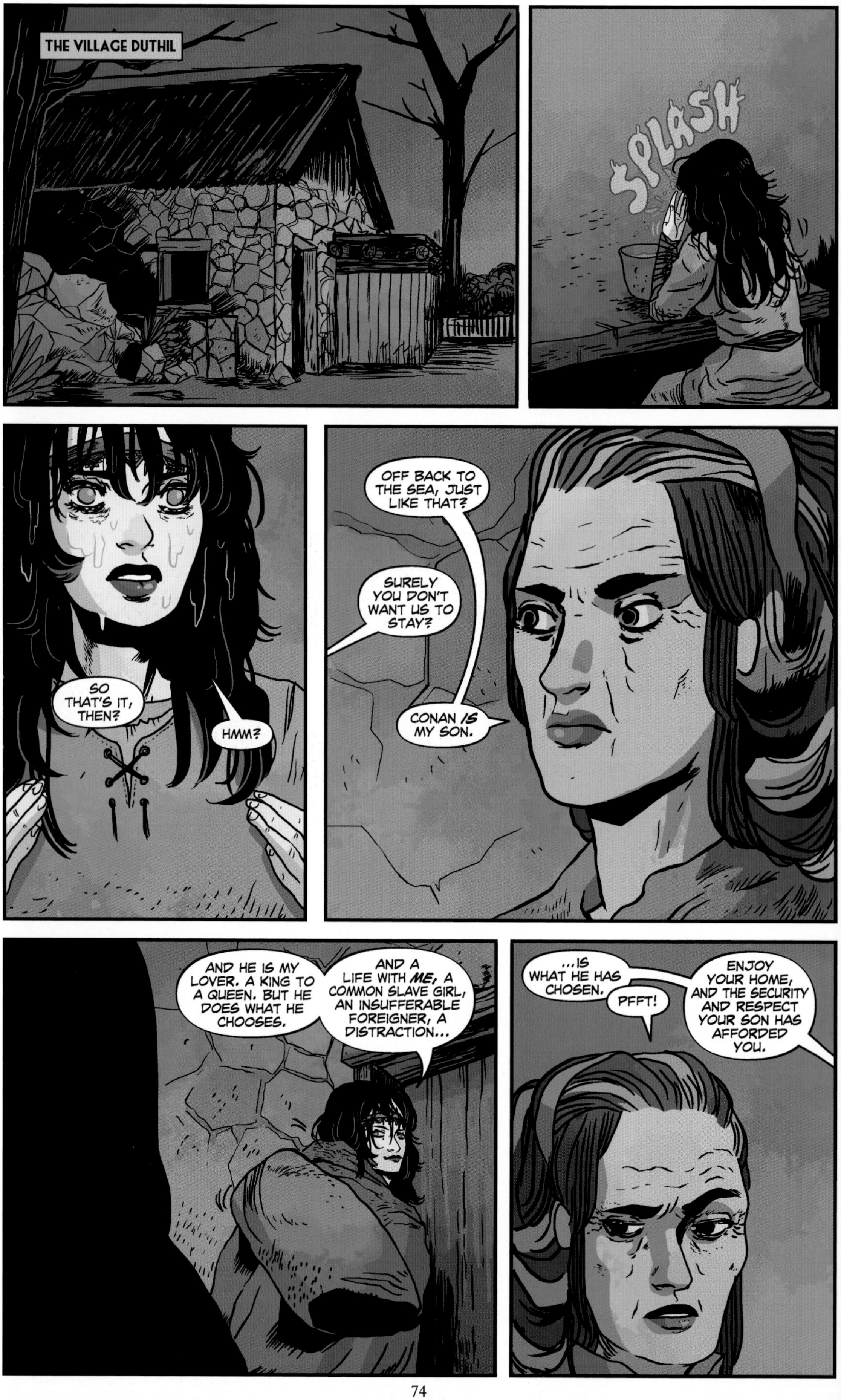
THE VILLAGE DUTHIL
SPLASH
SO THAT'S IT, THEN?
HMM?
OFF BACK TO THE SEA, JUST LIKE THAT?
SURELY YOU DON'T WANT US TO STAY?
CONAN IS MY SON.
AND HE IS MY LOVER. A KING TO A QUEEN. BUT HE DOES WHAT HE CHOOSES.
AND A LIFE WITH ME, A COMMON SLAVE GIRL, AN INSUFFERABLE FOREIGNER, A DISTRACTION...
...IS WHAT HE HAS CHOSEN.
PFFT!
ENJOY YOUR HOME, AND THE SECURITY AND RESPECT YOUR SON HAS AFFORDED YOU.

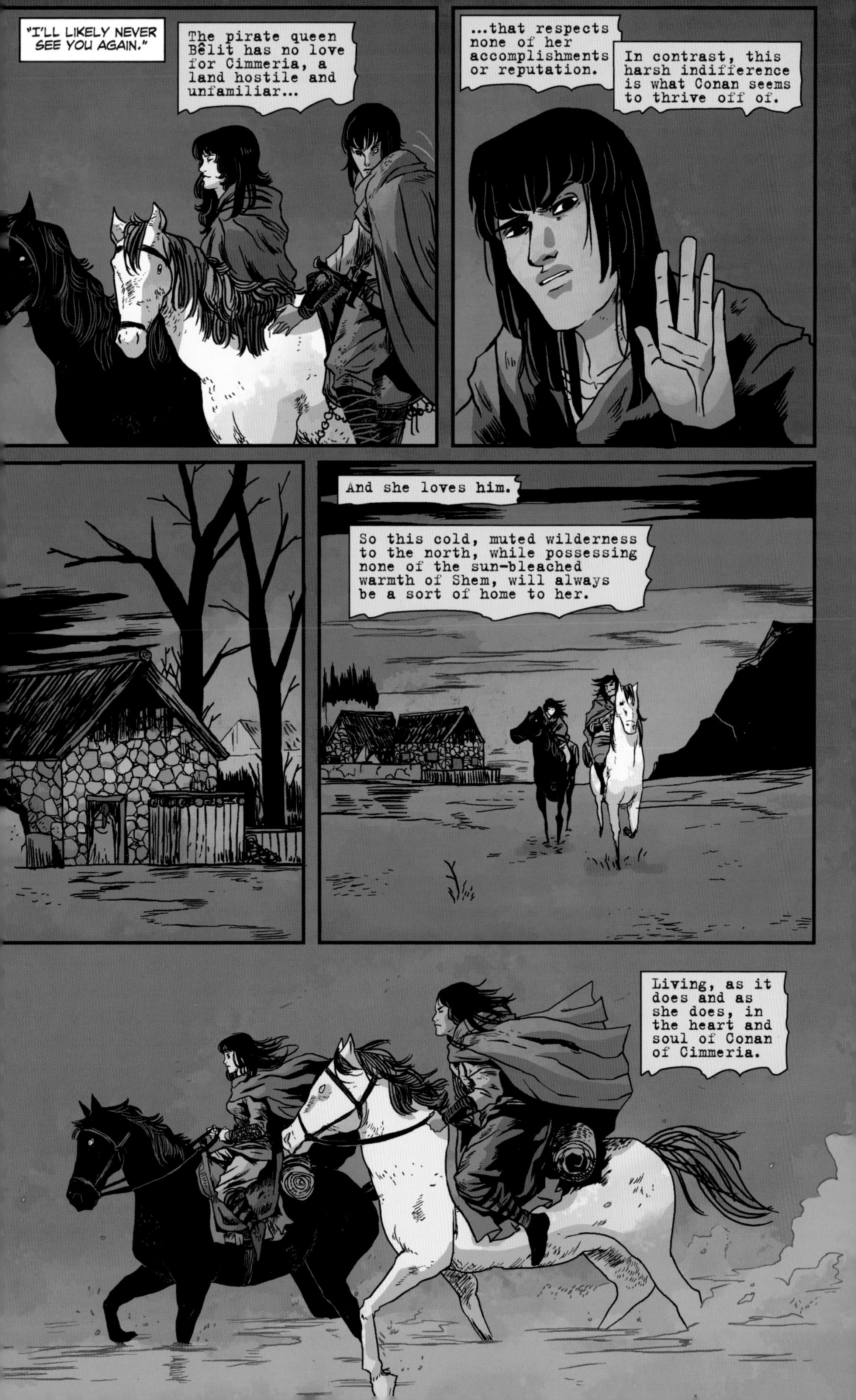
"I'LL LIKELY NEVER SEE YOU AGAIN."
The pirate queen Bêlit has no love for Cimmeria, a land hostile and unfamiliar...
...that respects none of her accomplishments or reputation.
In contrast, this harsh indifference is what Conan seems to thrive off of.
And she loves him.
So this cold, muted wilderness to the north, while possessing none of the sun-bleached warmth of Shem, will always be a sort of home to her.
Living, as it does and as she does, in the heart and soul of Conan of Cimmeria.

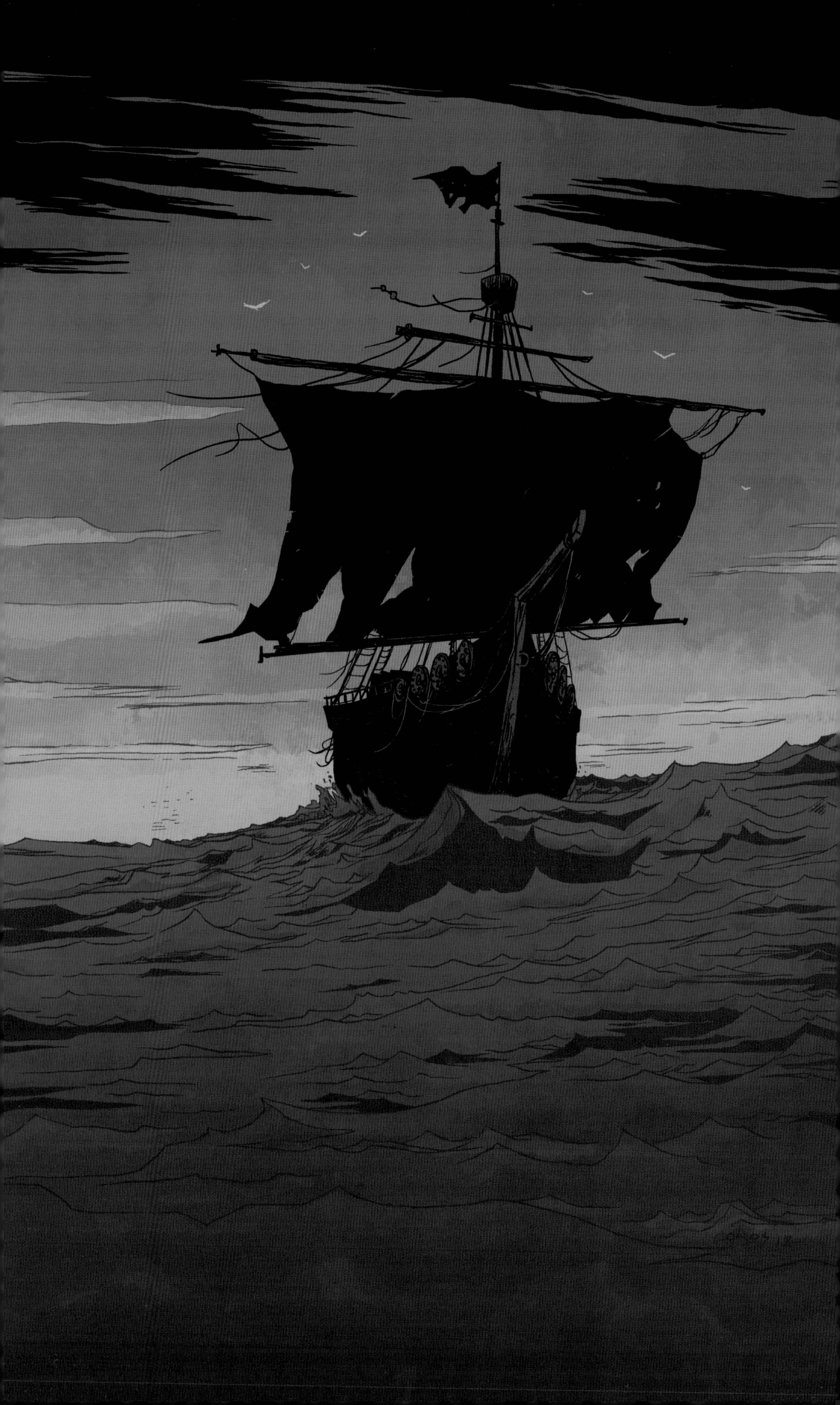

CHAPTER FOUR

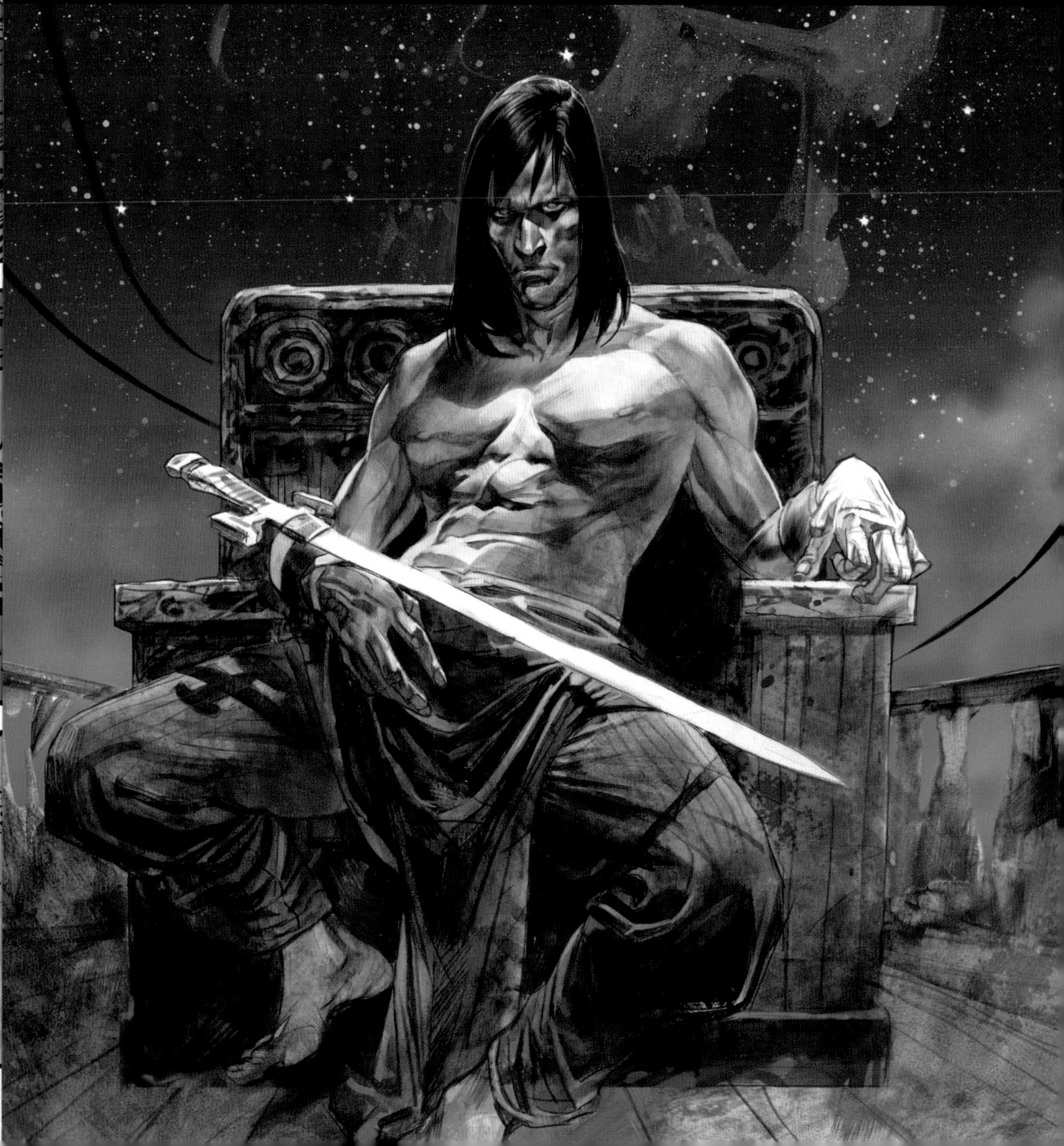

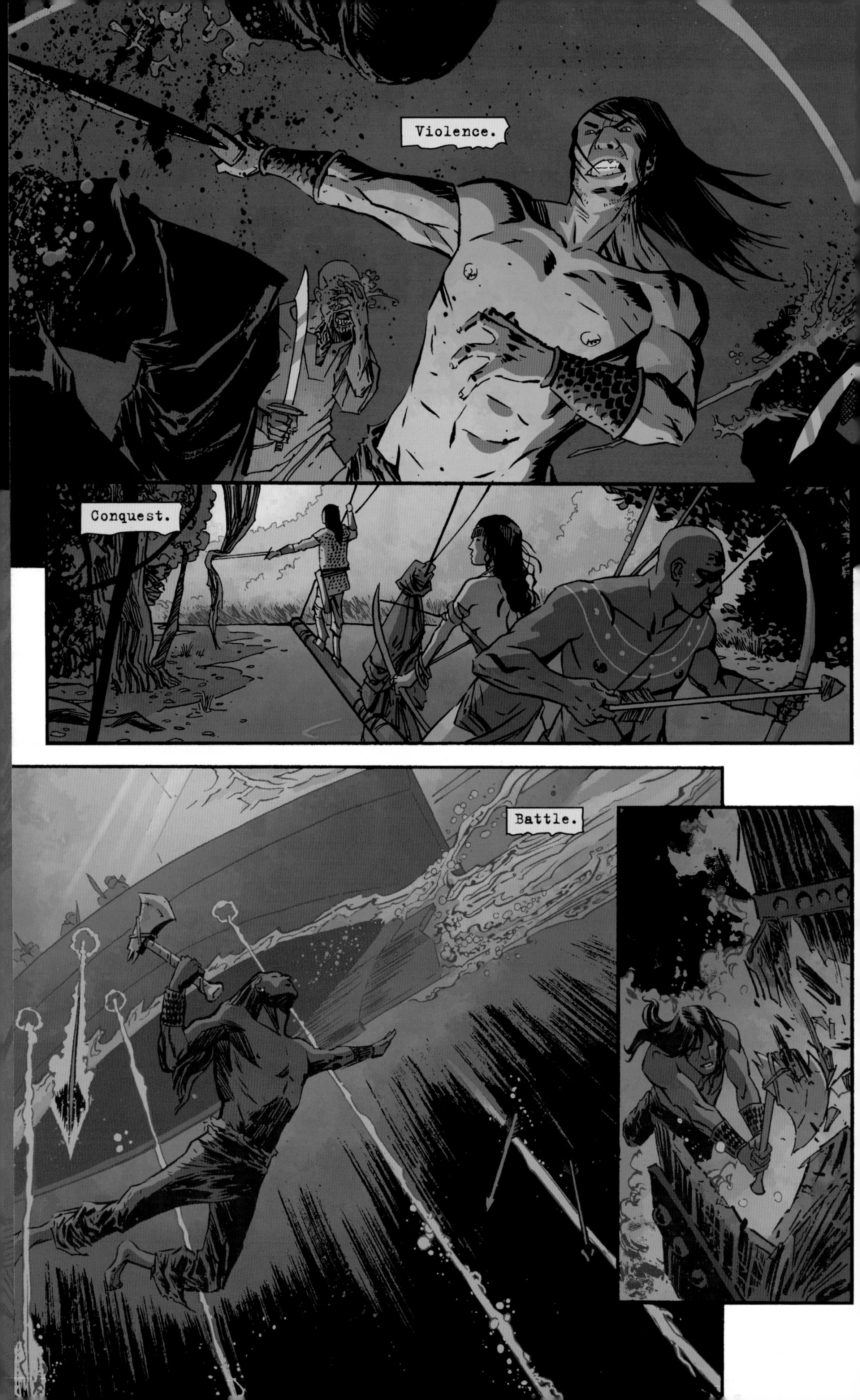
Violence.
Conquest.
Battle.

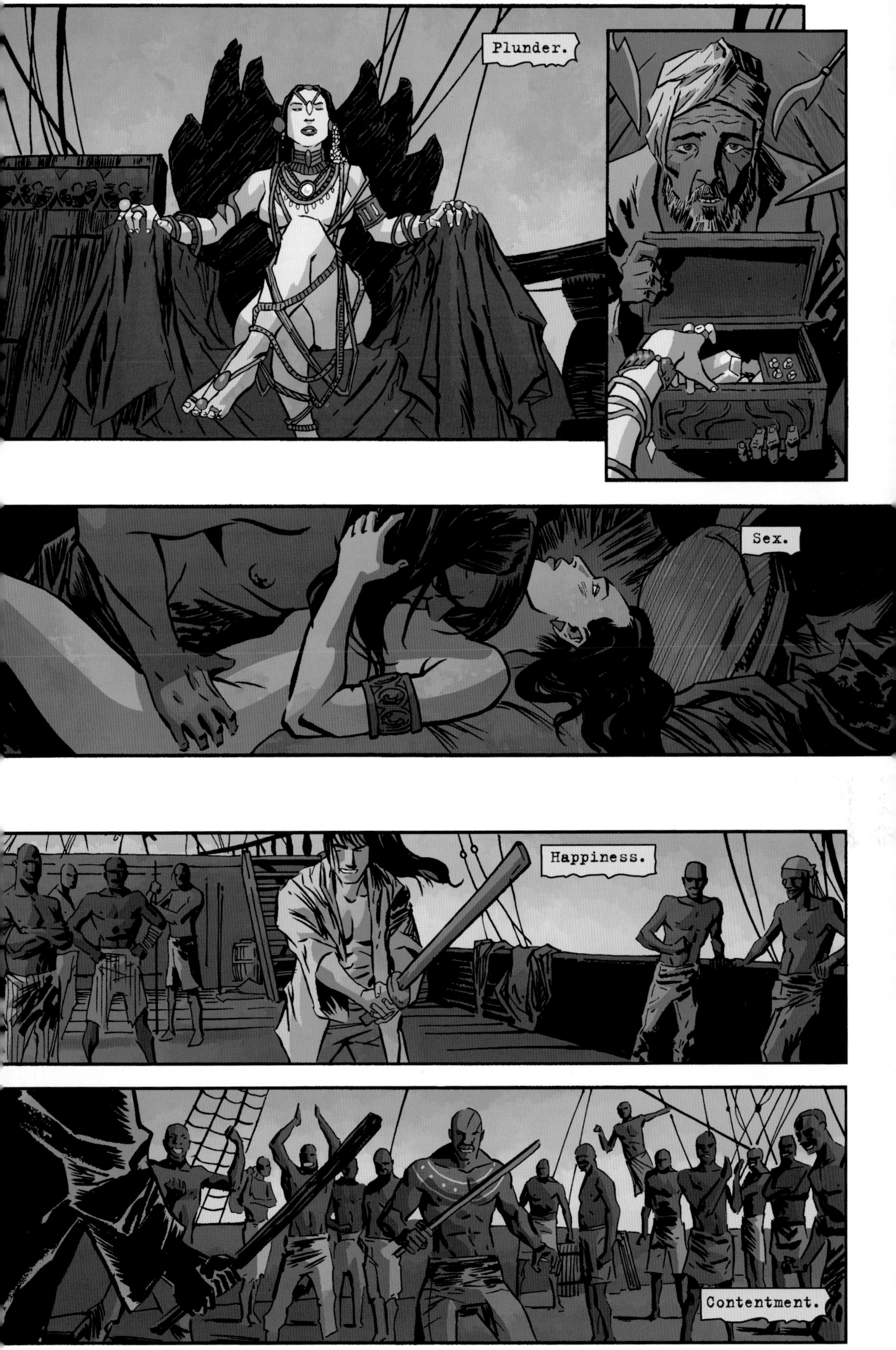
Plunder.
Sex.
Happiness.
Contentment.

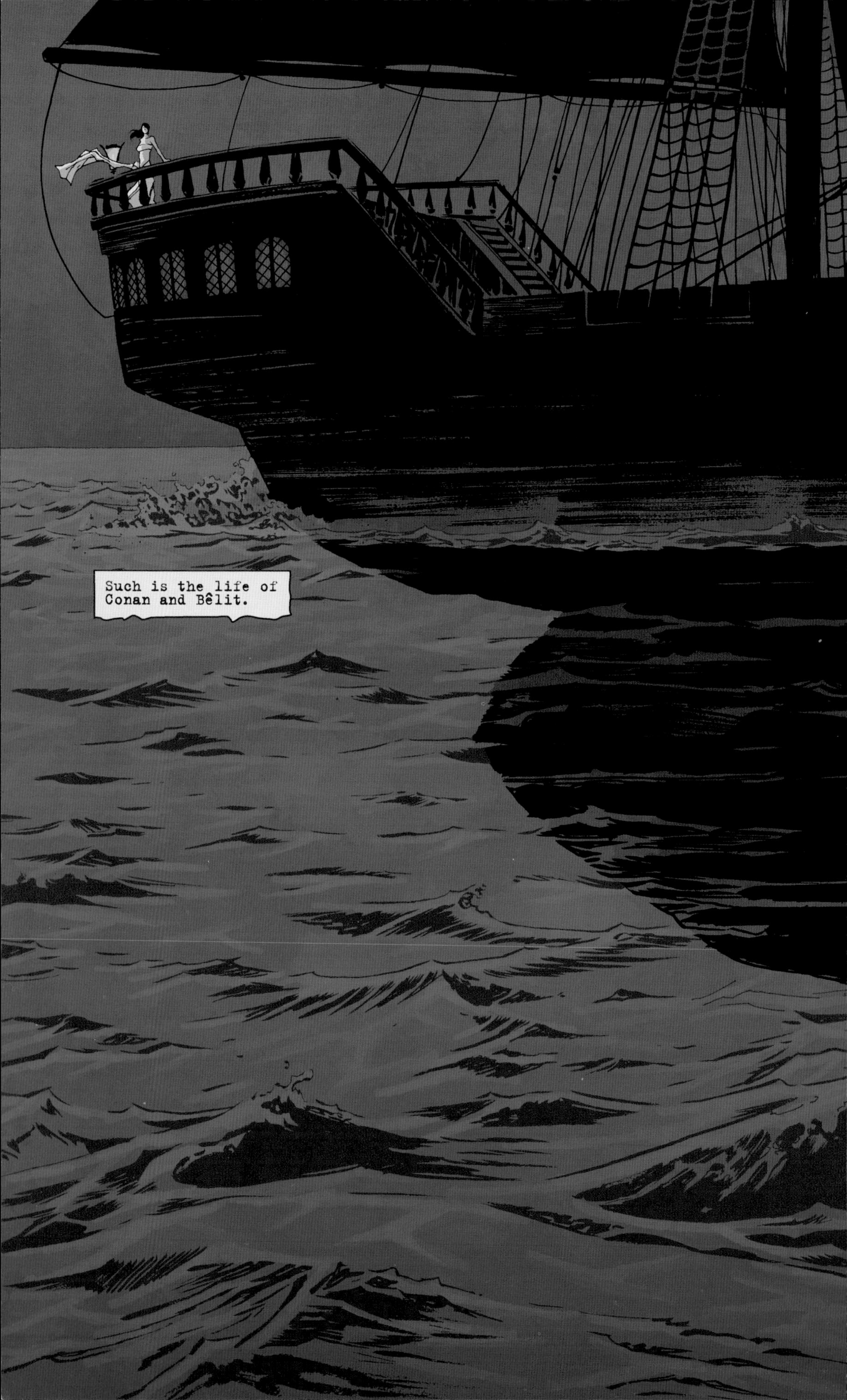
Such is the life of
Conan and Bêlit.

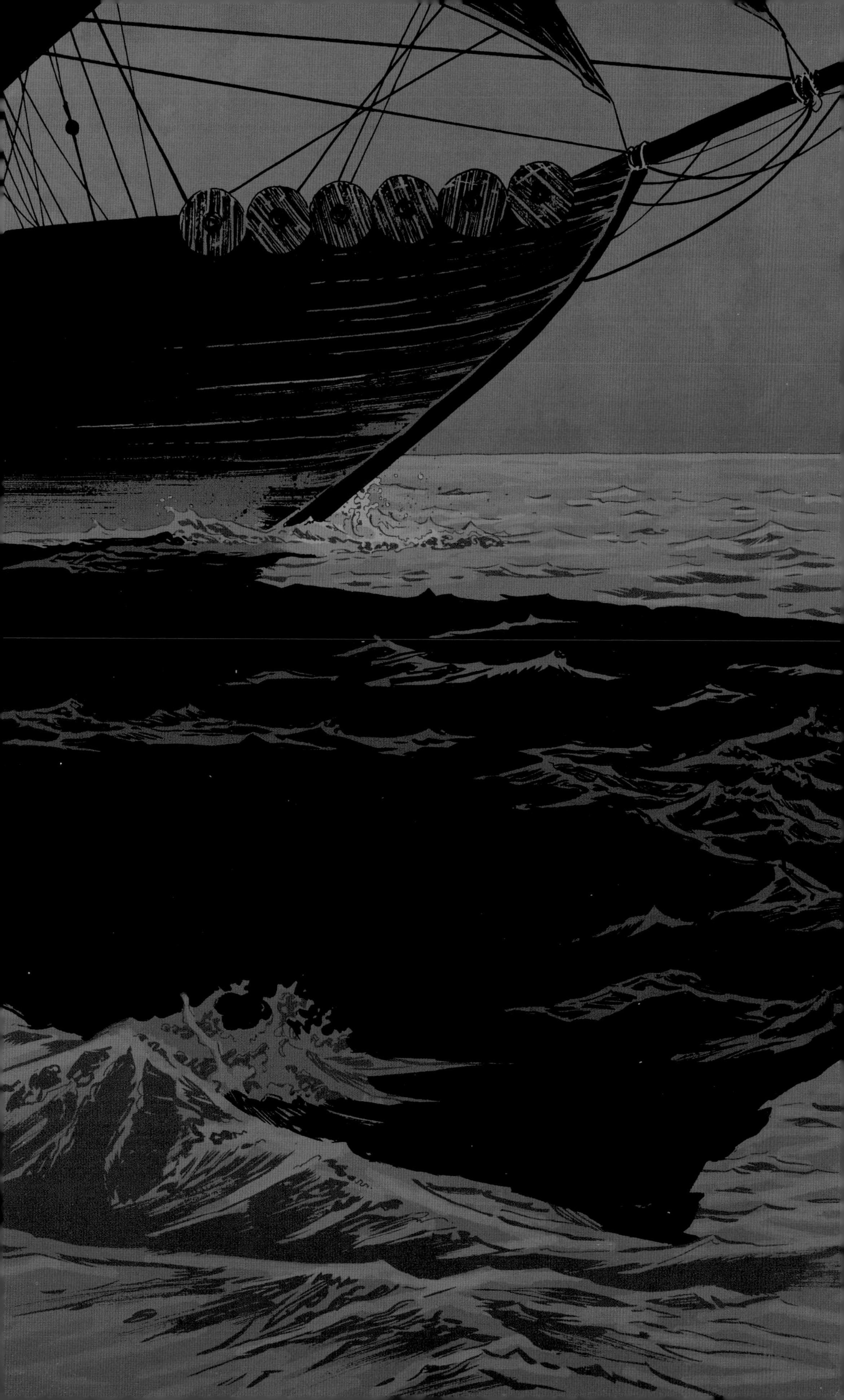

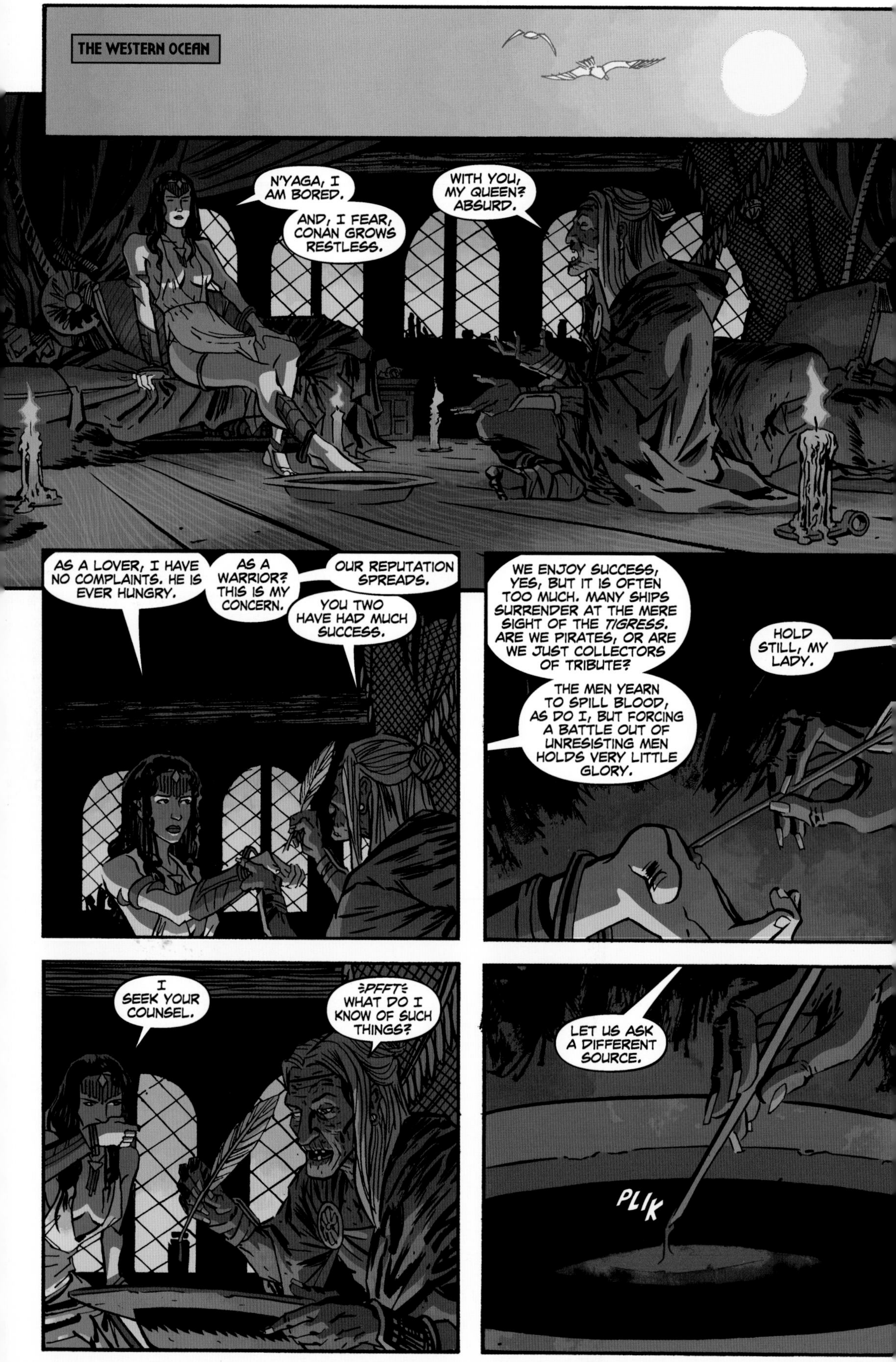
THE WESTERN OCEAN
N'YAGA, I AM BORED.
AND, I FEAR, CONAN GROWS RESTLESS.
WITH YOU, MY QUEEN? ABSURD.
AS A LOVER, I HAVE NO COMPLAINTS. HE IS EVER HUNGRY.
AS A WARRIOR? THIS IS MY CONCERN.
OUR REPUTATION SPREADS.
YOU TWO HAVE HAD MUCH SUCCESS.
WE ENJOY SUCCESS, YES, BUT IT IS OFTEN TOO MUCH. MANY SHIPS SURRENDER AT THE MERE SIGHT OF THE TIGRESS. ARE WE PIRATES, OR ARE WE JUST COLLECTORS OF TRIBUTE?
THE MEN YEARN TO SPILL BLOOD, AS DO I, BUT FORCING A BATTLE OUT OF UNRESISTING MEN HOLDS VERY LITTLE GLORY.
HOLD STILL, MY LADY.
I SEEK YOUR COUNSEL.
PFFT WHAT DO I KNOW OF SUCH THINGS?
LET US ASK A DIFFERENT SOURCE.
PLIK

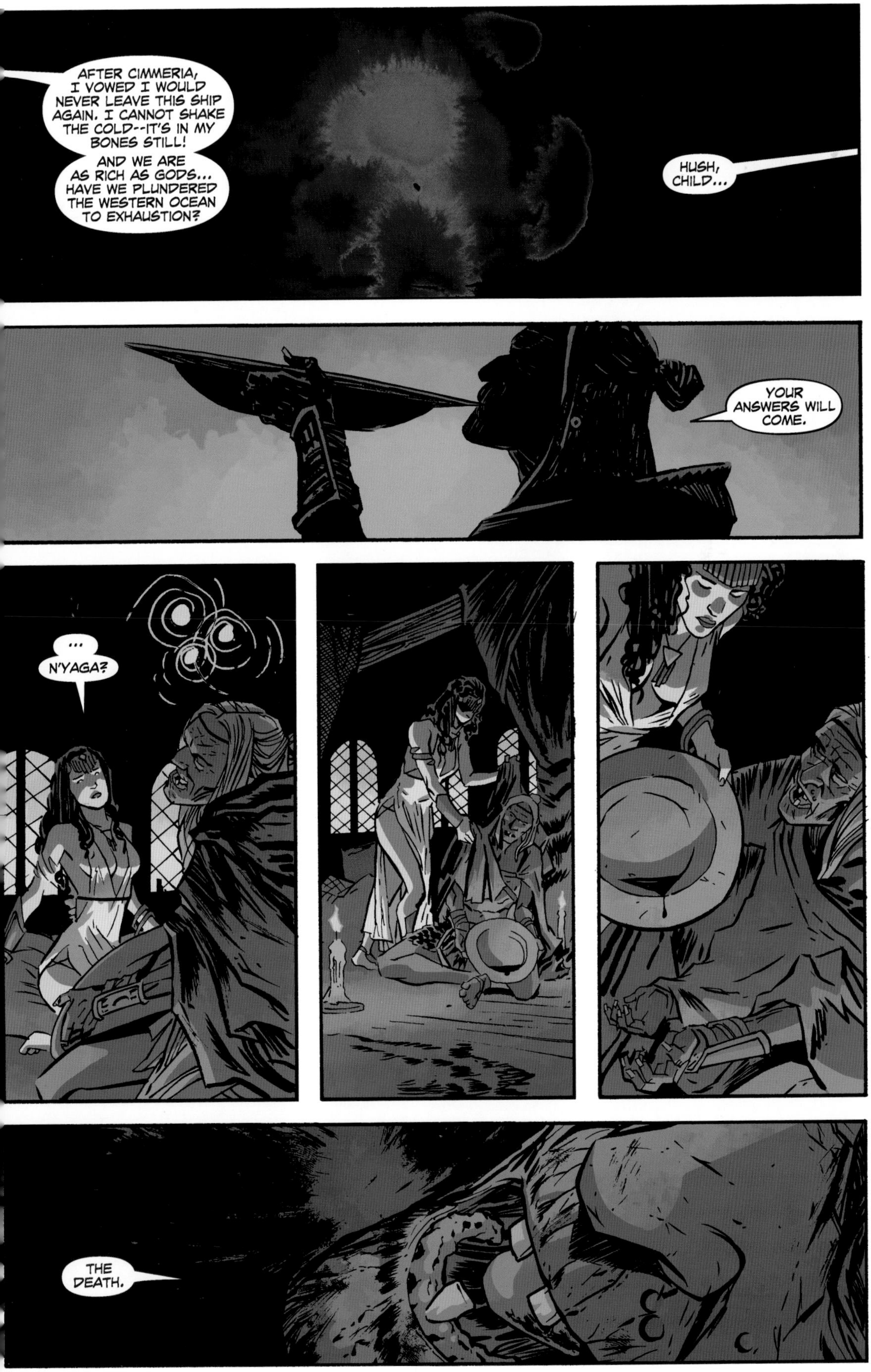
AFTER CIMMERIA, I VOWED I WOULD NEVER LEAVE THIS SHIP AGAIN. I CANNOT SHAKE THE COLD--IT'S IN MY BONES STILL!
AND WE ARE AS RICH AS GODS... HAVE WE PLUNDERED THE WESTERN OCEAN TO EXHAUSTION?
HUSH, CHILD...
YOUR ANSWERS WILL COME.
... N'YAGA?
THE DEATH.

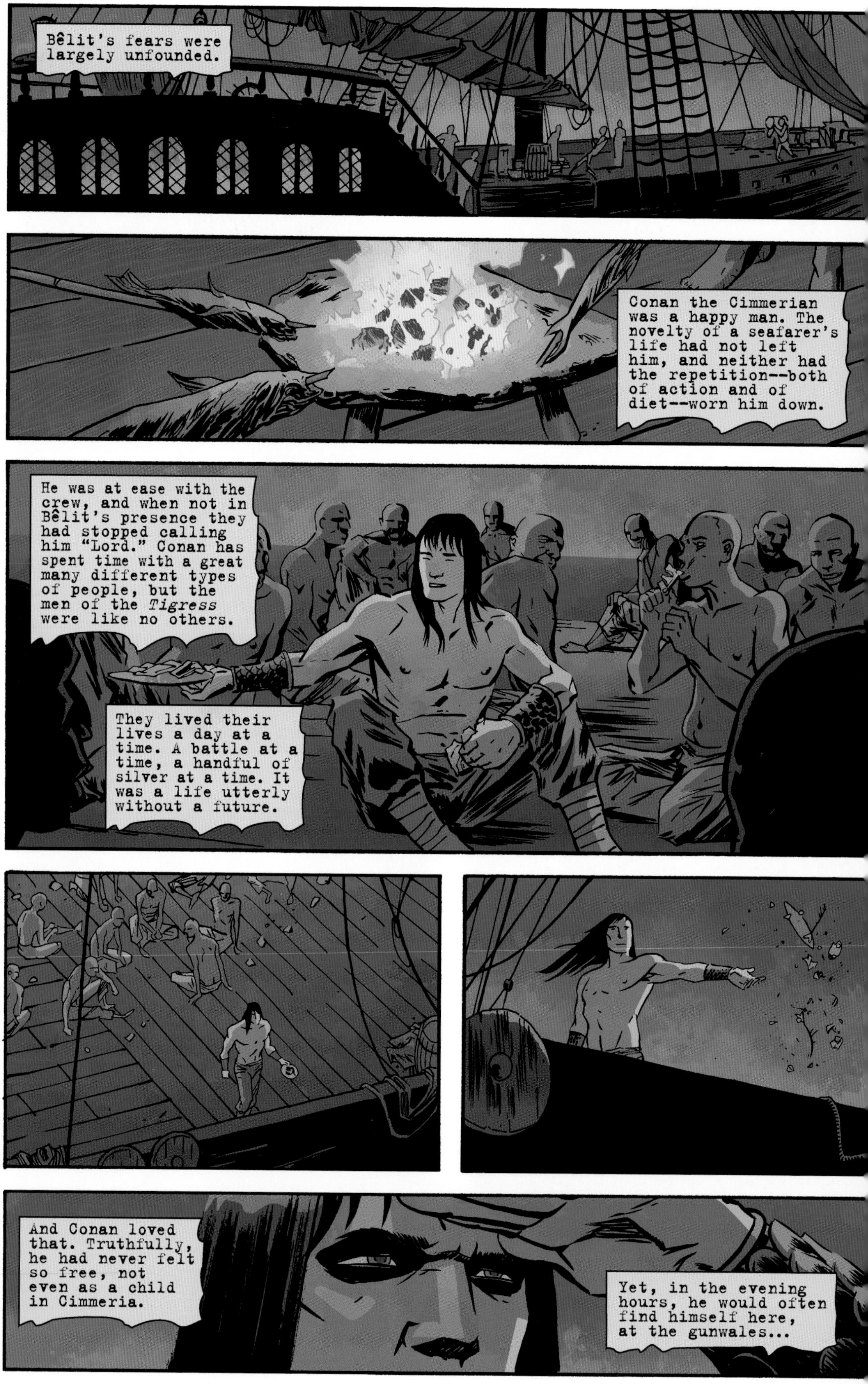
Bêlit's fears were largely unfounded.
Conan the Cimmerian was a happy man. The novelty of a seafarer's life had not left him, and neither had the repetition--both of action and of diet--worn him down.
He was at ease with the crew, and when not in Bêlit's presence they had stopped calling him "Lord." Conan has spent time with a great many different types of people, but the men of the *Tigress* were like no others.
They lived their lives a day at a time. A battle at a time, a handful of silver at a time. It was a life utterly without a future.
And Conan loved that. Truthfully, he had never felt so free, not even as a child in Cimmeria.
Yet, in the evening hours, he would often find himself here, at the gunwales...

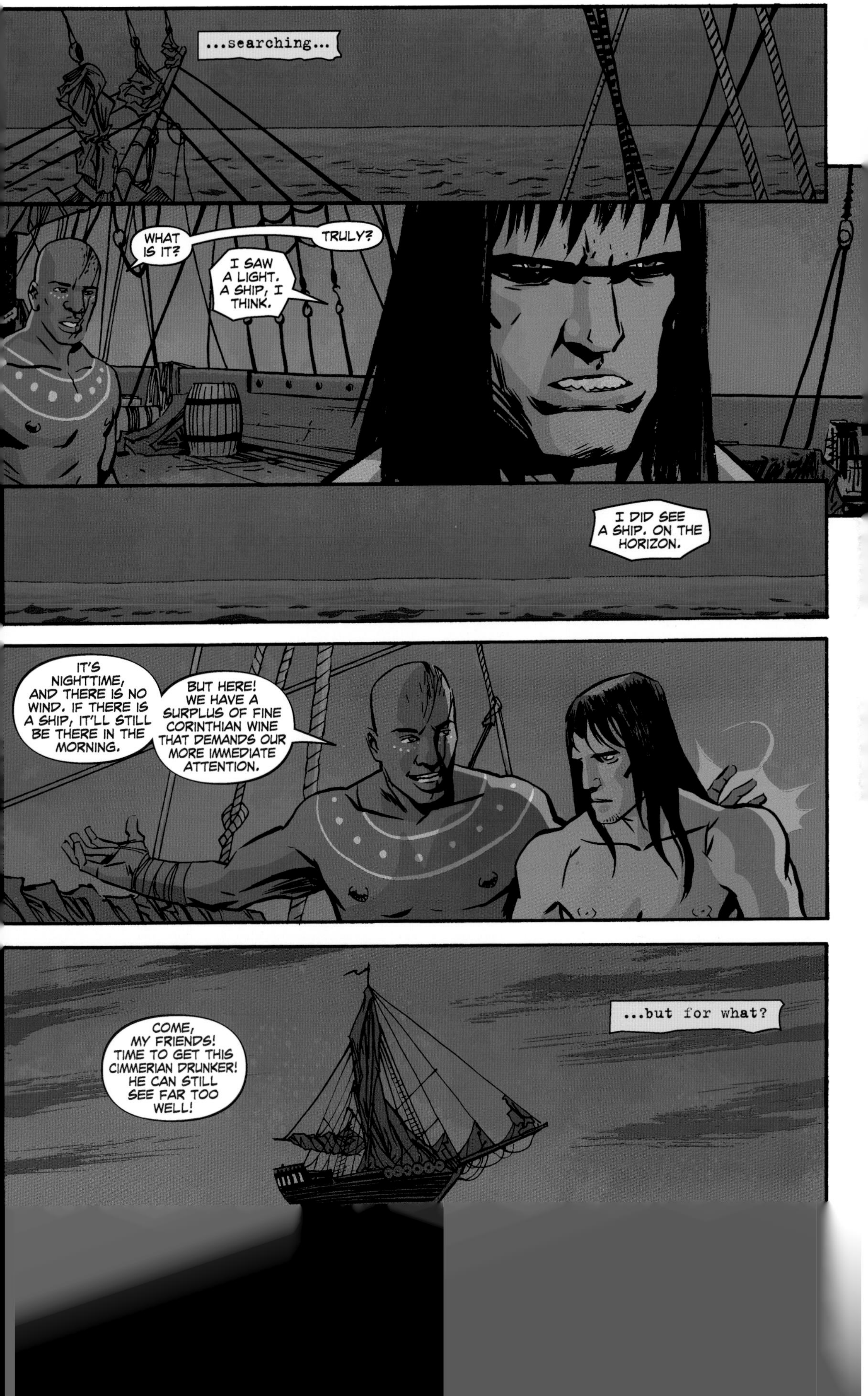
...searching...
WHAT IS IT?
TRULY?
I SAW A LIGHT. A SHIP, I THINK.
I DID SEE A SHIP. ON THE HORIZON.
IT'S NIGHTTIME, AND THERE IS NO WIND. IF THERE IS A SHIP, IT'LL STILL BE THERE IN THE MORNING.
BUT HERE! WE HAVE A SURPLUS OF FINE CORINTHIAN WINE THAT DEMANDS OUR MORE IMMEDIATE ATTENTION.
...but for what?
COME, MY FRIENDS! TIME TO GET THIS CIMMERIAN DRUNKER! HE CAN STILL SEE FAR TOO WELL!

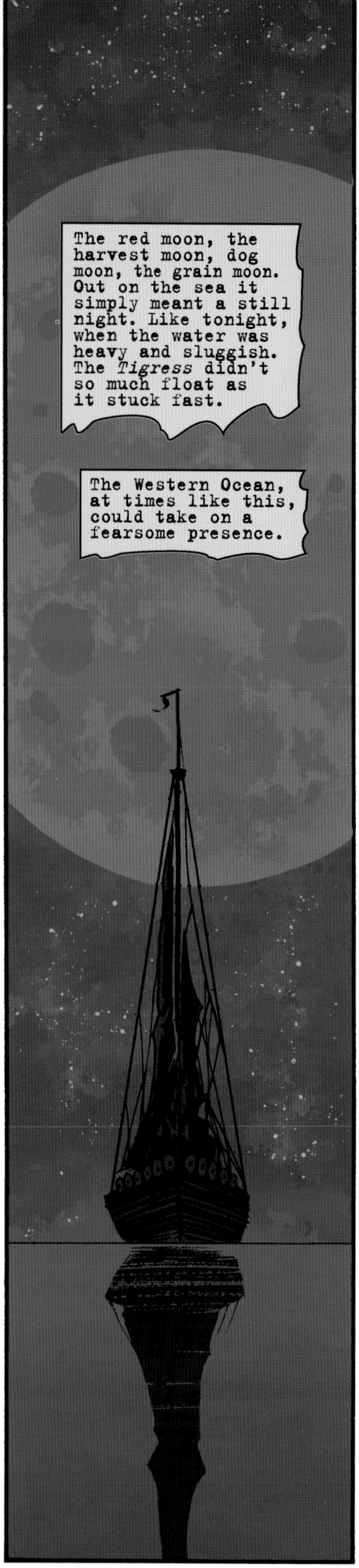
The red moon, the harvest moon, dog moon, the grain moon. Out on the sea it simply meant a still night. Like tonight, when the water was heavy and sluggish. The *Tigress* didn't so much float as it stuck fast.
The Western Ocean, at times like this, could take on a fearsome presence.

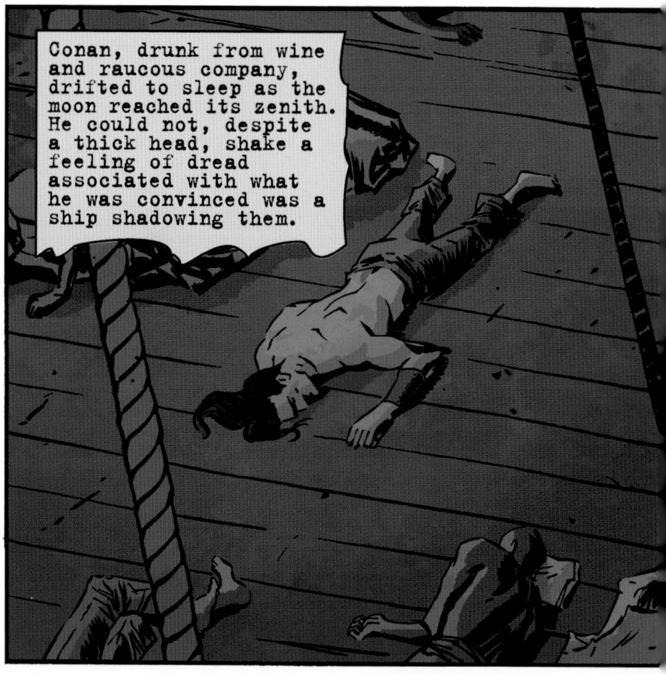
Conan, drunk from wine and raucous company, drifted to sleep as the moon reached its zenith. He could not, despite a thick head, shake a feeling of dread associated with what he was convinced was a ship shadowing them.

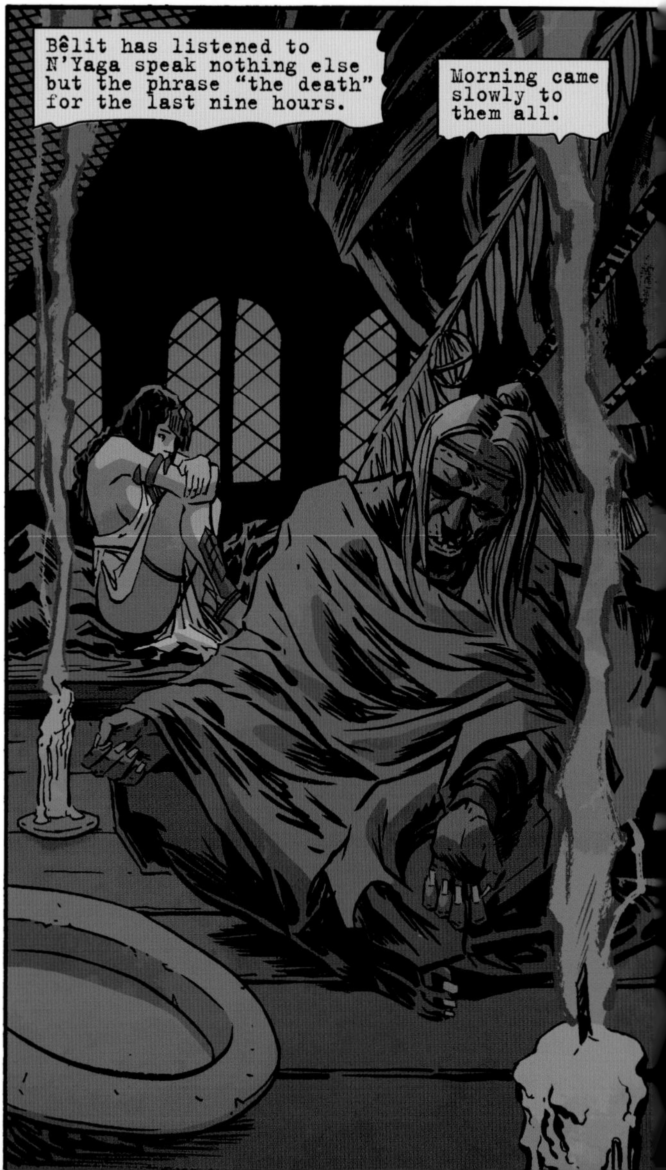
Bêlit has listened to N'Yaga speak nothing else but the phrase "the death" for the last nine hours.
Morning came slowly to them all.

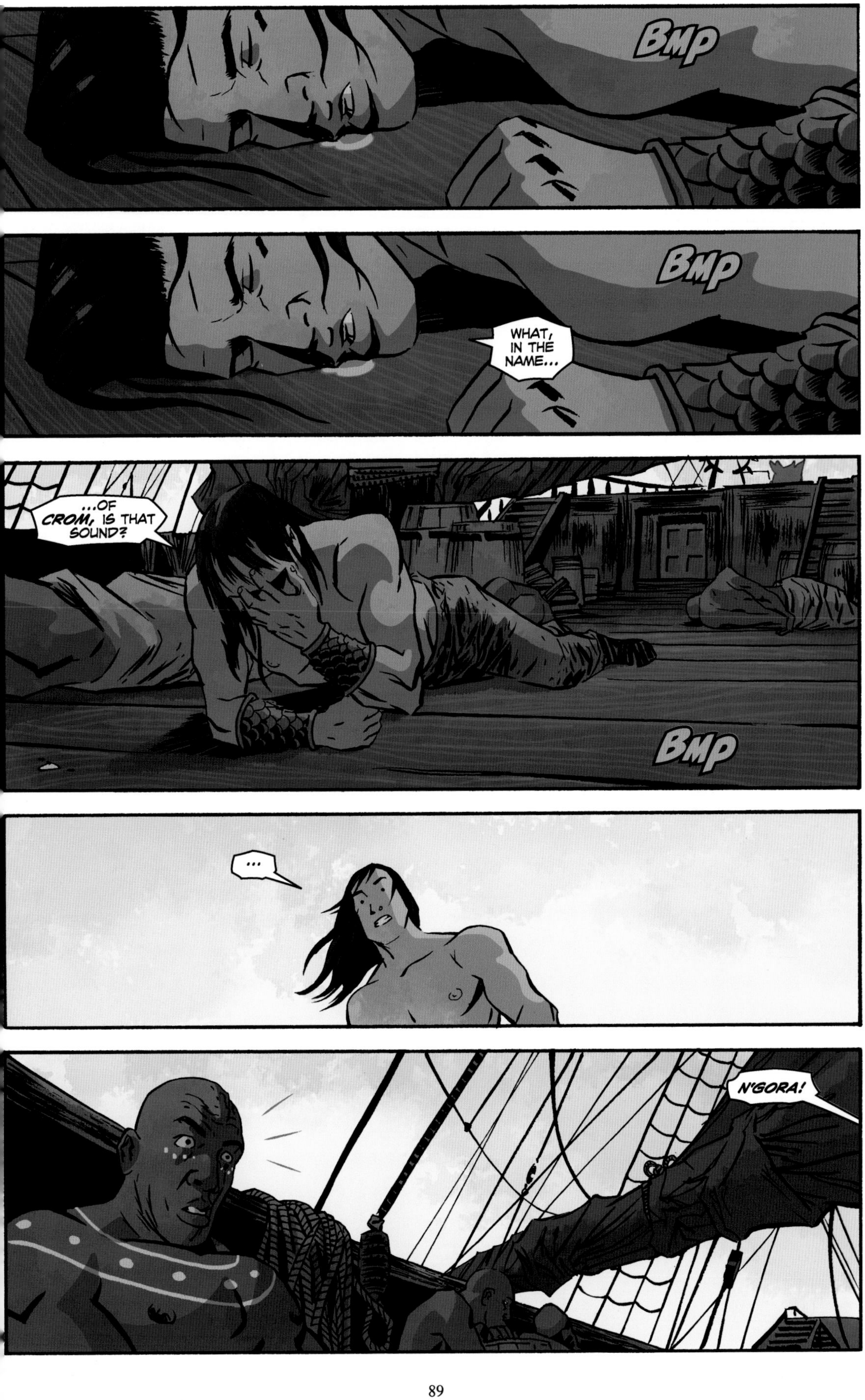
BMP
BMP
WHAT, IN THE NAME...
...OF CROM, IS THAT SOUND?
BMP
...
N'GORA!

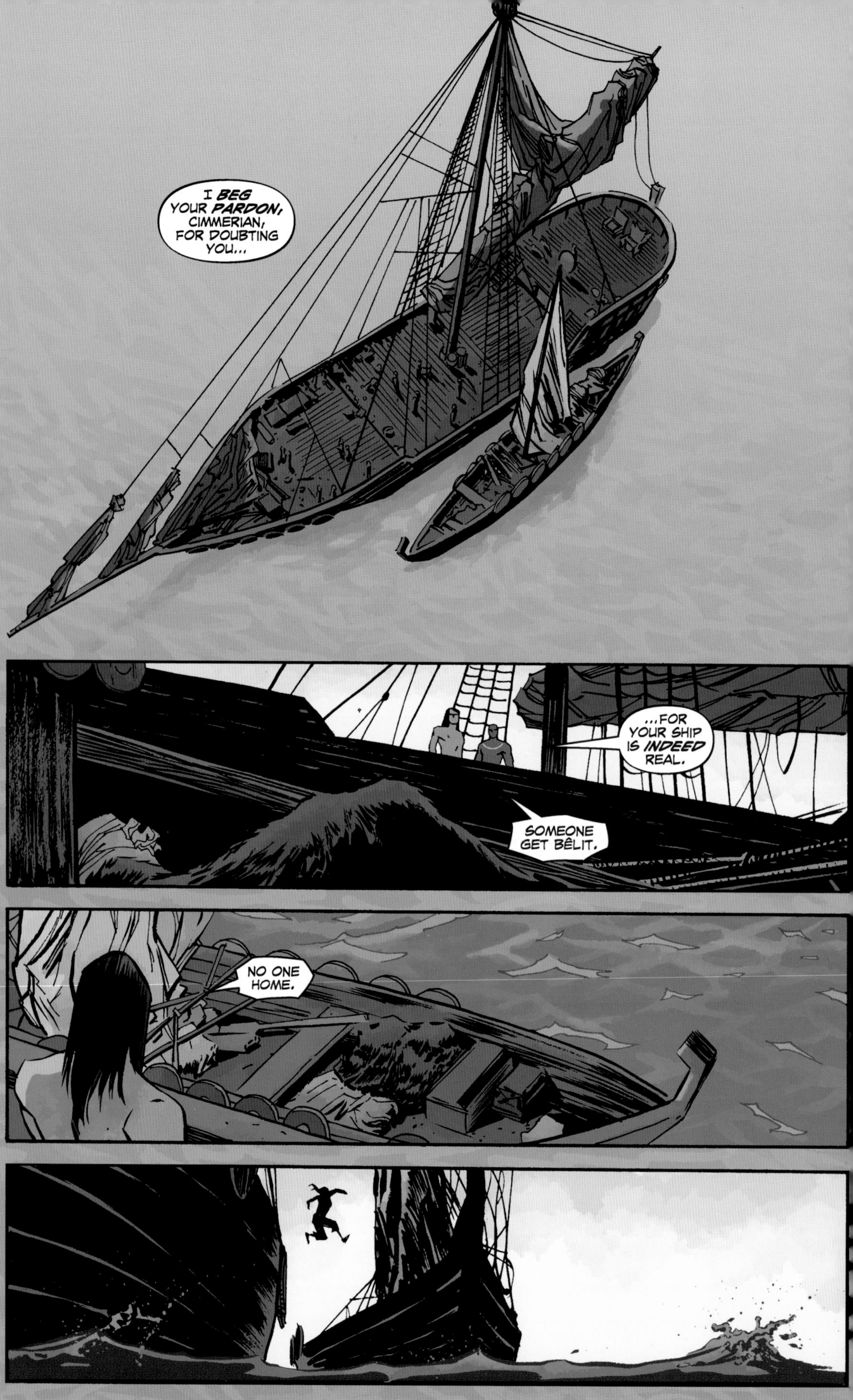
I BEG YOUR PARDON, CIMMERIAN, FOR DOUBTING YOU...
...FOR YOUR SHIP IS INDEED REAL.
SOMEONE GET BÊLIT.
NO ONE HOME.

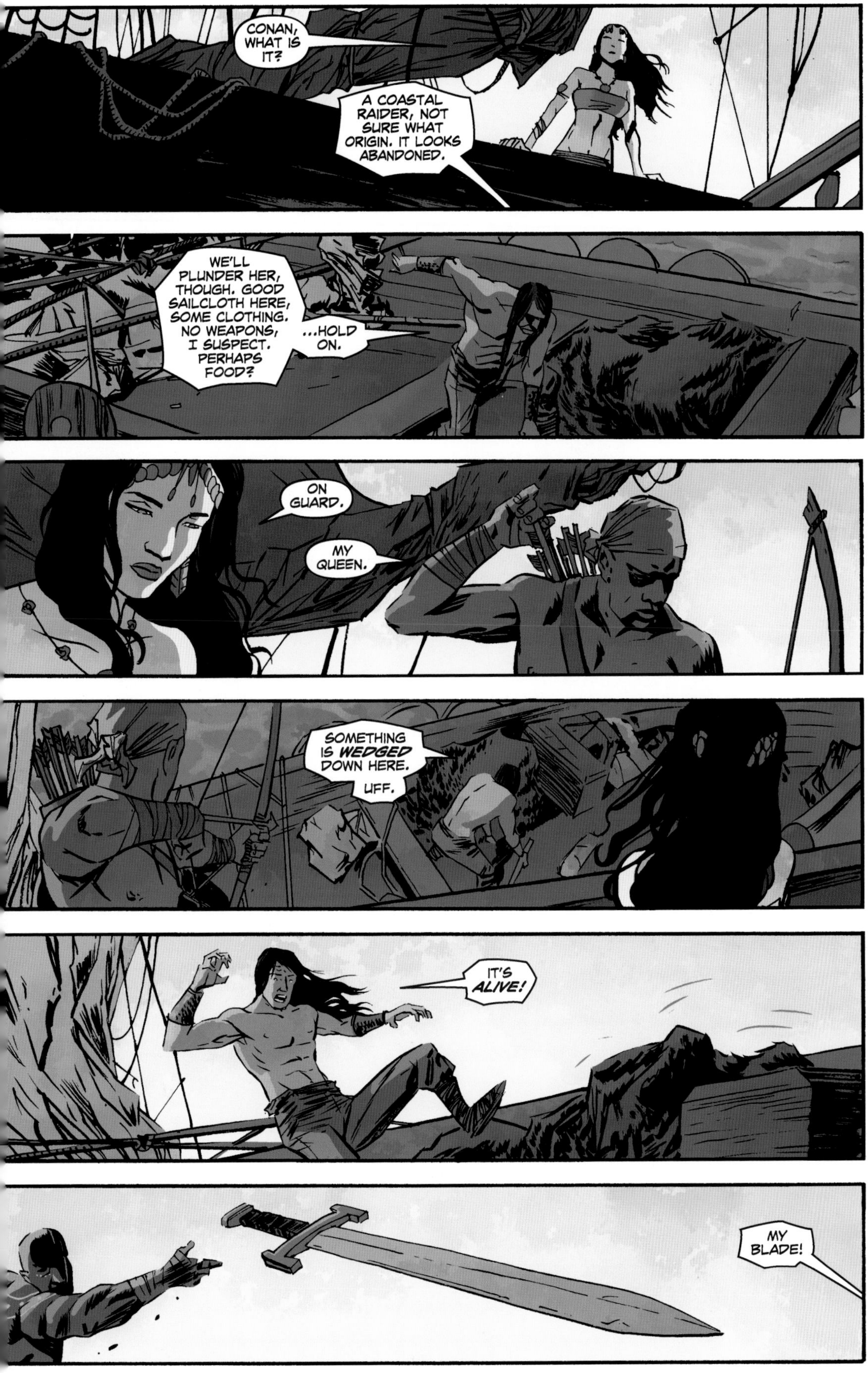
CONAN, WHAT IS IT?
A COASTAL RAIDER, NOT SURE WHAT ORIGIN. IT LOOKS ABANDONED.
WE'LL PLUNDER HER, THOUGH. GOOD SAILCLOTH HERE, SOME CLOTHING. NO WEAPONS, I SUSPECT. PERHAPS FOOD?
...HOLD ON.
ON GUARD.
MY QUEEN.
SOMETHING IS ***WEDGED*** DOWN HERE.
UFF.
IT'S ***ALIVE!***
MY BLADE!

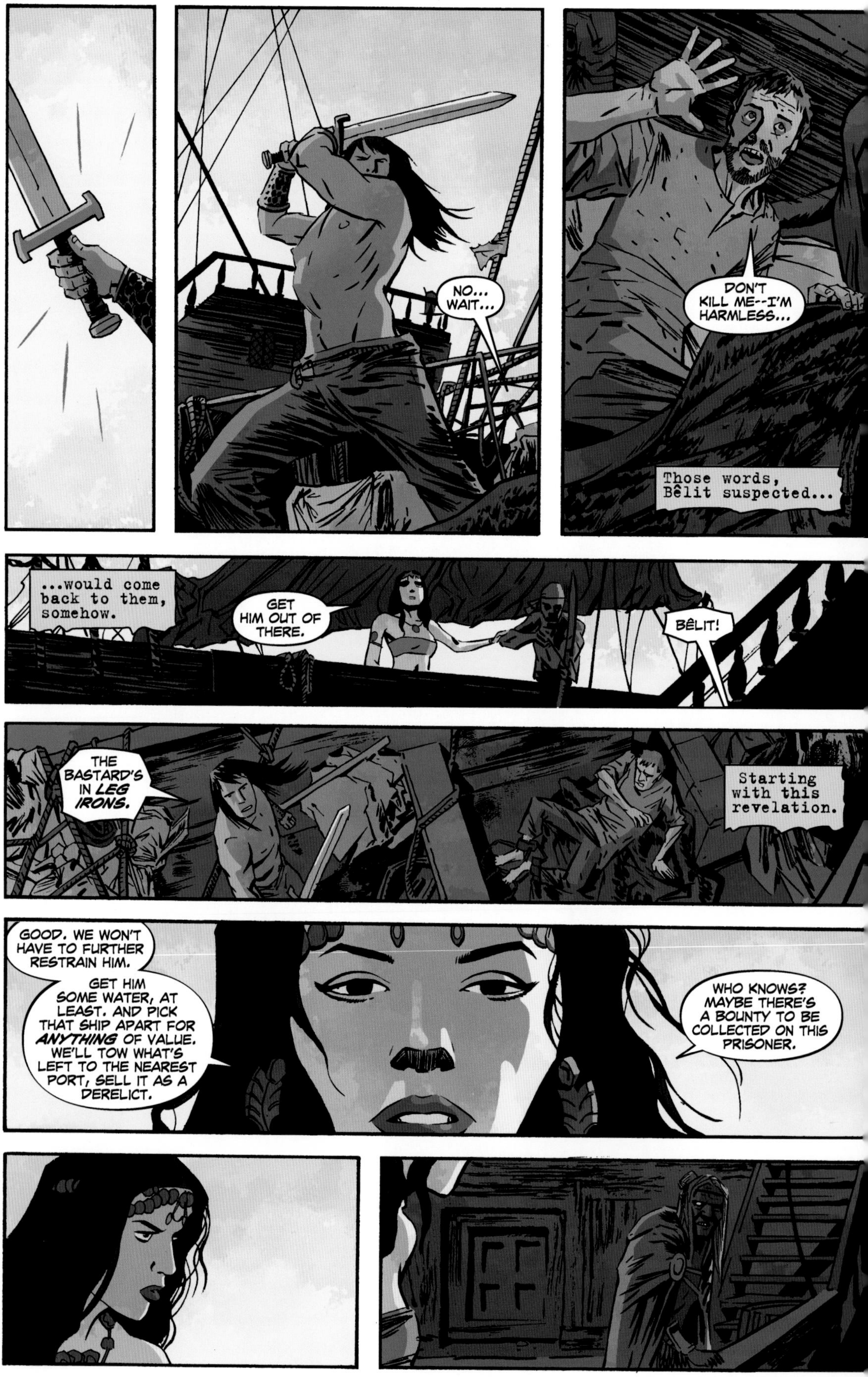
NO... WAIT...
DON'T KILL ME--I'M HARMLESS...
Those words, Bêlit suspected...
...would come back to them, somehow.
GET HIM OUT OF THERE.
BÊLIT!
THE BASTARD'S IN LEG IRONS.
Starting with this revelation.
GOOD. WE WON'T HAVE TO FURTHER RESTRAIN HIM.
GET HIM SOME WATER, AT LEAST. AND PICK THAT SHIP APART FOR ANYTHING OF VALUE. WE'LL TOW WHAT'S LEFT TO THE NEAREST PORT, SELL IT AS A DERELICT.
WHO KNOWS? MAYBE THERE'S A BOUNTY TO BE COLLECTED ON THIS PRISONER.

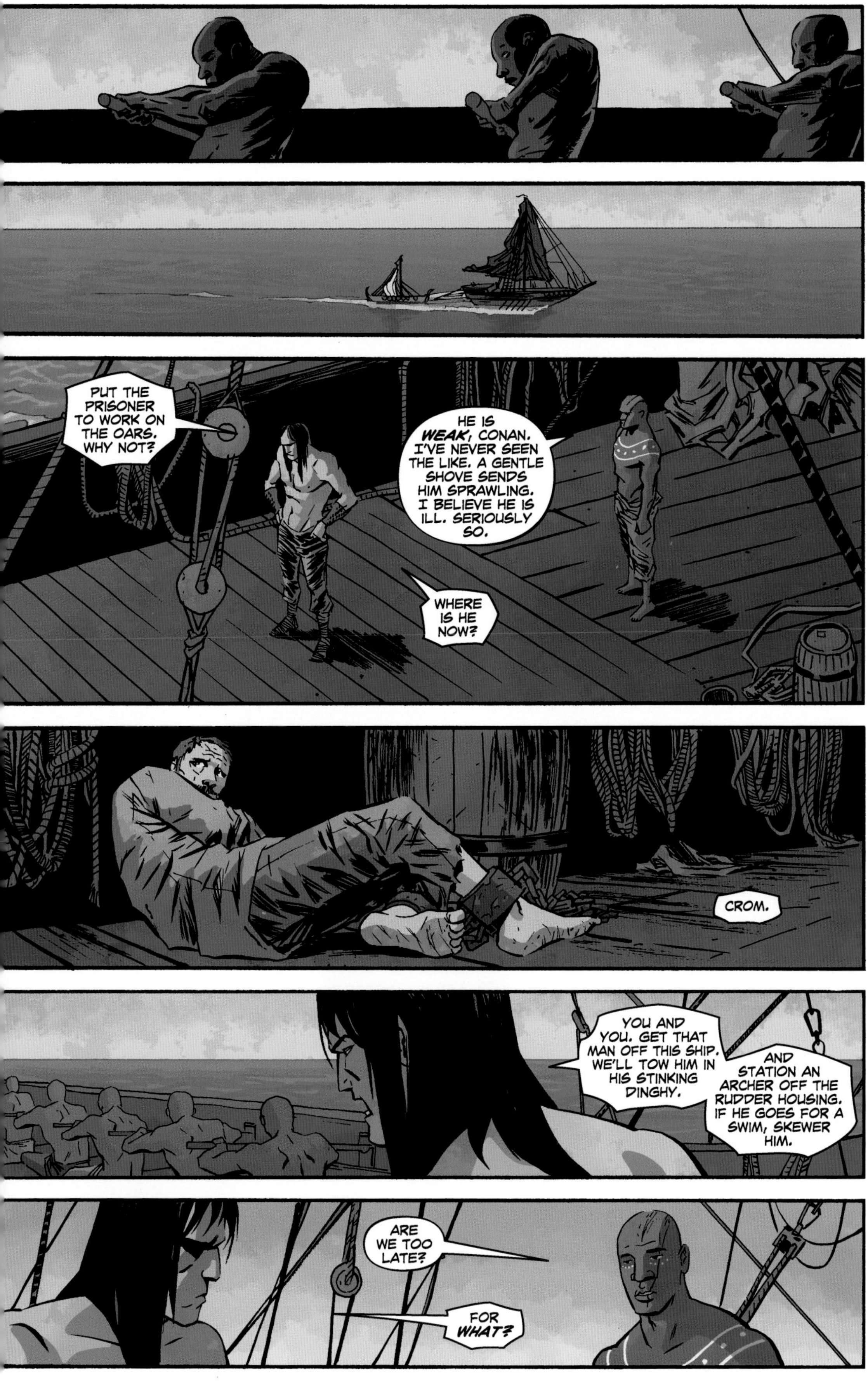
PUT THE PRISONER TO WORK ON THE OARS. WHY NOT?
HE IS *WEAK*, CONAN. I'VE NEVER SEEN THE LIKE. A GENTLE SHOVE SENDS HIM SPRAWLING. I BELIEVE HE IS ILL. SERIOUSLY SO.
WHERE IS HE NOW?
CROM.
YOU AND YOU. GET THAT MAN OFF THIS SHIP. WE'LL TOW HIM IN HIS STINKING DINGHY.
AND STATION AN ARCHER OFF THE RUDDER HOUSING. IF HE GOES FOR A SWIM, SKEWER HIM.
ARE WE TOO LATE?
FOR *WHAT?*

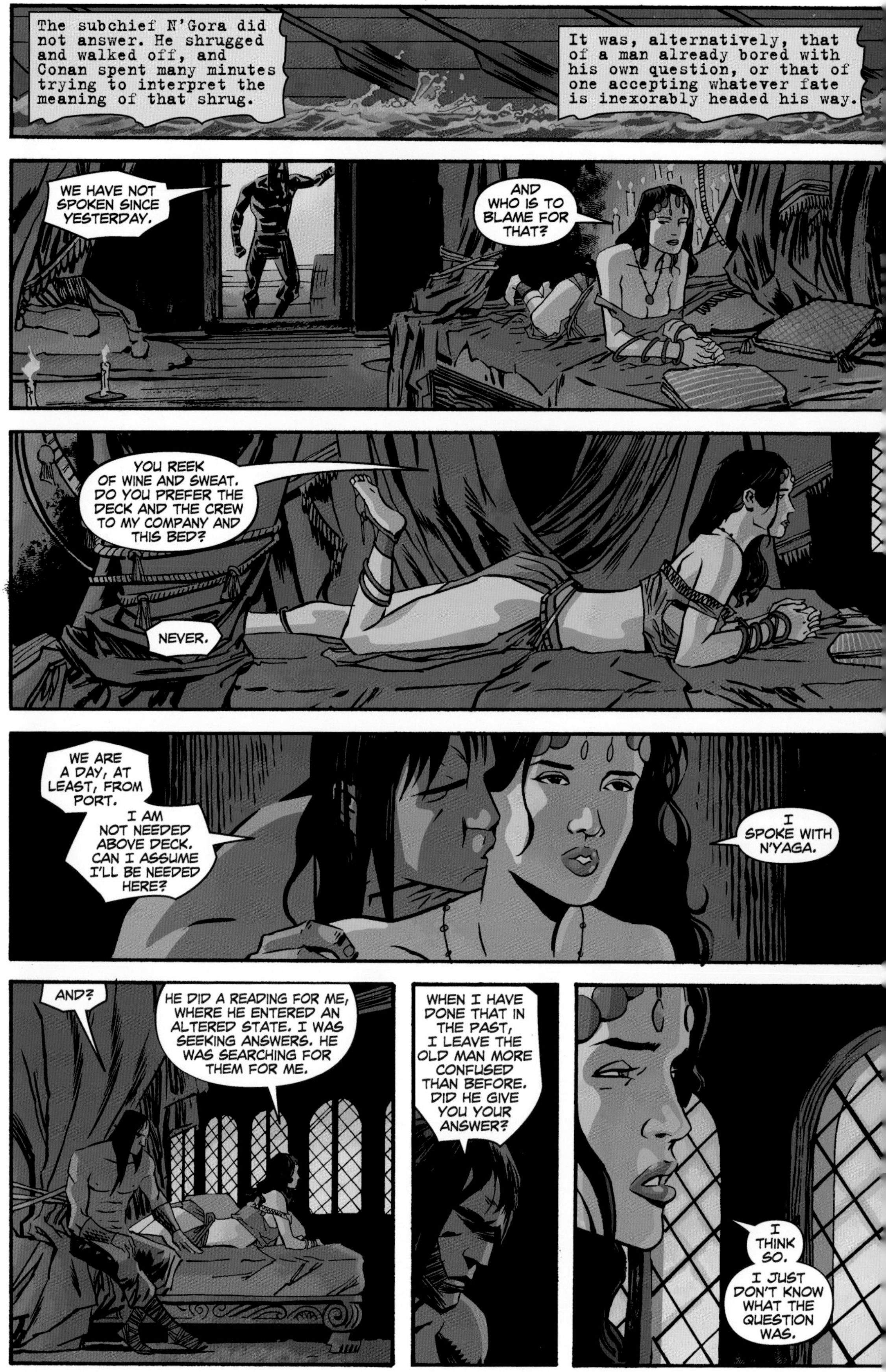
The subchief N'Gora did not answer. He shrugged and walked off, and Conan spent many minutes trying to interpret the meaning of that shrug.
It was, alternatively, that of a man already bored with his own question, or that of one accepting whatever fate is inexorably headed his way.
WE HAVE NOT SPOKEN SINCE YESTERDAY.
AND WHO IS TO BLAME FOR THAT?
YOU REEK OF WINE AND SWEAT. DO YOU PREFER THE DECK AND THE CREW TO MY COMPANY AND THIS BED?
NEVER.
WE ARE A DAY, AT LEAST, FROM PORT.
I AM NOT NEEDED ABOVE DECK. CAN I ASSUME I'LL BE NEEDED HERE?
I SPOKE WITH N'YAGA.
AND?
HE DID A READING FOR ME, WHERE HE ENTERED AN ALTERED STATE. I WAS SEEKING ANSWERS. HE WAS SEARCHING FOR THEM FOR ME.
WHEN I HAVE DONE THAT IN THE PAST, I LEAVE THE OLD MAN MORE CONFUSED THAN BEFORE. DID HE GIVE YOU YOUR ANSWER?
I THINK SO.
I JUST DON'T KNOW WHAT THE QUESTION WAS.

YOU SPEAK IN RIDDLES, LIKE N'YAGA.

CONAN, I THINK BACK TO YOU IN CIMMERIA. YOU SEEMED TO COME ALIVE, MORE ALIVE THAN I SEE YOU HERE. YET, YOU RETURNED WITH ME TO THE *TIGRESS*.

WHY?

CIMMERIA IS FAMILIAR. A FAMILIAR SURROUNDING CAN BE A COMFORT, AND CAN ALSO MAKE ONE WEAK.

I AM HERE TO BE WITH YOU. BUT ALSO TO SEE SIGHTS THAT MOST CIMMERIANS COULD NOT DREAM UP. NOT EVEN WITH A *BARREL* OF N'GORA'S RANCID WINE.

WHAT DOES THIS HAVE TO DO WITH N'YAGA?

WHAT DID HE SAY TO YOU?

NOTHING. NONSENSE, A RIDDLE, LIKE YOU SAY.

WHAT DO YOU MAKE OF THAT FUGITIVE?

WHAT'S TO SAY? HE COULD BE A CRIMINAL, OR AN ESCAPED SLAVE. HE COULD EARN US A NICE BOUNTY, OR WE'LL HAVE A FIGHT ON OUR HANDS. I WON'T HAND OVER A SLAVE.

N'GORA CLAIMS HE'S SICK.

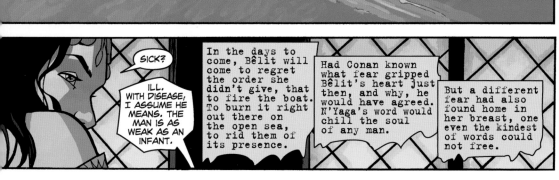

SICK?

ILL. WITH DISEASE, I ASSUME HE MEANS. THE MAN IS AS WEAK AS AN INFANT.

In the days to come, Bêlit will come to regret the order she didn't give, that to fire the boat. To burn it right out there on the open sea, to rid them of its presence.

Had Conan known what fear gripped Bêlit's heart just then, and why, he would have agreed. N'Yaga's word would chill the soul of any man.

But a different fear had also found home in her breast, one even the kindest of words could not free.

YOU WILL STAY WITH ME TONIGHT.

For a woman who, from childhood, has cultivated a strength and power to rival a king, this fear and doubt are unwelcome intruders, ones she is determined to chase off.

And under the specter of death, life and passion are that much more intense.

But the dark cloud remains, a roiling bundle of anxiety and fear. She wonders if Conan can sense it. She quickens her breath, and feels the press of his body in response.

N'Yaga's words haunt her so.

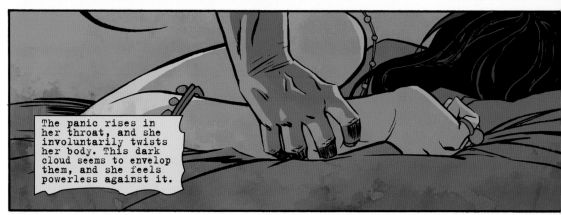

The panic rises in her throat, and she involuntarily twists her body. This dark cloud seems to envelop them, and she feels powerless against it.

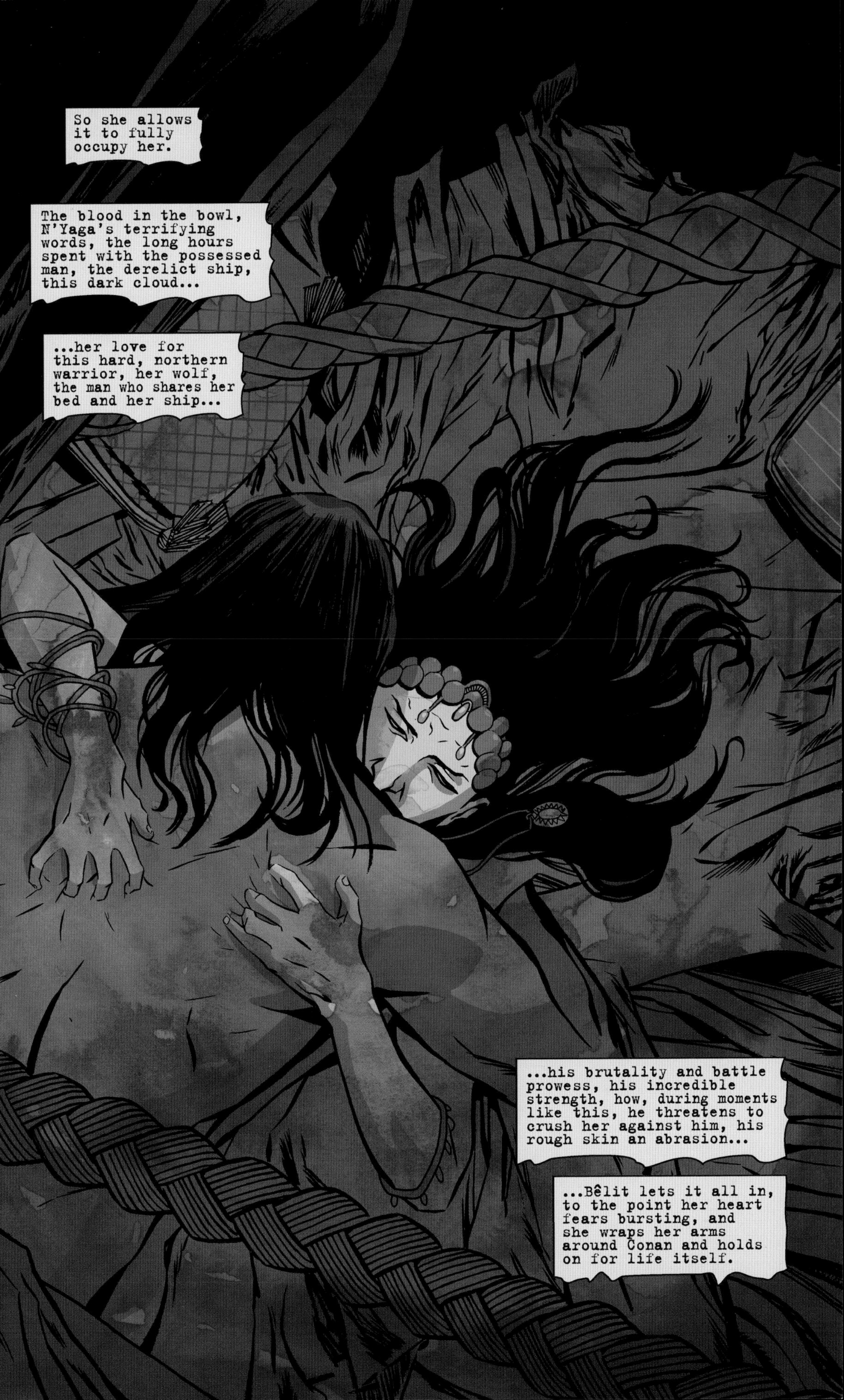
So she allows it to fully occupy her.
The blood in the bowl, N'Yaga's terrifying words, the long hours spent with the possessed man, the derelict ship, this dark cloud...
...her love for this hard, northern warrior, her wolf, the man who shares her bed and her ship...
...his brutality and battle prowess, his incredible strength, how, during moments like this, he threatens to crush her against him, his rough skin an abrasion...
...Bêlit lets it all in, to the point her heart fears bursting, and she wraps her arms around Conan and holds on for life itself.

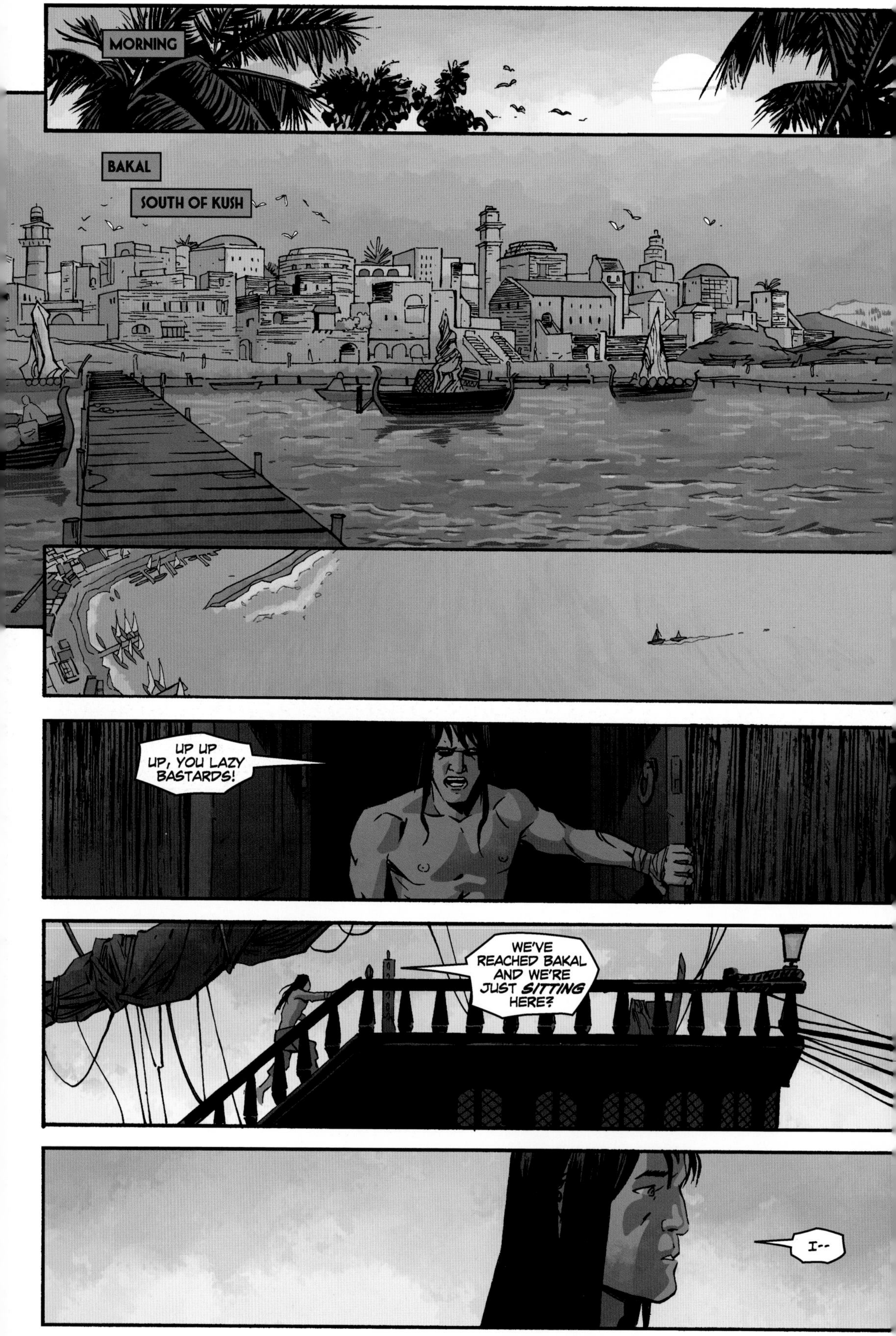
MORNING
BAKAL
SOUTH OF KUSH
UP UP UP, YOU LAZY BASTARDS!
WE'VE REACHED BAKAL AND WE'RE JUST *SITTING* HERE?
I--

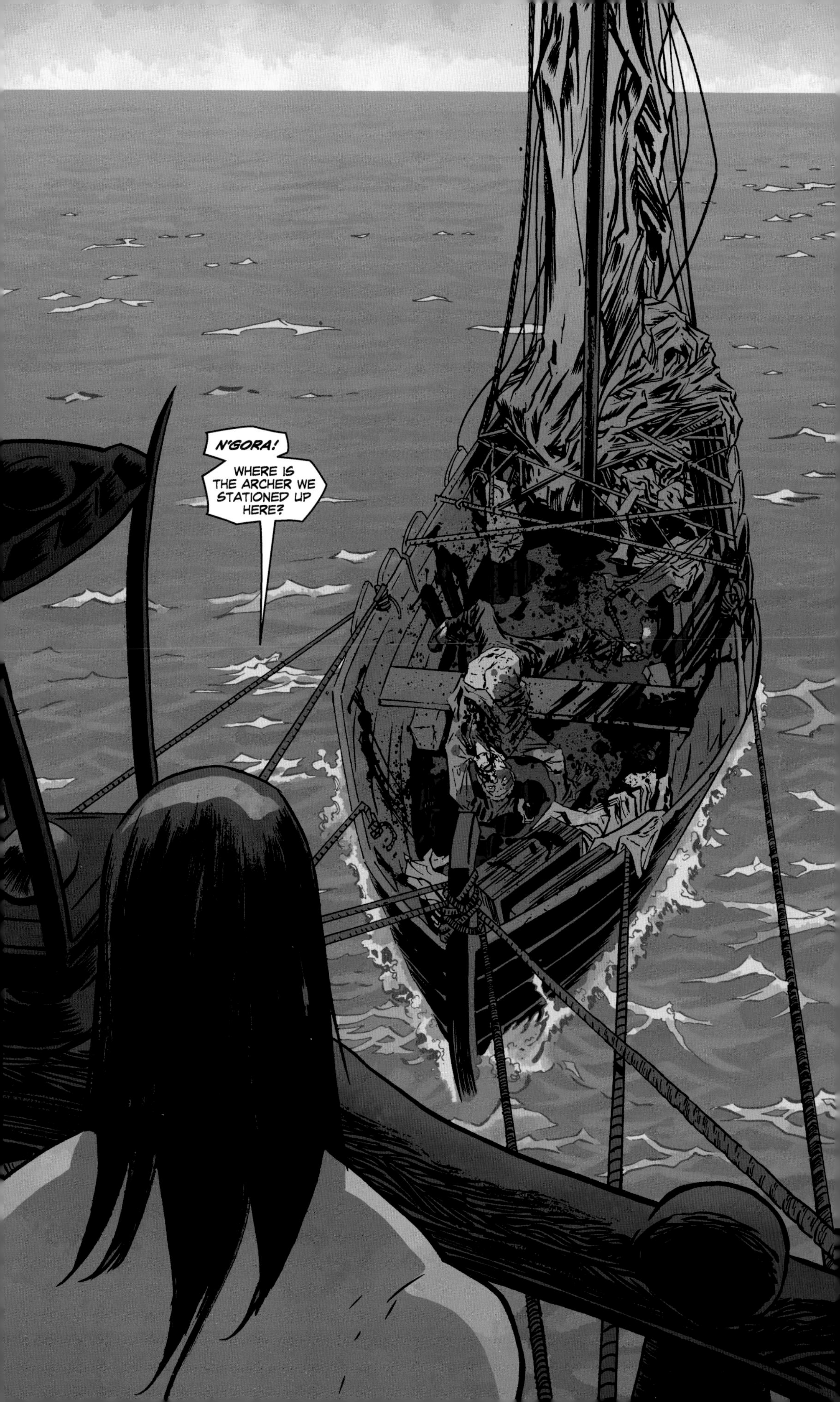
N'GORA!
WHERE IS THE ARCHER WE STATIONED UP HERE?

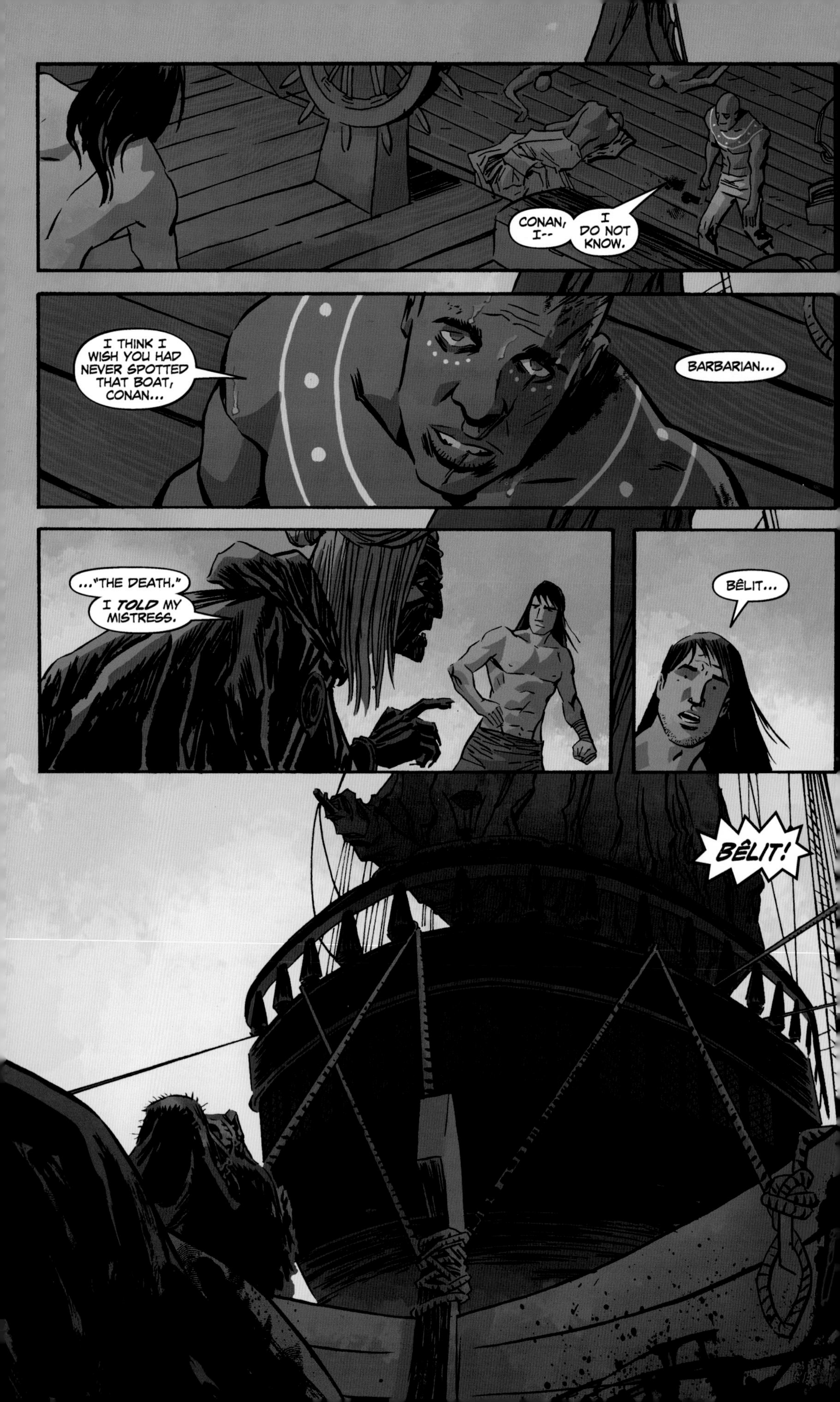
CONAN, I--
I DO NOT KNOW.
I THINK I WISH YOU HAD NEVER SPOTTED THAT BOAT, CONAN...
BARBARIAN...
..."THE DEATH." I TOLD MY MISTRESS.
BÊLIT...
BÊLIT!

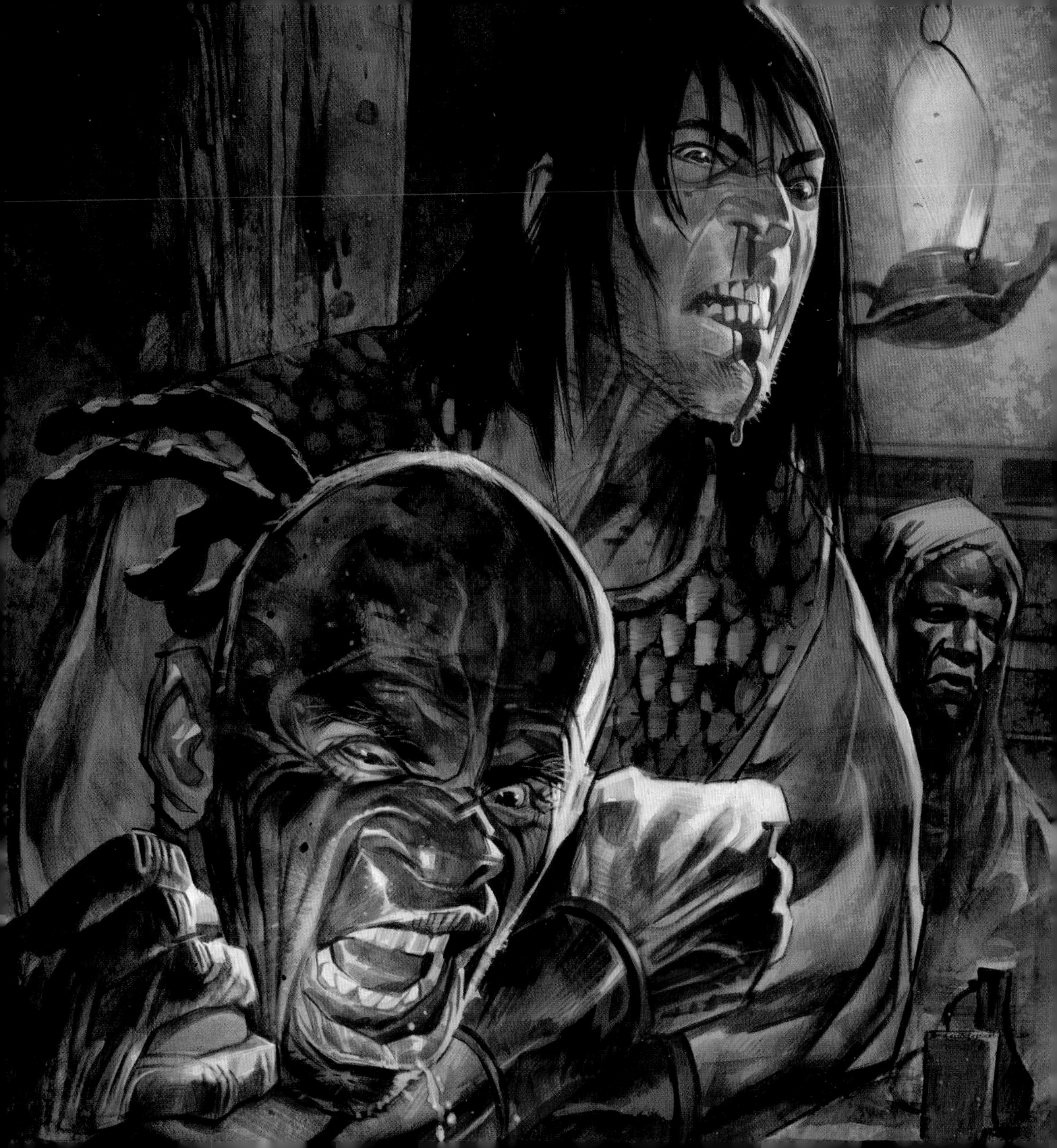

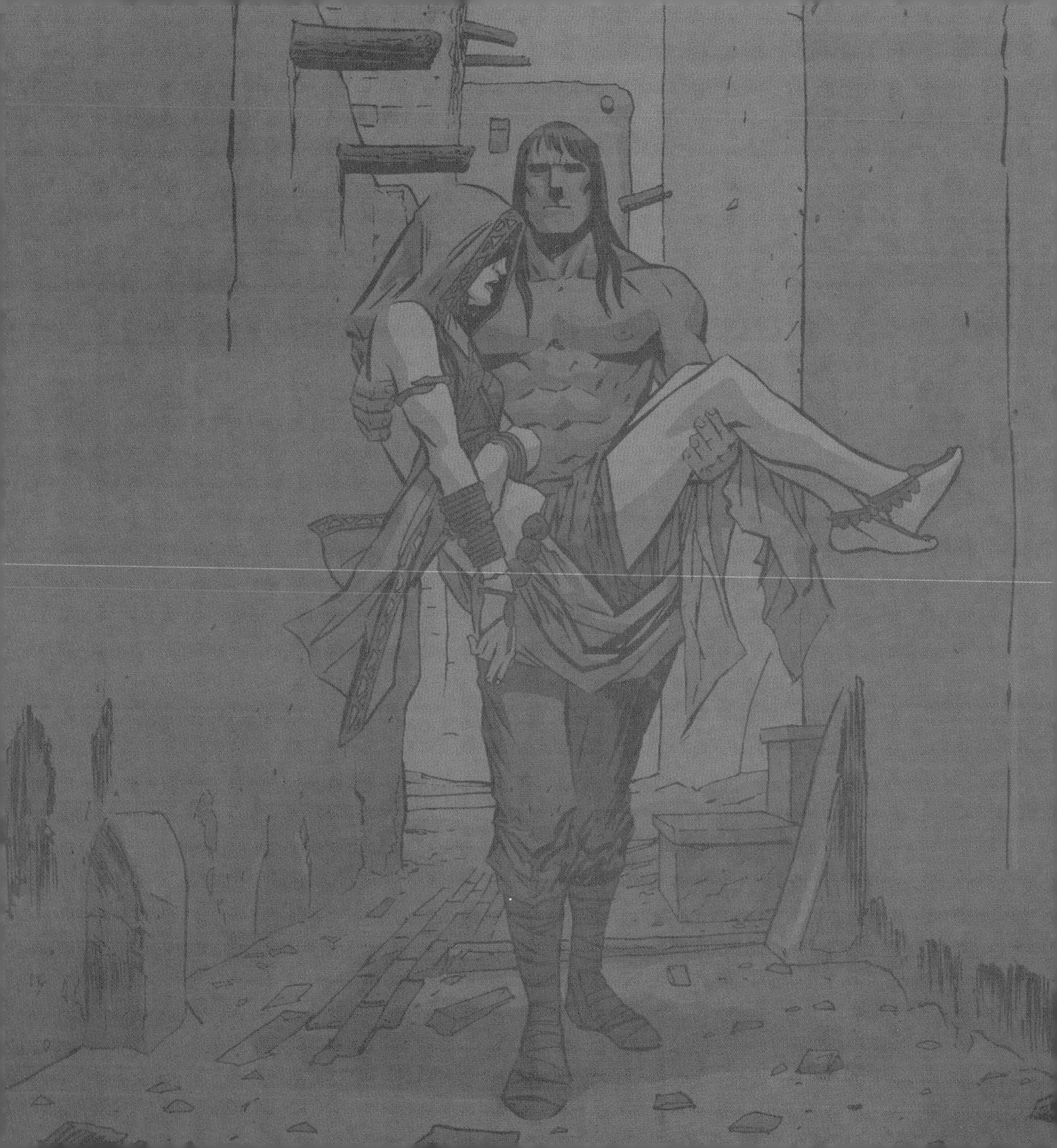

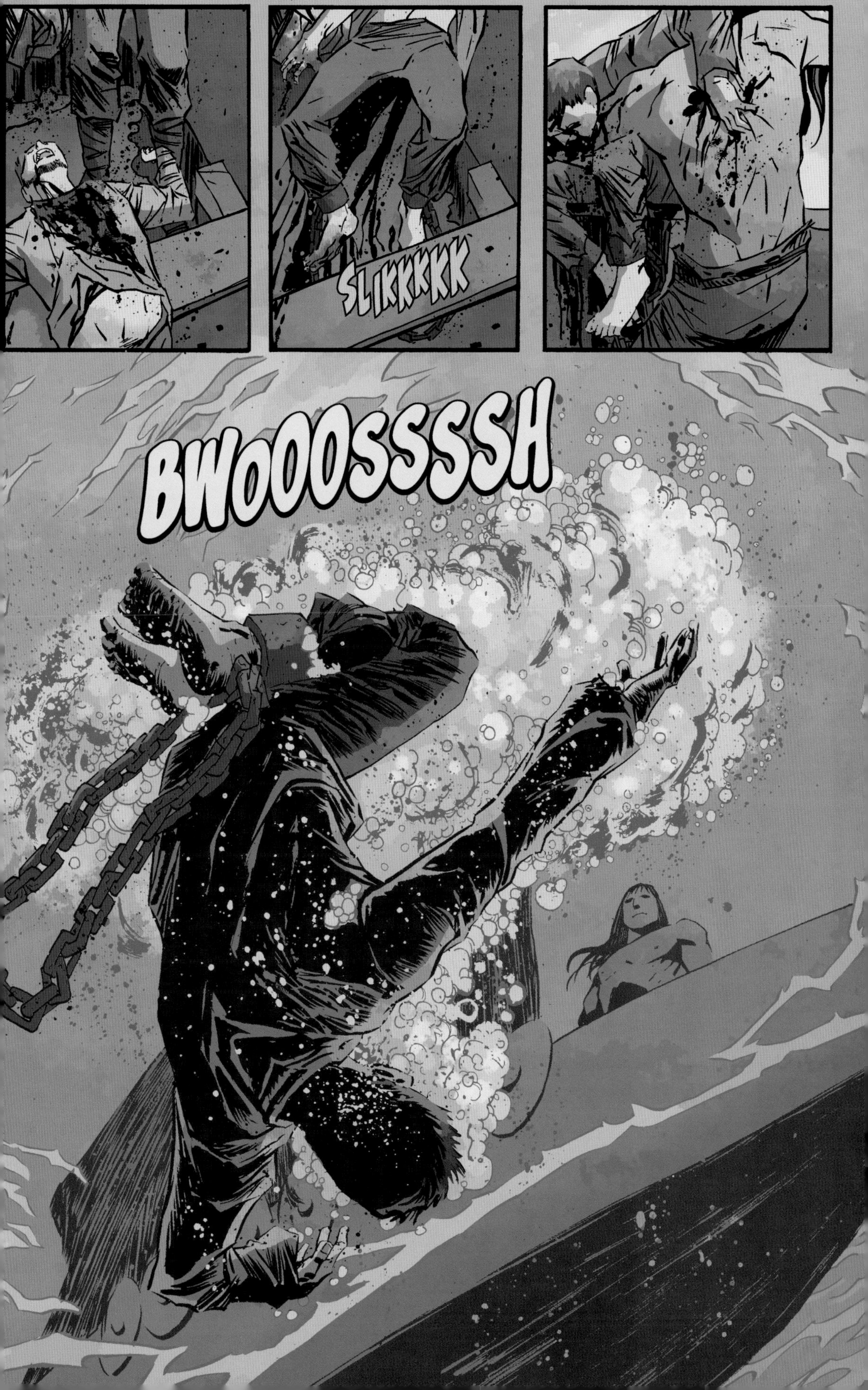
SLIKKKKK
BWOOOSSSSH

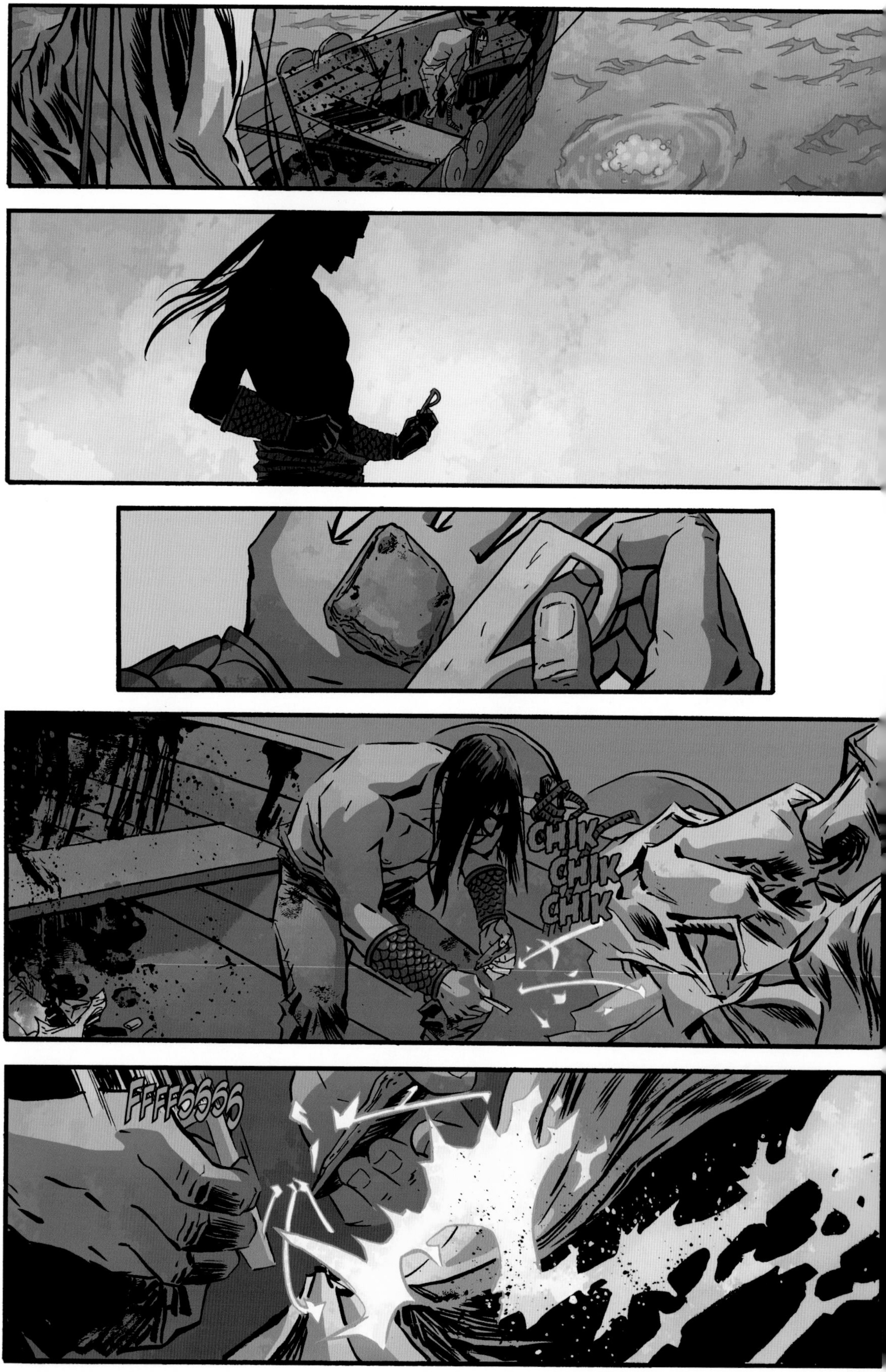
CHIK
CHIK
CHIK
FFFFSSSS

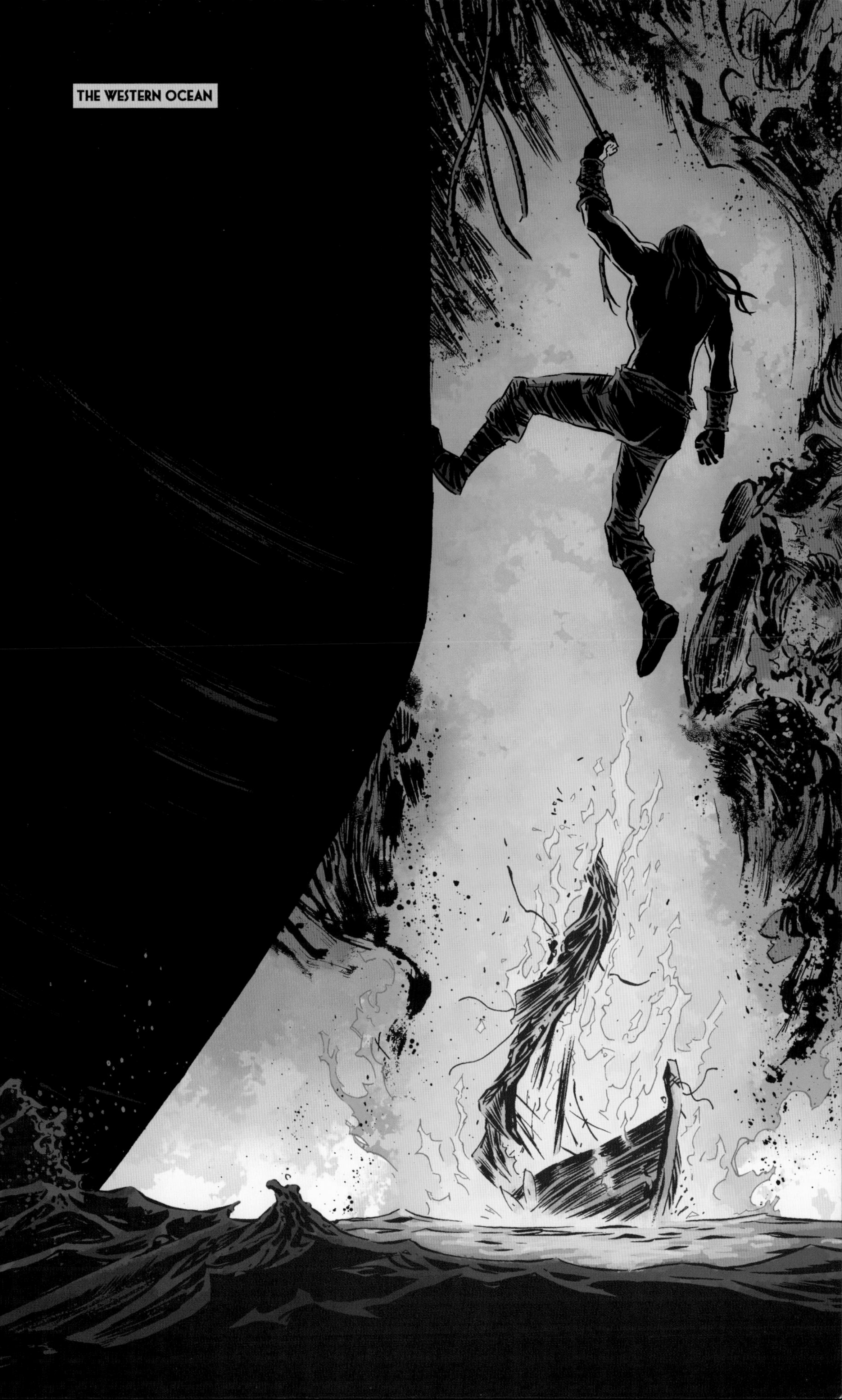
THE WESTERN OCEAN

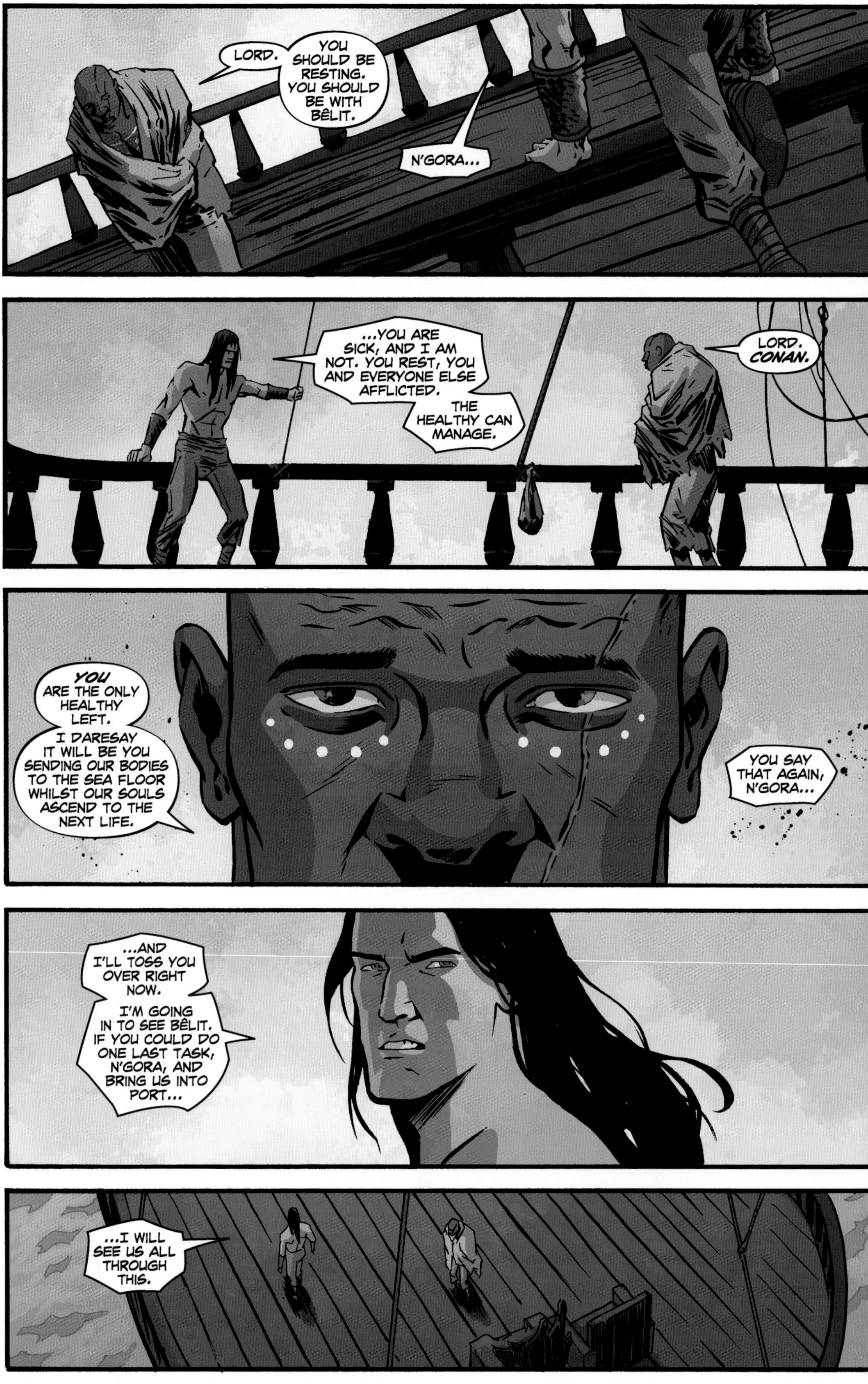
LORD.
YOU SHOULD BE RESTING. YOU SHOULD BE WITH BÊLIT.
N'GORA...
LORD. CONAN.
...YOU ARE SICK, AND I AM NOT. YOU REST, YOU AND EVERYONE ELSE AFFLICTED.
THE HEALTHY CAN MANAGE.
YOU ARE THE ONLY HEALTHY LEFT.
I DARESAY IT WILL BE YOU SENDING OUR BODIES TO THE SEA FLOOR WHILST OUR SOULS ASCEND TO THE NEXT LIFE.
YOU SAY THAT AGAIN, N'GORA...
...AND I'LL TOSS YOU OVER RIGHT NOW.
I'M GOING IN TO SEE BÊLIT. IF YOU COULD DO ONE LAST TASK, N'GORA, AND BRING US INTO PORT...
...I WILL SEE US ALL THROUGH THIS.

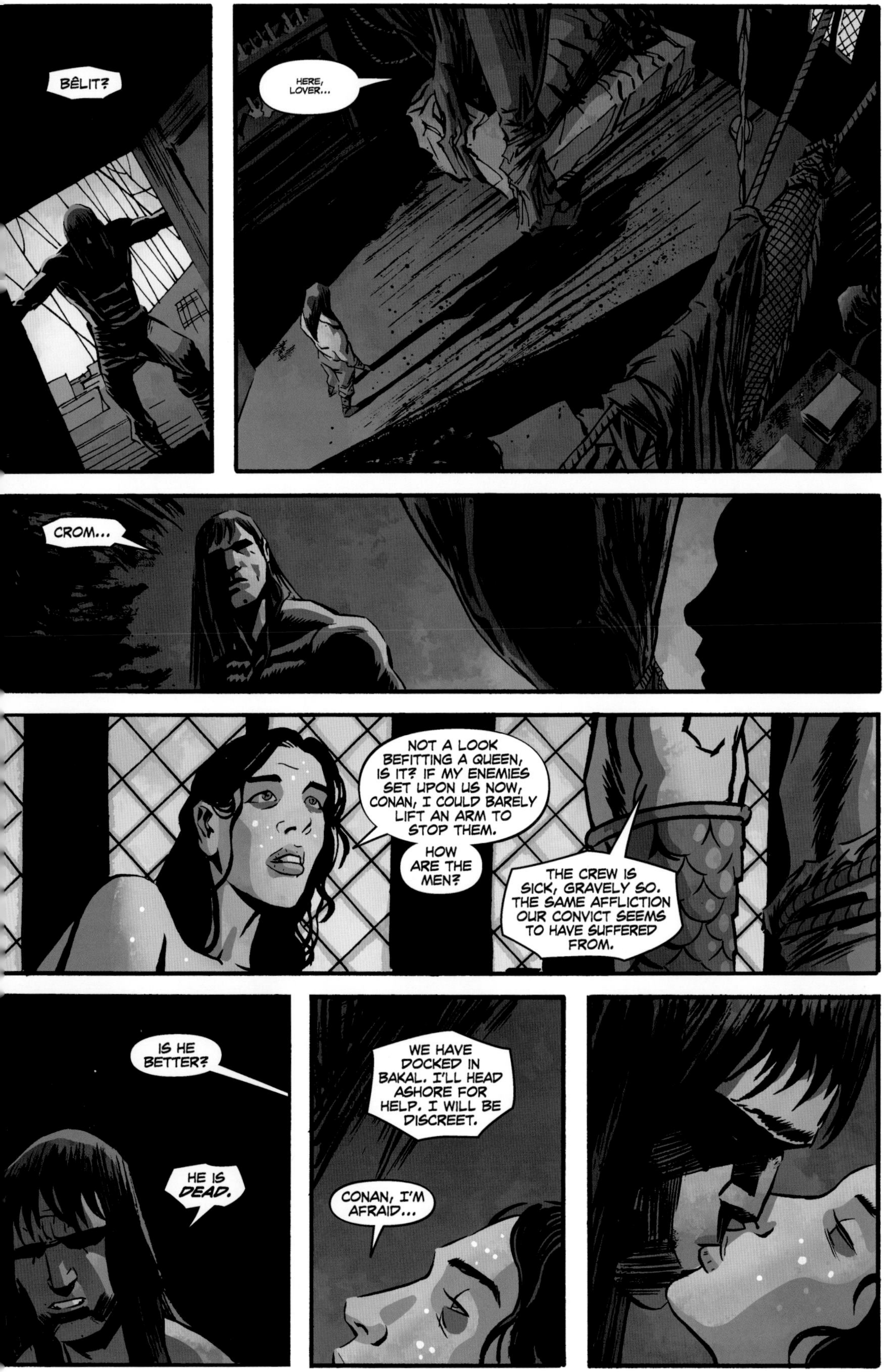
BÊLIT?
HERE, LOVER...
CROM...
NOT A LOOK BEFITTING A QUEEN, IS IT? IF MY ENEMIES SET UPON US NOW, CONAN, I COULD BARELY LIFT AN ARM TO STOP THEM.
HOW ARE THE MEN?
THE CREW IS SICK, GRAVELY SO. THE SAME AFFLICTION OUR CONVICT SEEMS TO HAVE SUFFERED FROM.
IS HE BETTER?
HE IS *DEAD.*
WE HAVE DOCKED IN BAKAL. I'LL HEAD ASHORE FOR HELP. I WILL BE DISCREET.
CONAN, I'M AFRAID...

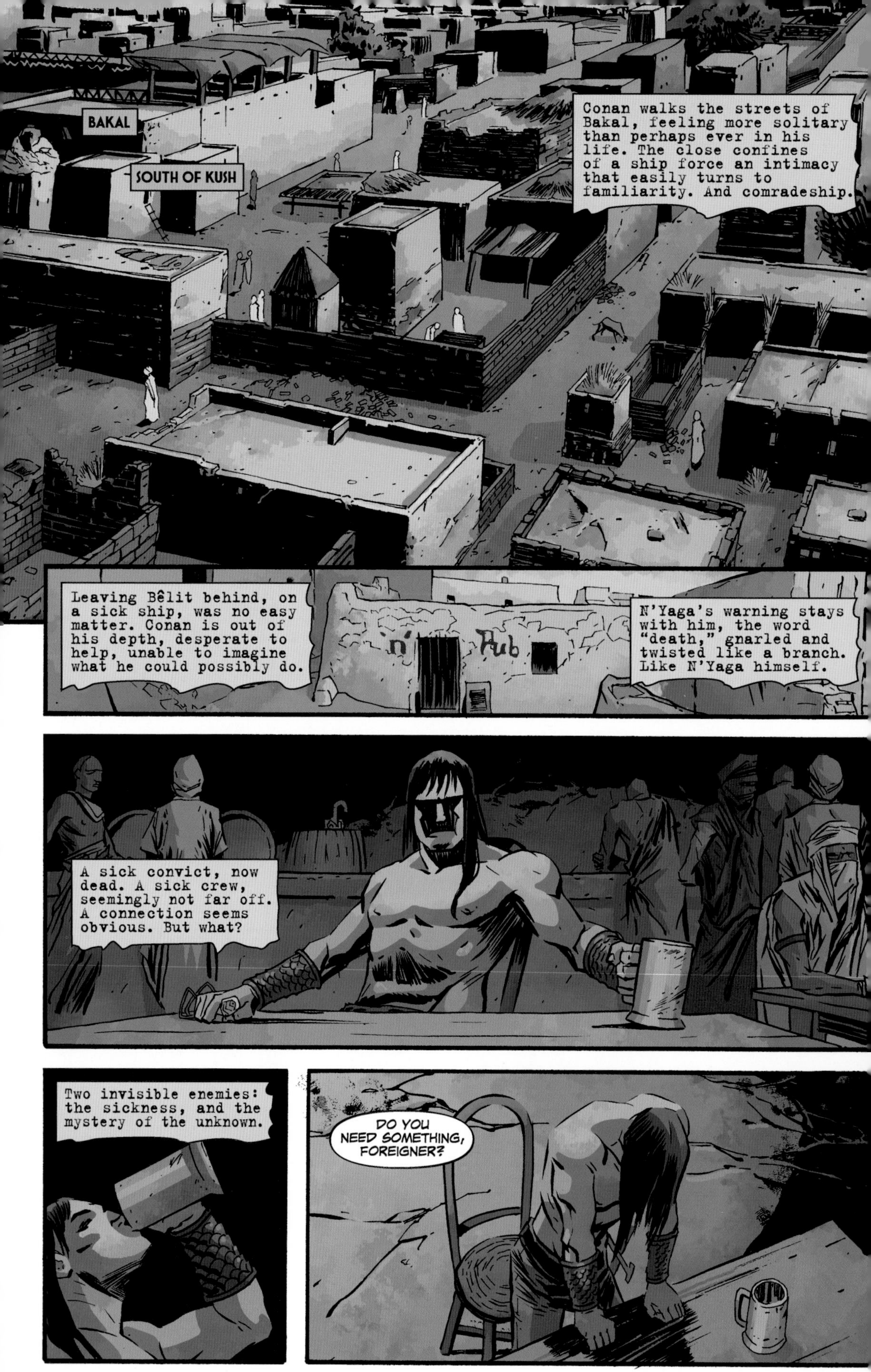
BAKAL
SOUTH OF KUSH
Conan walks the streets of Bakal, feeling more solitary than perhaps ever in his life. The close confines of a ship force an intimacy that easily turns to familiarity. And comradeship.
Leaving Bêlit behind, on a sick ship, was no easy matter. Conan is out of his depth, desperate to help, unable to imagine what he could possibly do.
N'Yaga's warning stays with him, the word "death," gnarled and twisted like a branch. Like N'Yaga himself.
A sick convict, now dead. A sick crew, seemingly not far off. A connection seems obvious. But what?
Two invisible enemies: the sickness, and the mystery of the unknown.
DO YOU NEED SOMETHING, FOREIGNER?

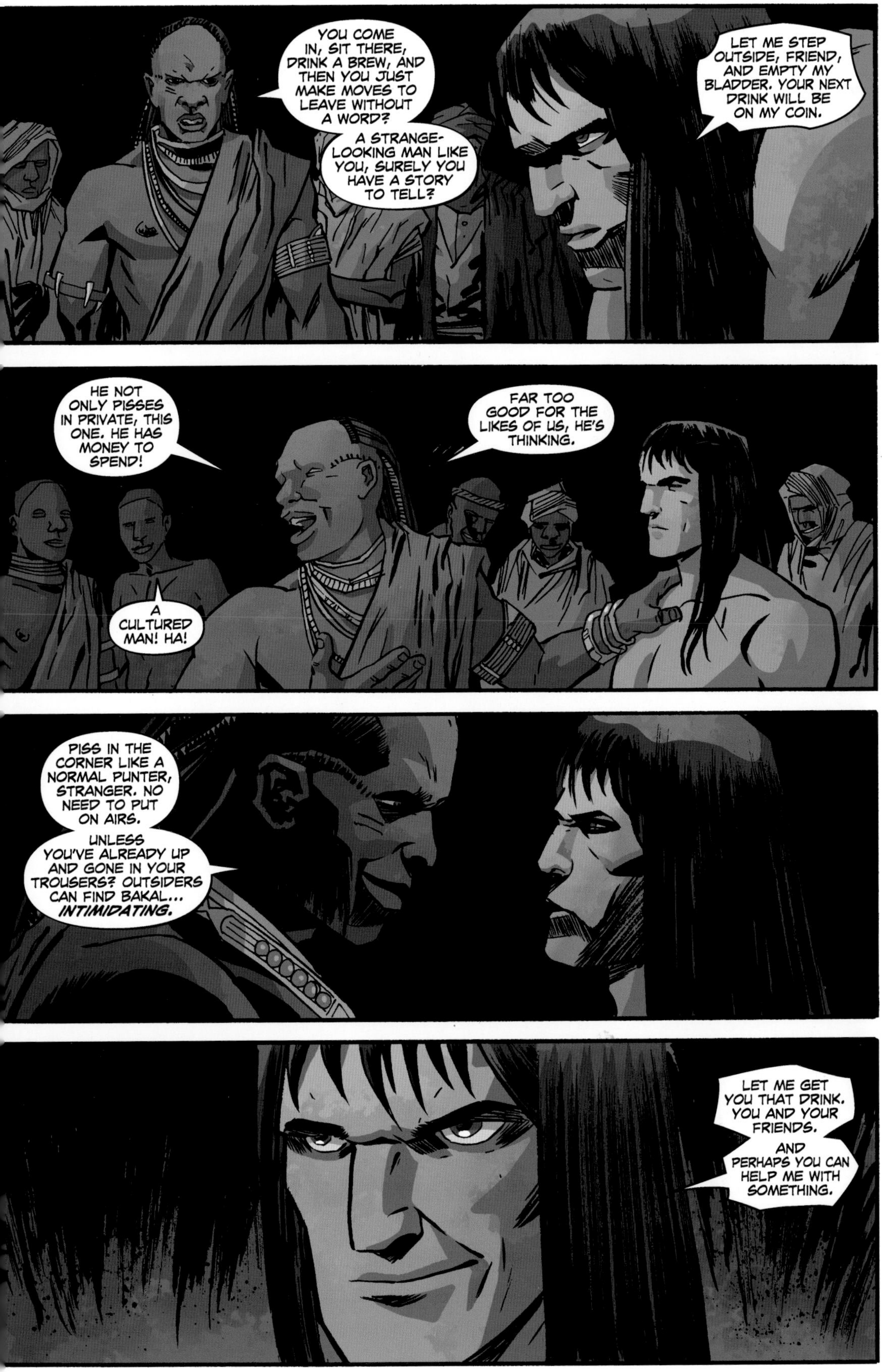
YOU COME IN, SIT THERE, DRINK A BREW, AND THEN YOU JUST MAKE MOVES TO LEAVE WITHOUT A WORD?
A STRANGE-LOOKING MAN LIKE YOU, SURELY YOU HAVE A STORY TO TELL?
LET ME STEP OUTSIDE, FRIEND, AND EMPTY MY BLADDER. YOUR NEXT DRINK WILL BE ON MY COIN.
HE NOT ONLY PISSES IN PRIVATE, THIS ONE. HE HAS MONEY TO SPEND!
FAR TOO GOOD FOR THE LIKES OF US, HE'S THINKING.
A CULTURED MAN! HA!
PISS IN THE CORNER LIKE A NORMAL PUNTER, STRANGER. NO NEED TO PUT ON AIRS.
UNLESS YOU'VE ALREADY UP AND GONE IN YOUR TROUSERS? OUTSIDERS CAN FIND BAKAL... *INTIMIDATING.*
LET ME GET YOU THAT DRINK. YOU AND YOUR FRIENDS.
AND PERHAPS YOU CAN HELP ME WITH SOMETHING.

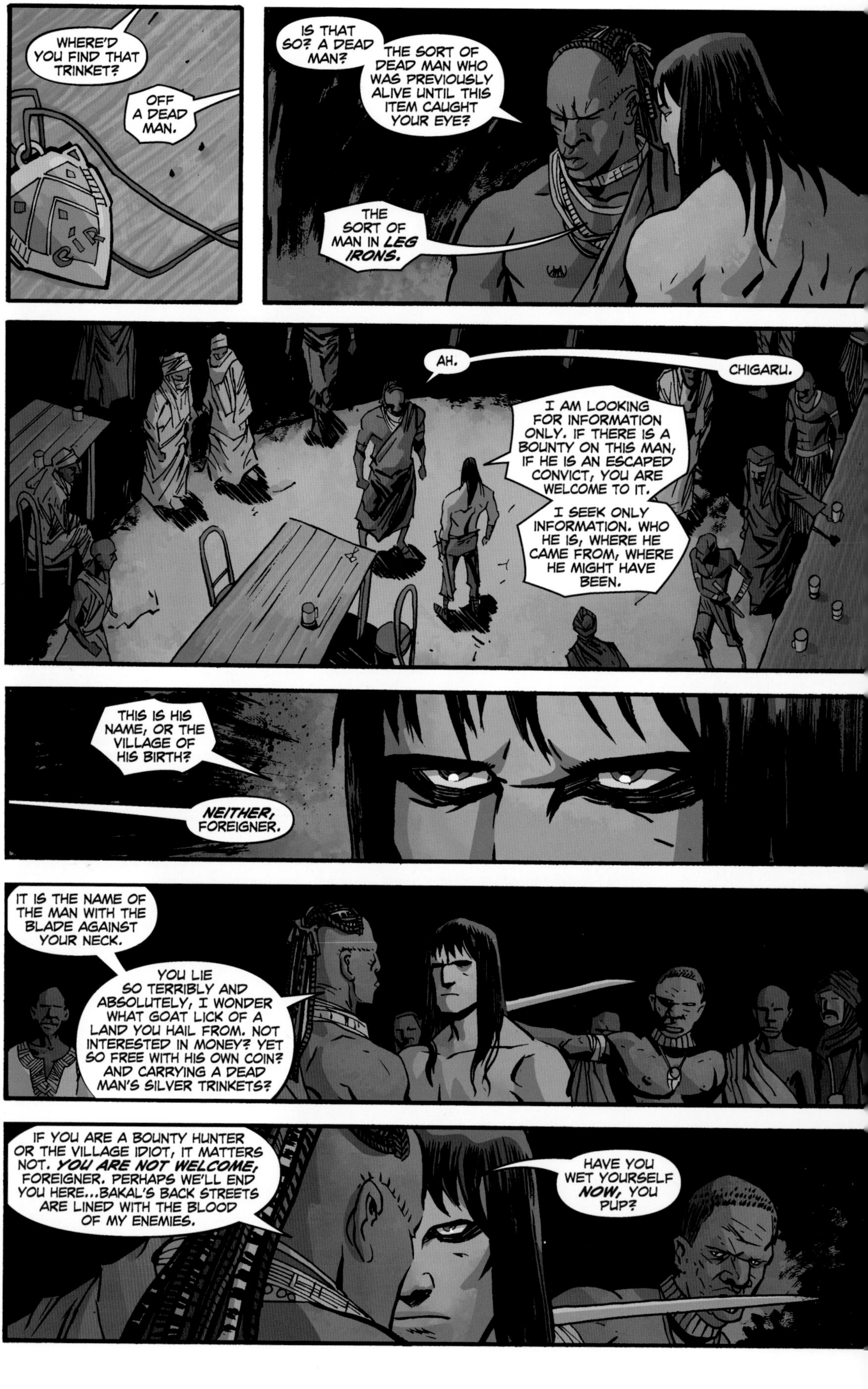
WHERE'D YOU FIND THAT TRINKET?
OFF A DEAD MAN.
IS THAT SO? A DEAD MAN?
THE SORT OF DEAD MAN WHO WAS PREVIOUSLY ALIVE UNTIL THIS ITEM CAUGHT YOUR EYE?
THE SORT OF MAN IN *LEG IRONS.*
AH.
CHIGARU.
I AM LOOKING FOR INFORMATION ONLY. IF THERE IS A BOUNTY ON THIS MAN, IF HE IS AN ESCAPED CONVICT, YOU ARE WELCOME TO IT.
I SEEK ONLY INFORMATION. WHO HE IS, WHERE HE CAME FROM, WHERE HE MIGHT HAVE BEEN.
THIS IS HIS NAME, OR THE VILLAGE OF HIS BIRTH?
NEITHER, FOREIGNER.
IT IS THE NAME OF THE MAN WITH THE BLADE AGAINST YOUR NECK.
YOU LIE SO TERRIBLY AND ABSOLUTELY, I WONDER WHAT GOAT LICK OF A LAND YOU HAIL FROM. NOT INTERESTED IN MONEY? YET SO FREE WITH HIS OWN COIN? AND CARRYING A DEAD MAN'S SILVER TRINKETS?
IF YOU ARE A BOUNTY HUNTER OR THE VILLAGE IDIOT, IT MATTERS NOT. *YOU ARE NOT WELCOME,* FOREIGNER. PERHAPS WE'LL END YOU HERE...BAKAL'S BACK STREETS ARE LINED WITH THE BLOOD OF MY ENEMIES.
HAVE YOU WET YOURSELF *NOW,* YOU PUP?

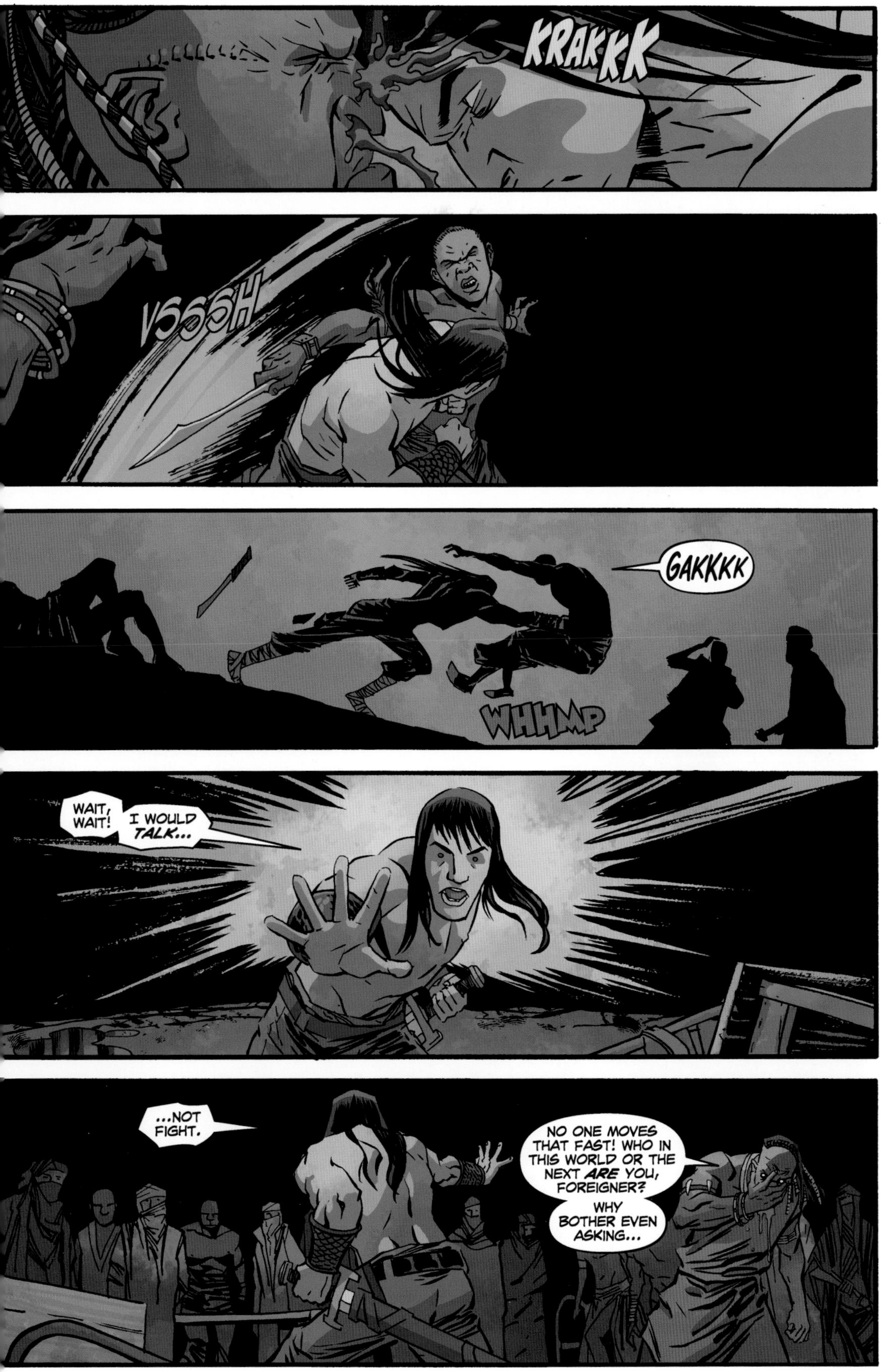
KRAKKK
VSSSH
GAKKKK
WHHMP
WAIT, WAIT!
I WOULD *TALK*...
...NOT FIGHT.
NO ONE MOVES THAT FAST! WHO IN THIS WORLD OR THE NEXT *ARE* YOU, FOREIGNER?
WHY BOTHER EVEN ASKING...

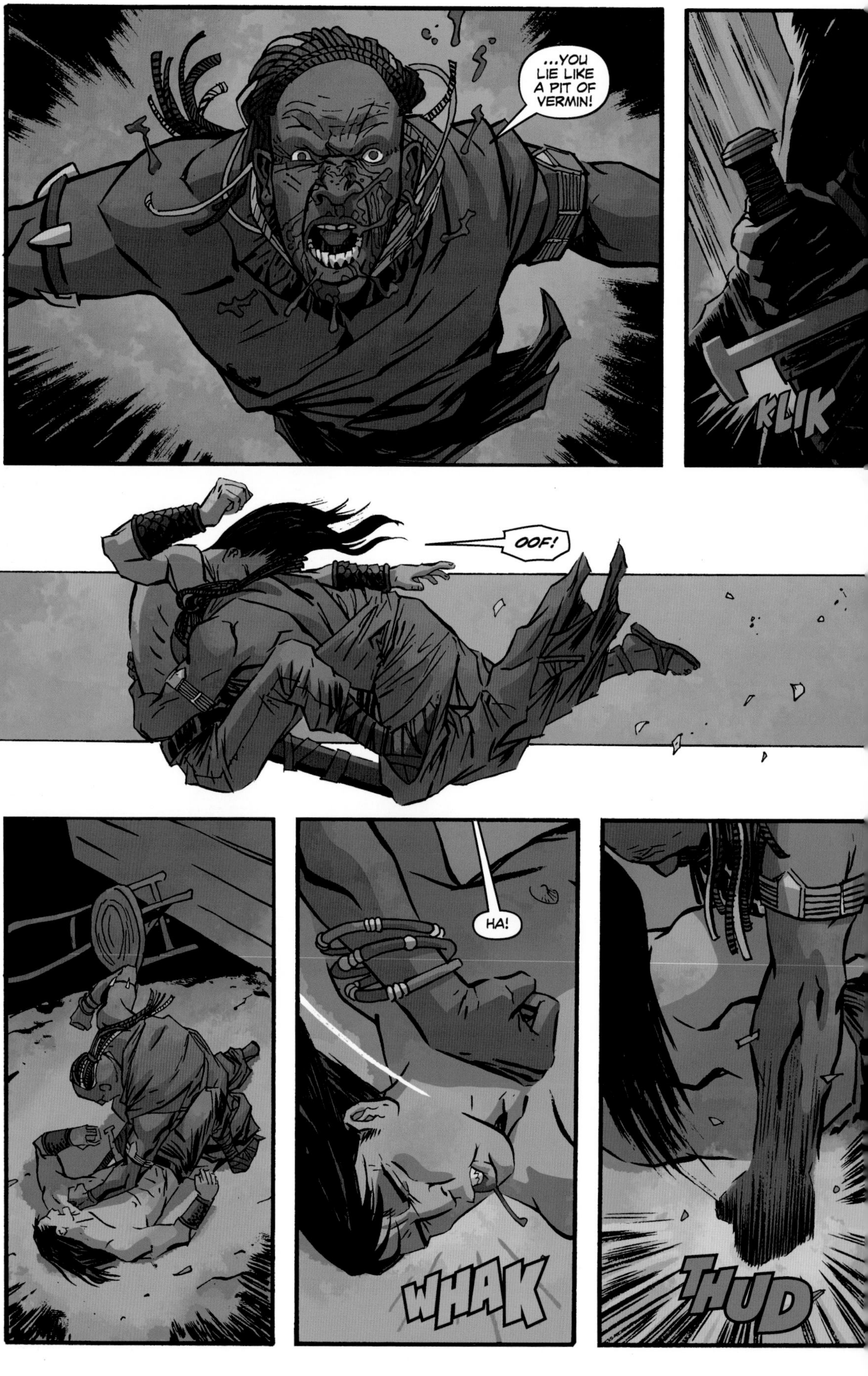
...YOU LIE LIKE A PIT OF VERMIN!
KLIK
OOF!
HA!
WHAK
THUD

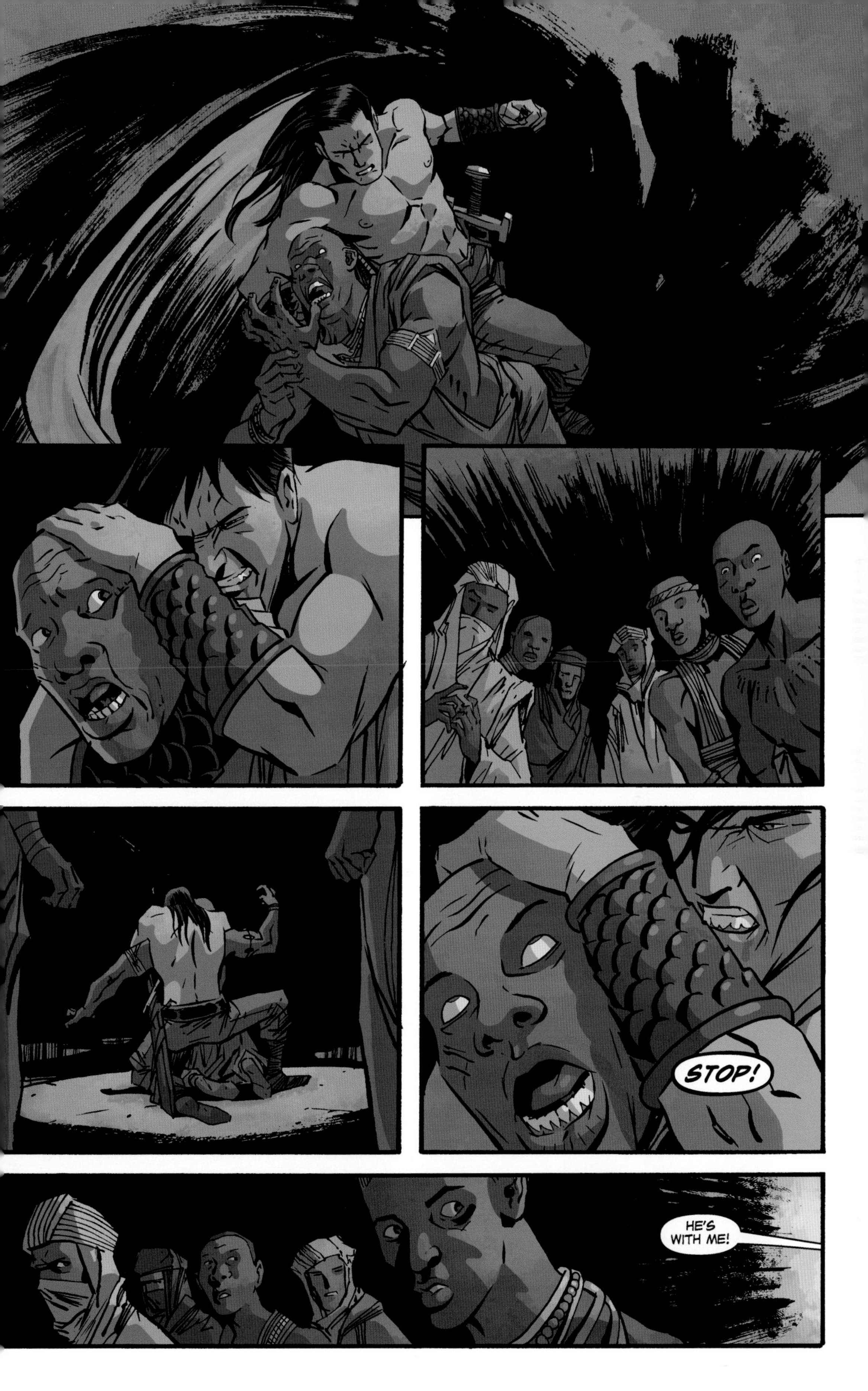
STOP!
HE'S WITH ME!

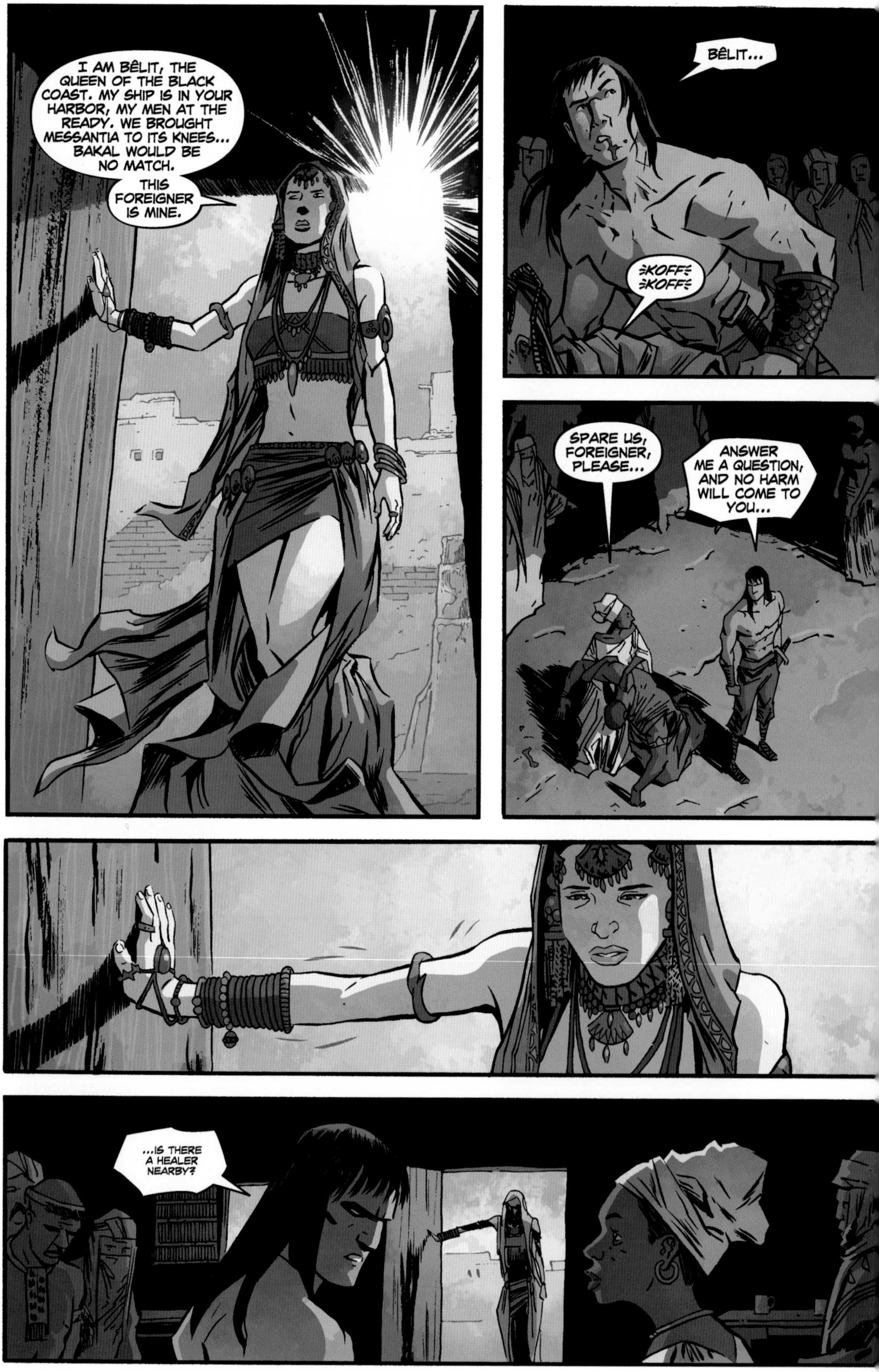
I AM BÊLIT, THE QUEEN OF THE BLACK COAST. MY SHIP IS IN YOUR HARBOR, MY MEN AT THE READY. WE BROUGHT MESSANTIA TO ITS KNEES... BAKAL WOULD BE NO MATCH.
THIS FOREIGNER IS MINE.
BÊLIT...
KOFF KOFF
SPARE US, FOREIGNER, PLEASE...
ANSWER ME A QUESTION, AND NO HARM WILL COME TO YOU...
...IS THERE A HEALER NEARBY?

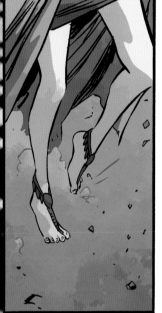

CONAN...

I GOT YOU.

HOW MUCH FURTHER?

THE HEALER IS SOME DISTANCE FURTHER, UP THAT HILL.

I CAN'T MAKE IT...

YOU CAN. YOU MUST.

CONAN, MY LOVE... CARRY ME BACK TO THE SHIP, BACK TO MY *TIGRESS.* MAKE ME MY TEA, AND PUT ME TO BED.

AND THEN YOU SHOULD GO.

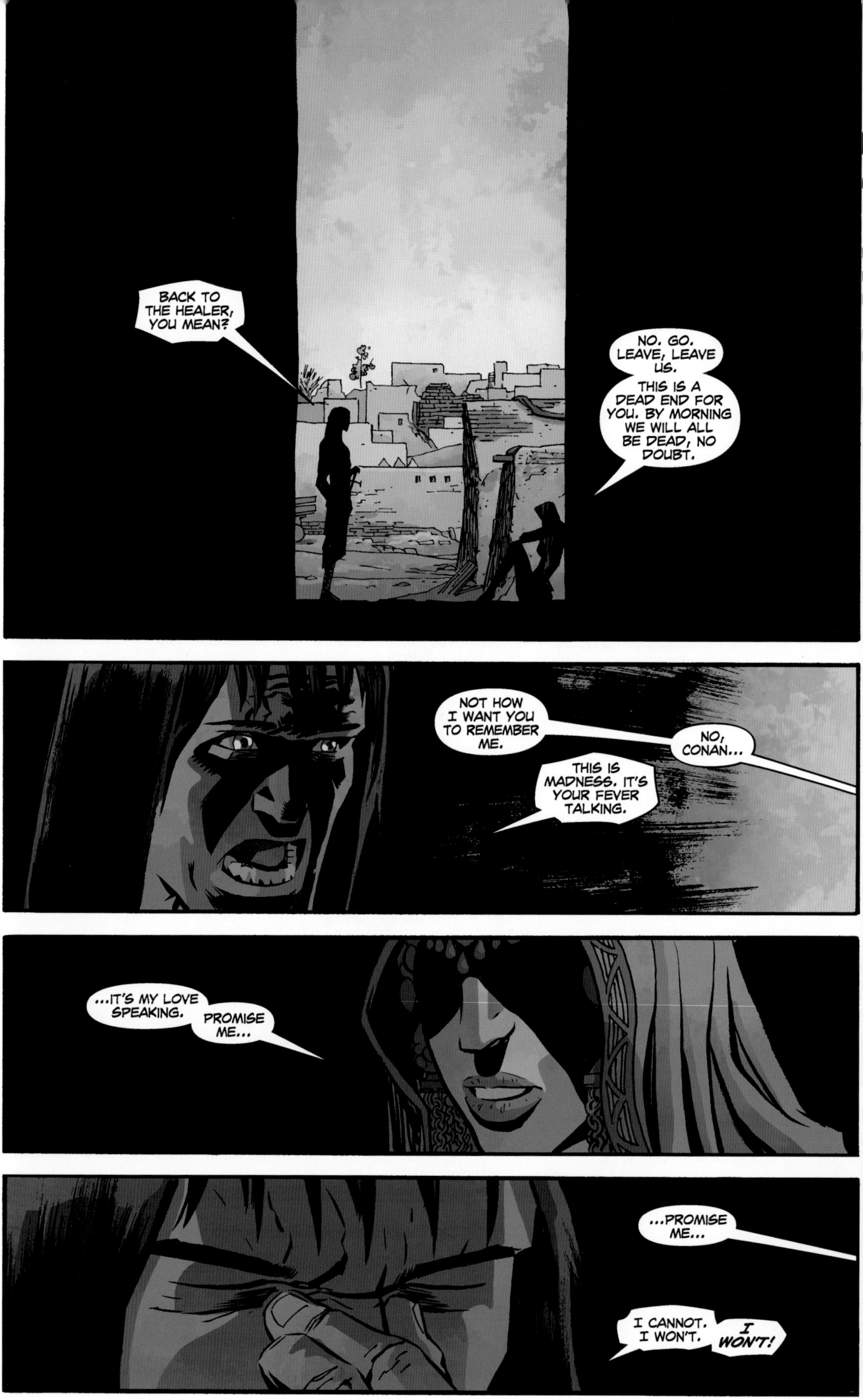
BACK TO THE HEALER, YOU MEAN?
NO. GO. LEAVE, LEAVE US.
THIS IS A DEAD END FOR YOU. BY MORNING WE WILL ALL BE DEAD, NO DOUBT.
NOT HOW I WANT YOU TO REMEMBER ME.
NO, CONAN...
THIS IS MADNESS. IT'S YOUR FEVER TALKING.
...IT'S MY LOVE SPEAKING.
PROMISE ME...
...PROMISE ME...
I CANNOT. I WON'T.
I WON'T!

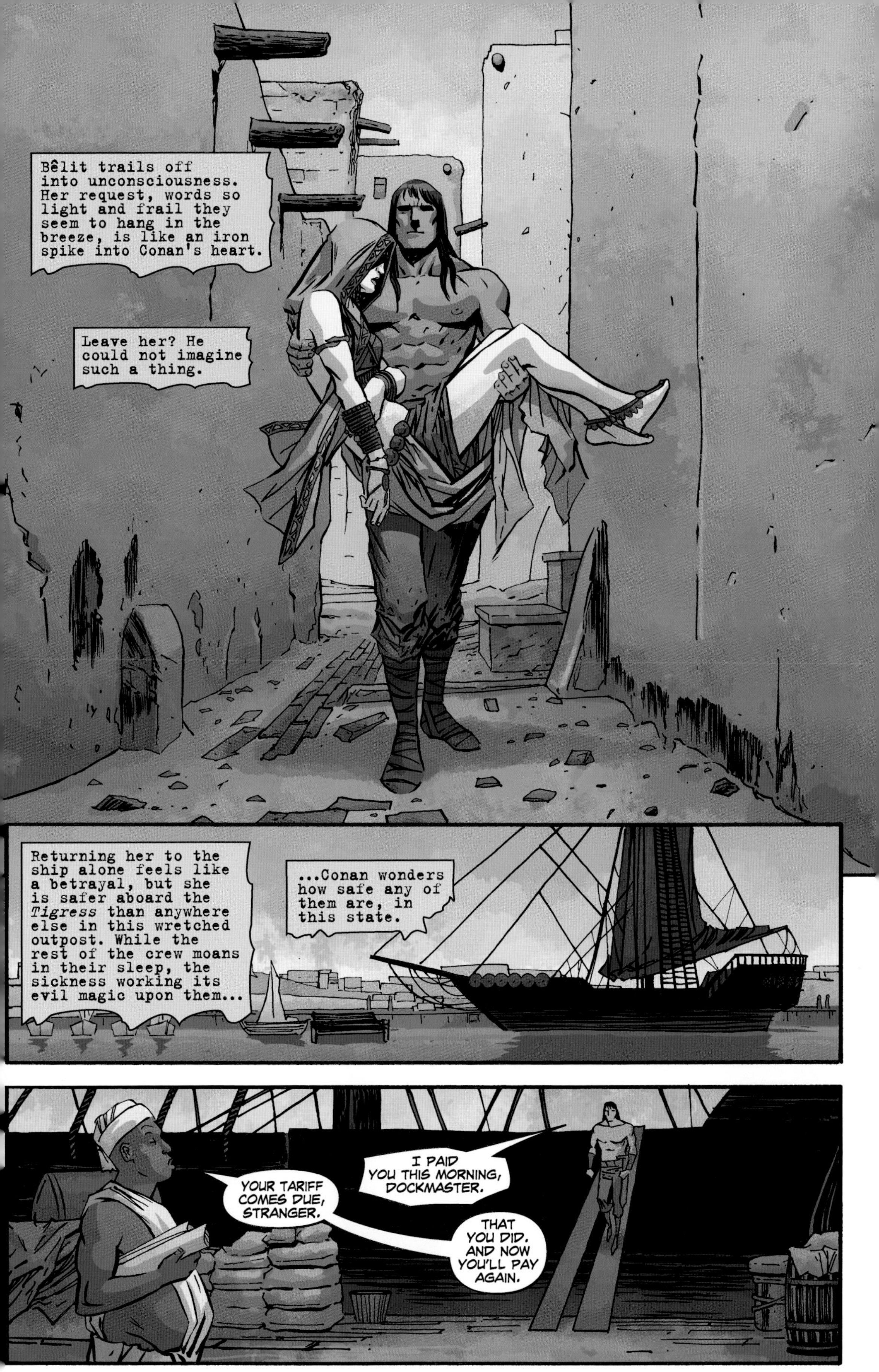
Bêlit trails off into unconsciousness. Her request, words so light and frail they seem to hang in the breeze, is like an iron spike into Conan's heart.
Leave her? He could not imagine such a thing.
Returning her to the ship alone feels like a betrayal, but she is safer aboard the *Tigress* than anywhere else in this wretched outpost. While the rest of the crew moans in their sleep, the sickness working its evil magic upon them...
...Conan wonders how safe any of them are, in this state.
YOUR TARIFF COMES DUE, STRANGER.
I PAID YOU THIS MORNING, DOCKMASTER.
THAT YOU DID. AND NOW YOU'LL PAY AGAIN.

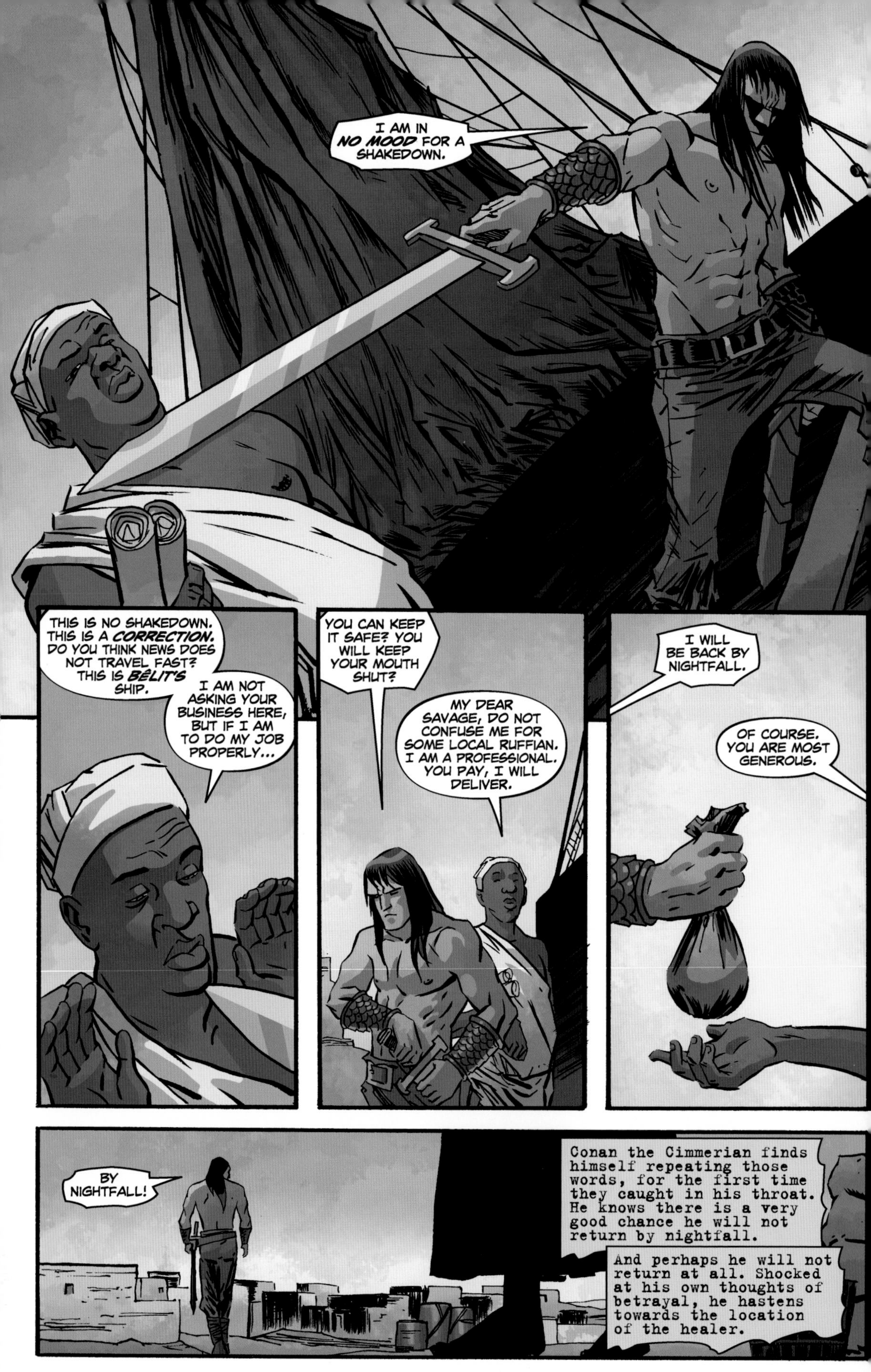
I AM IN NO MOOD FOR A SHAKEDOWN.
THIS IS NO SHAKEDOWN. THIS IS A CORRECTION. DO YOU THINK NEWS DOES NOT TRAVEL FAST? THIS IS BÊLIT'S SHIP.
I AM NOT ASKING YOUR BUSINESS HERE, BUT IF I AM TO DO MY JOB PROPERLY...
YOU CAN KEEP IT SAFE? YOU WILL KEEP YOUR MOUTH SHUT?
MY DEAR SAVAGE, DO NOT CONFUSE ME FOR SOME LOCAL RUFFIAN. I AM A PROFESSIONAL. YOU PAY, I WILL DELIVER.
I WILL BE BACK BY NIGHTFALL.
OF COURSE. YOU ARE MOST GENEROUS.
BY NIGHTFALL!
Conan the Cimmerian finds himself repeating those words, for the first time they caught in his throat. He knows there is a very good chance he will not return by nightfall.
And perhaps he will not return at all. Shocked at his own thoughts of betrayal, he hastens towards the location of the healer.

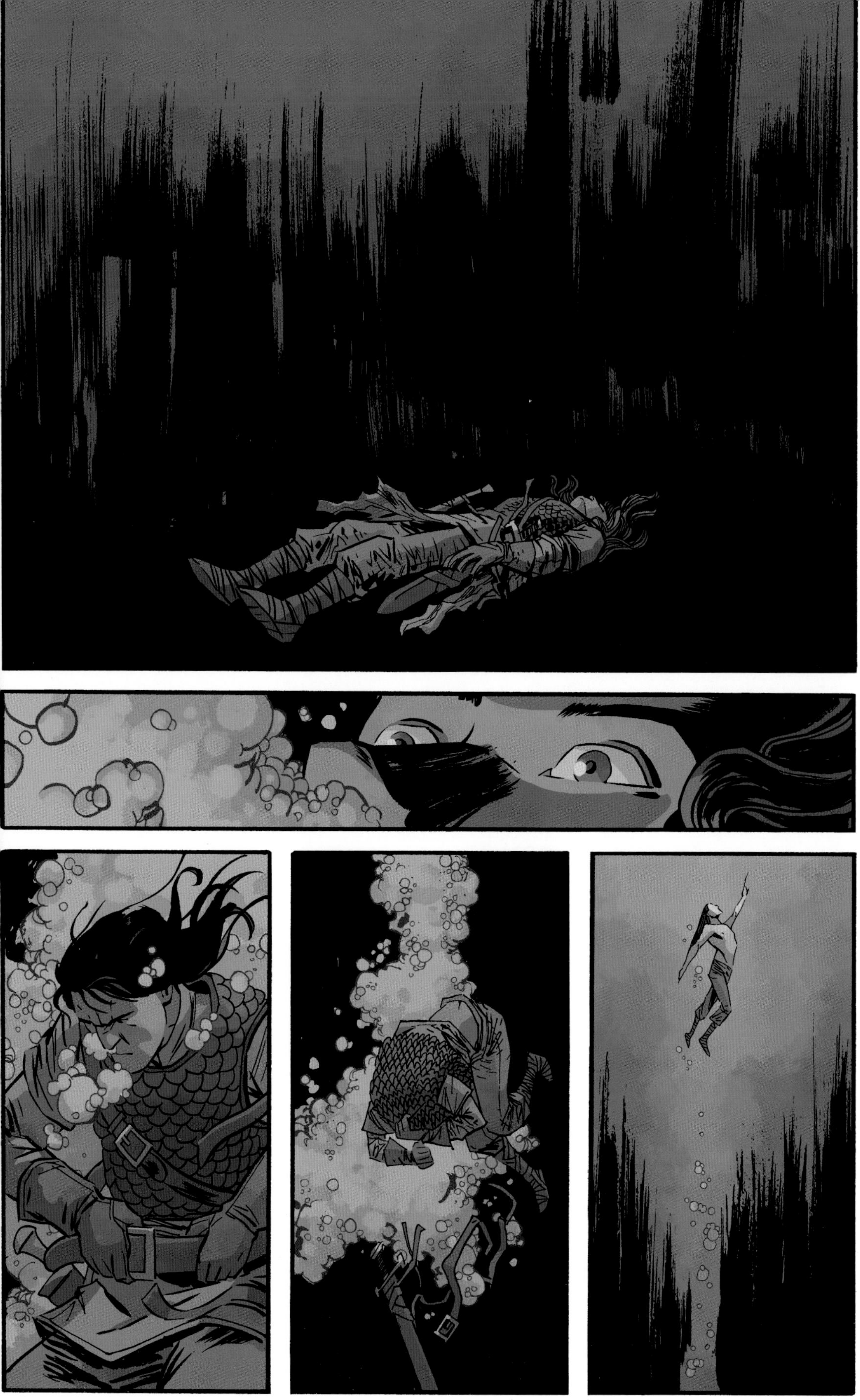

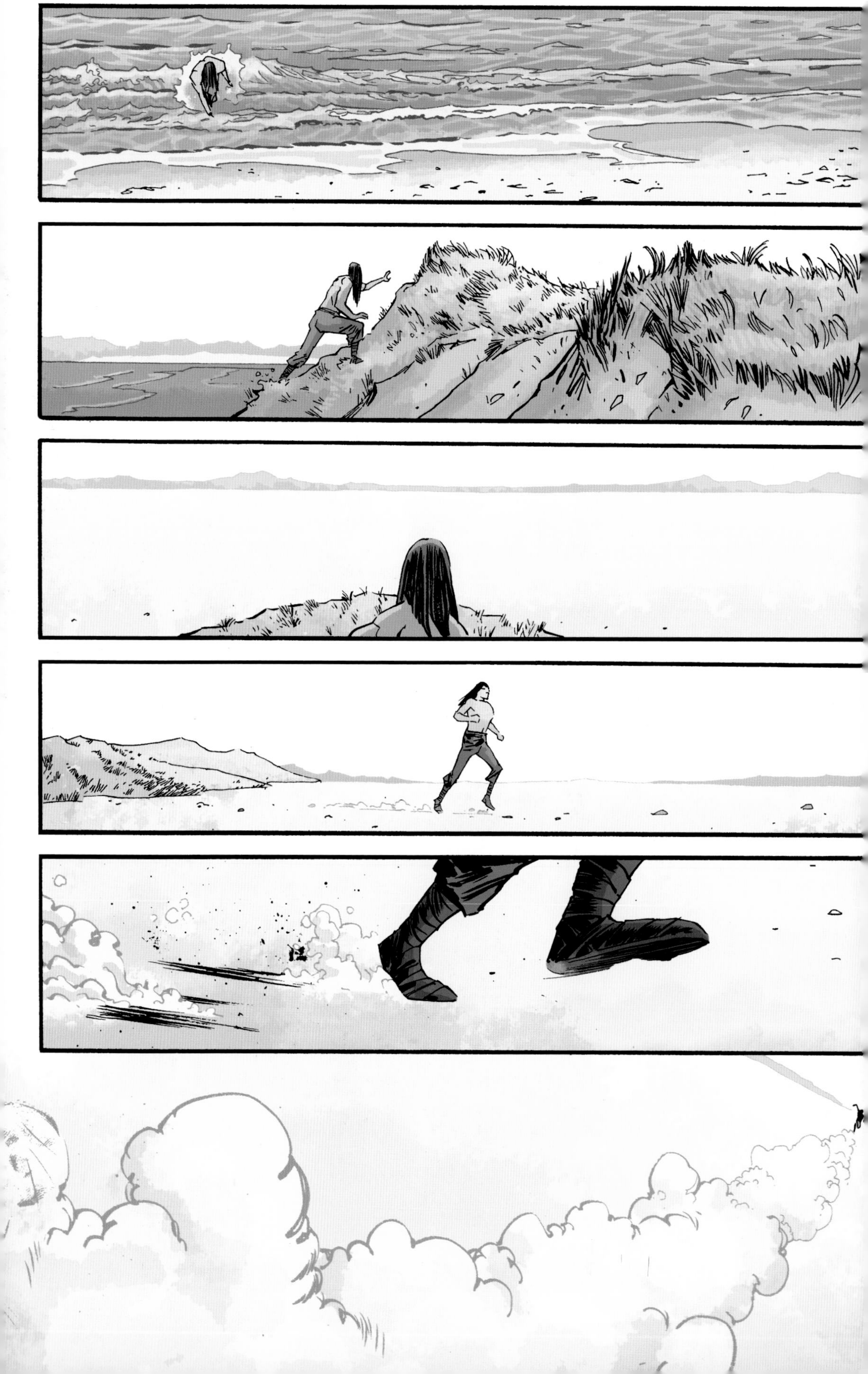

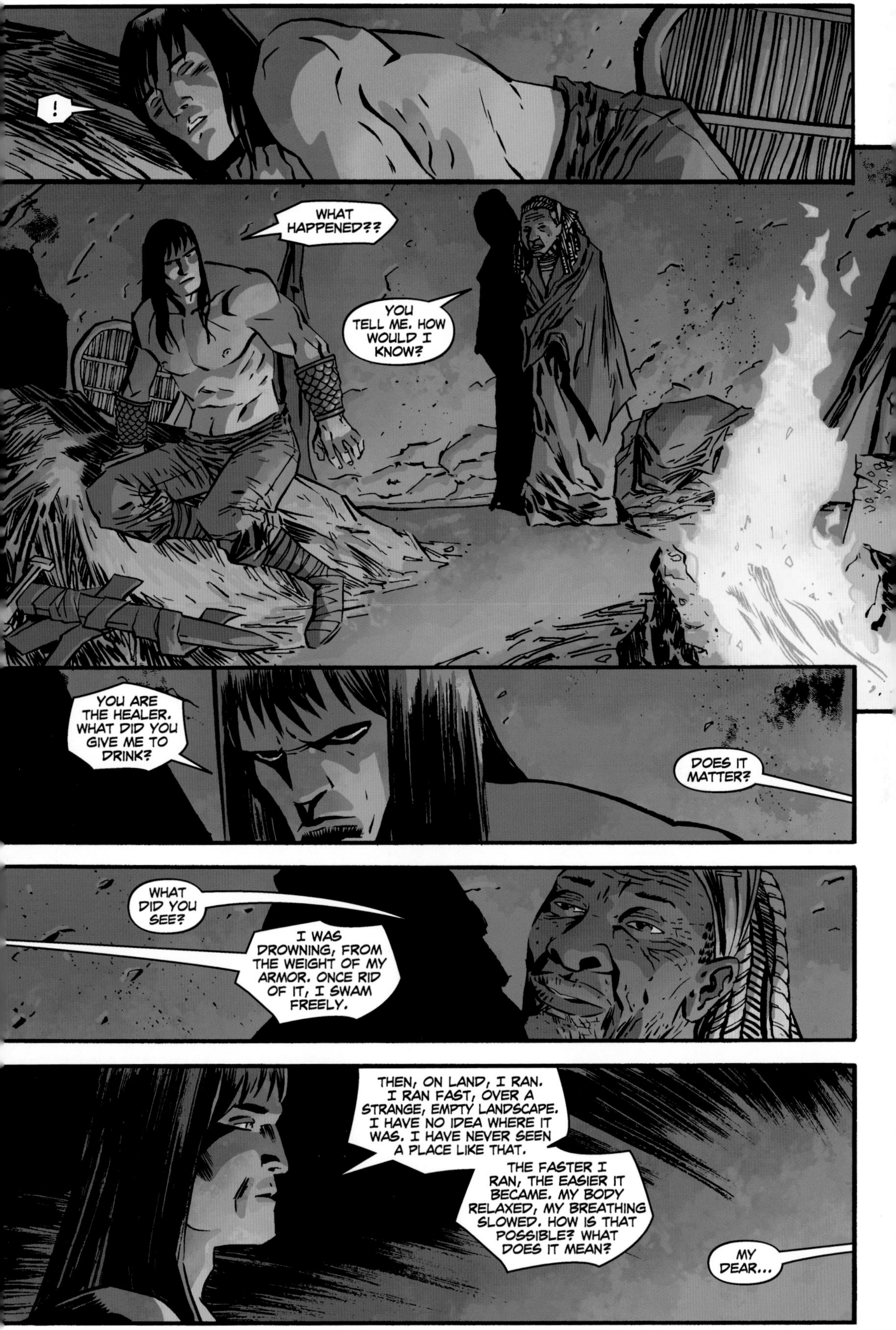
!
WHAT HAPPENED??
YOU TELL ME. HOW WOULD I KNOW?
YOU ARE THE HEALER. WHAT DID YOU GIVE ME TO DRINK?
DOES IT MATTER?
WHAT DID YOU SEE?
I WAS DROWNING, FROM THE WEIGHT OF MY ARMOR. ONCE RID OF IT, I SWAM FREELY.
THEN, ON LAND, I RAN. I RAN FAST, OVER A STRANGE, EMPTY LANDSCAPE. I HAVE NO IDEA WHERE IT WAS. I HAVE NEVER SEEN A PLACE LIKE THAT.
THE FASTER I RAN, THE EASIER IT BECAME. MY BODY RELAXED, MY BREATHING SLOWED. HOW IS THAT POSSIBLE? WHAT DOES IT MEAN?
MY DEAR...

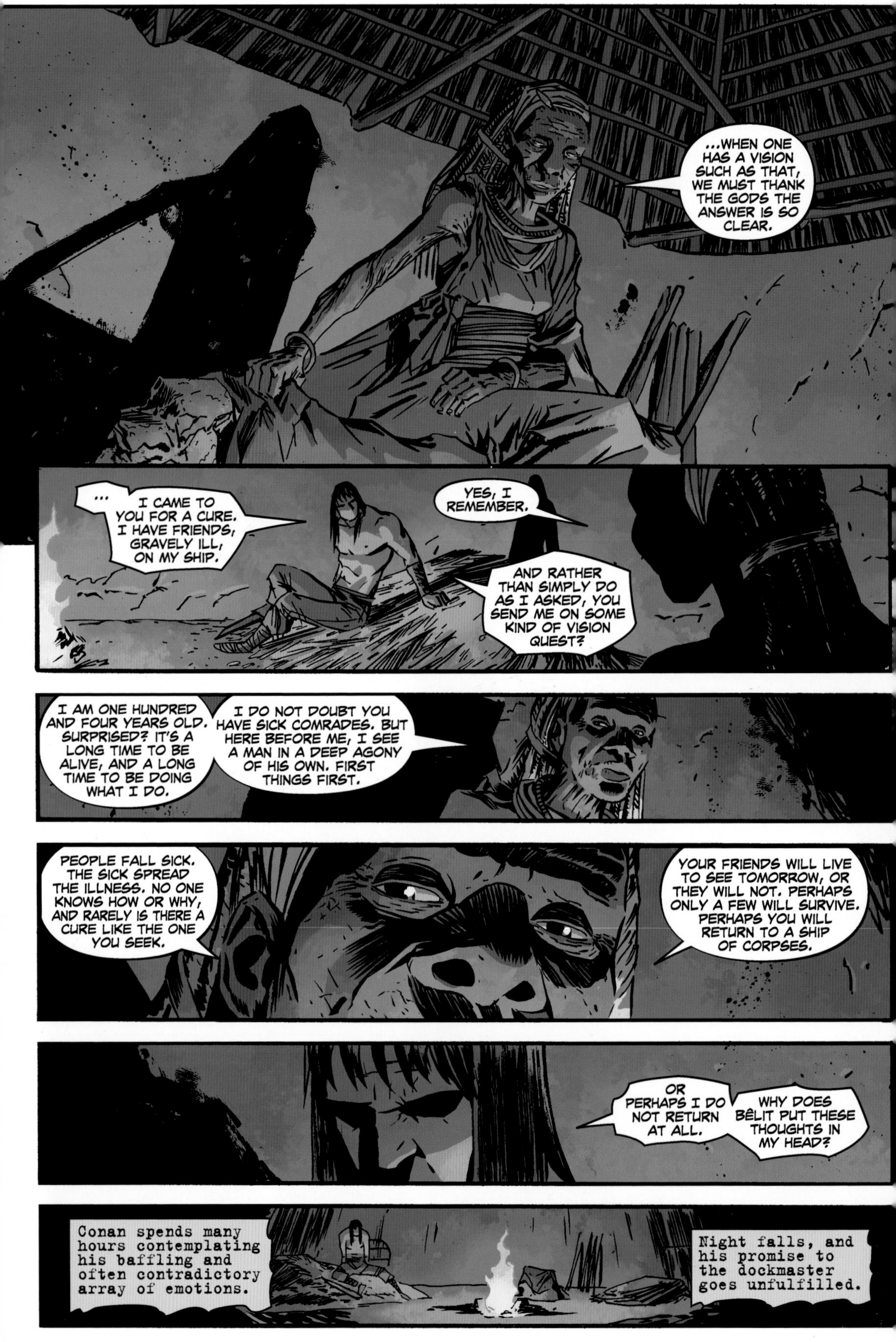
...WHEN ONE HAS A VISION SUCH AS THAT, WE MUST THANK THE GODS THE ANSWER IS SO CLEAR.
... I CAME TO YOU FOR A CURE. I HAVE FRIENDS, GRAVELY ILL, ON MY SHIP.
YES, I REMEMBER.
AND RATHER THAN SIMPLY DO AS I ASKED, YOU SEND ME ON SOME KIND OF VISION QUEST?
I AM ONE HUNDRED AND FOUR YEARS OLD. SURPRISED? IT'S A LONG TIME TO BE ALIVE, AND A LONG TIME TO BE DOING WHAT I DO.
I DO NOT DOUBT YOU HAVE SICK COMRADES. BUT HERE BEFORE ME, I SEE A MAN IN A DEEP AGONY OF HIS OWN. FIRST THINGS FIRST.
PEOPLE FALL SICK. THE SICK SPREAD THE ILLNESS. NO ONE KNOWS HOW OR WHY, AND RARELY IS THERE A CURE LIKE THE ONE YOU SEEK.
YOUR FRIENDS WILL LIVE TO SEE TOMORROW, OR THEY WILL NOT. PERHAPS ONLY A FEW WILL SURVIVE. PERHAPS YOU WILL RETURN TO A SHIP OF CORPSES.
OR PERHAPS I DO NOT RETURN AT ALL.
WHY DOES BÊLIT PUT THESE THOUGHTS IN MY HEAD?
Conan spends many hours contemplating his baffling and often contradictory array of emotions.
Night falls, and his promise to the dockmaster goes unfulfilled.

What of his promises to Bêlit?

For whatever reason, he cannot recall ever making any. Theirs was--is--a romance very much about the present, the simple pleasures of the day to day.

By some whim of fate, he remains healthy. If he were to return to the *Tigress*, perhaps he too would fall sick.

As a young boy in Cimmeria, he dreamed of seeing the world. He is not yet twenty-five years old. Is this it? Are the dusty streets of Bakal to be the end of his journey?

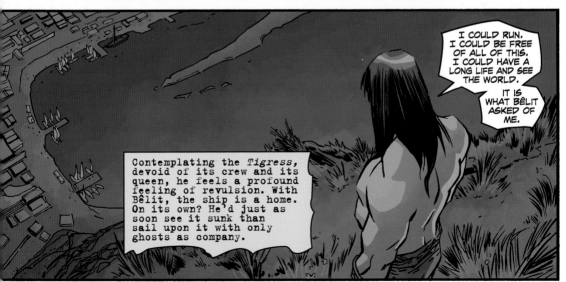

I COULD RUN. I COULD BE FREE OF ALL OF THIS. I COULD HAVE A LONG LIFE AND SEE THE WORLD.

IT IS WHAT BÊLIT ASKED OF ME.

Contemplating the *Tigress*, devoid of its crew and its queen, he feels a profound feeling of revulsion. With Bêlit, the ship is a home. On its own? He'd just as soon see it sunk than sail upon it with only ghosts as company.

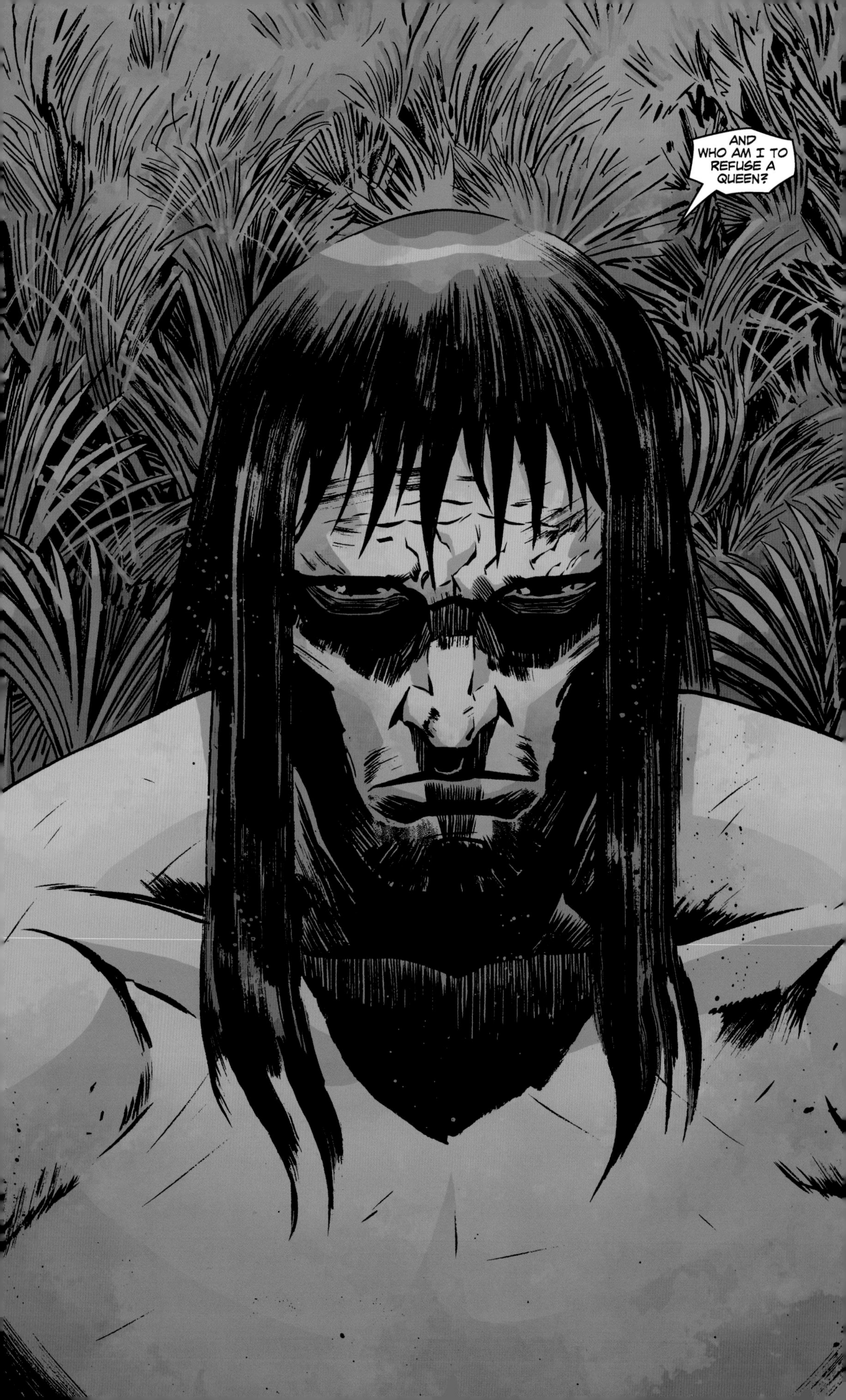
AND WHO AM I TO REFUSE A QUEEN?

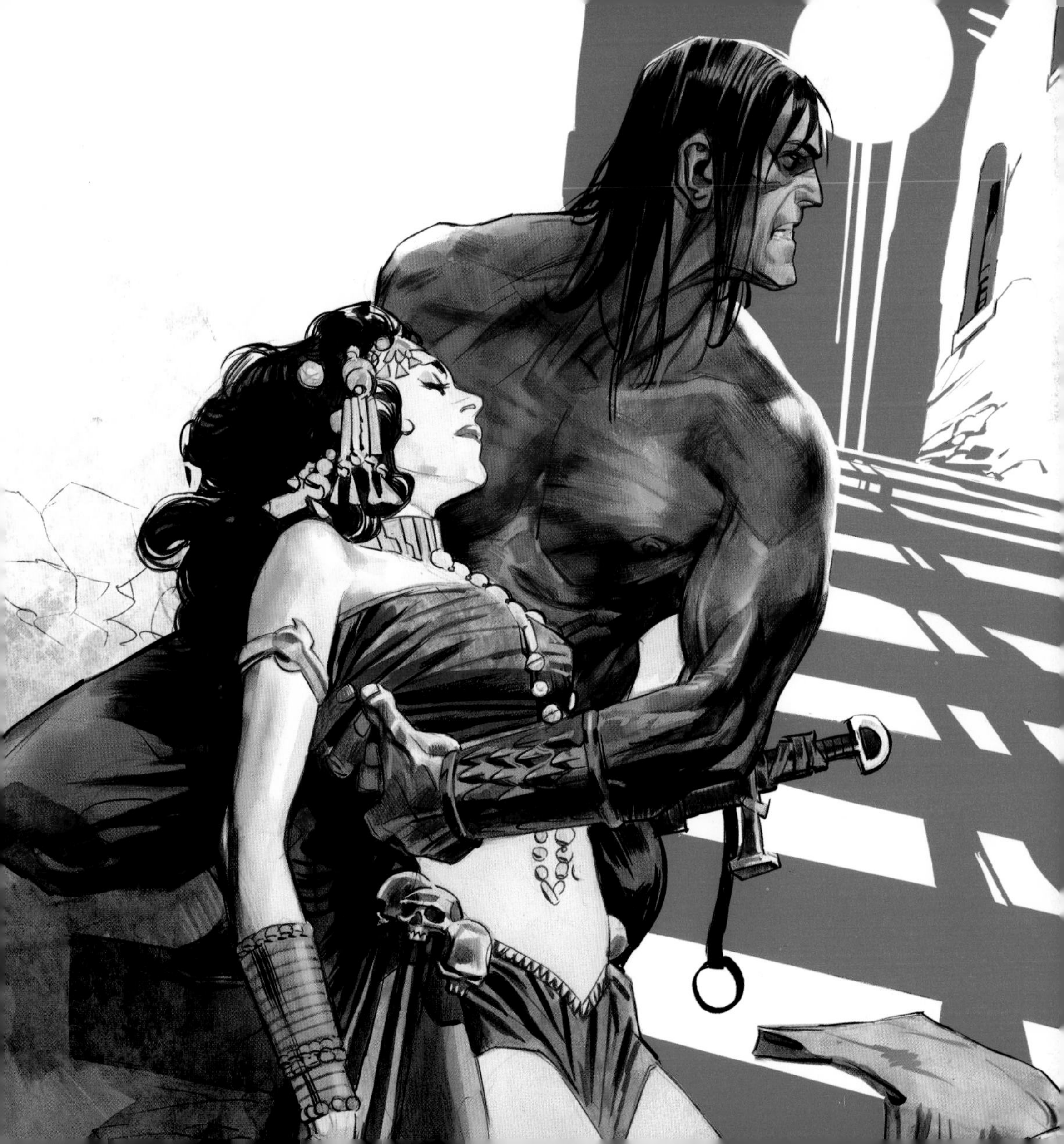

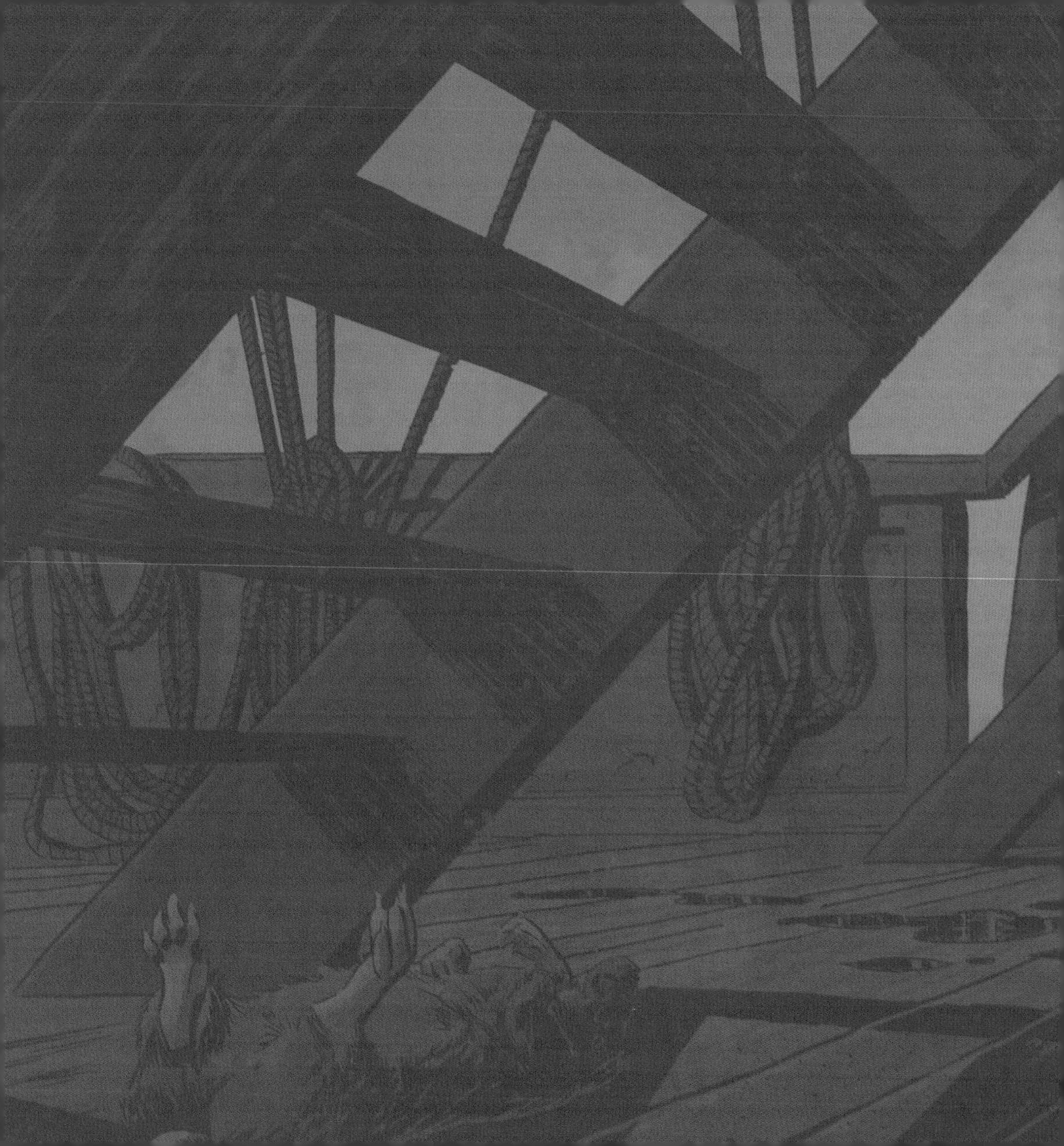

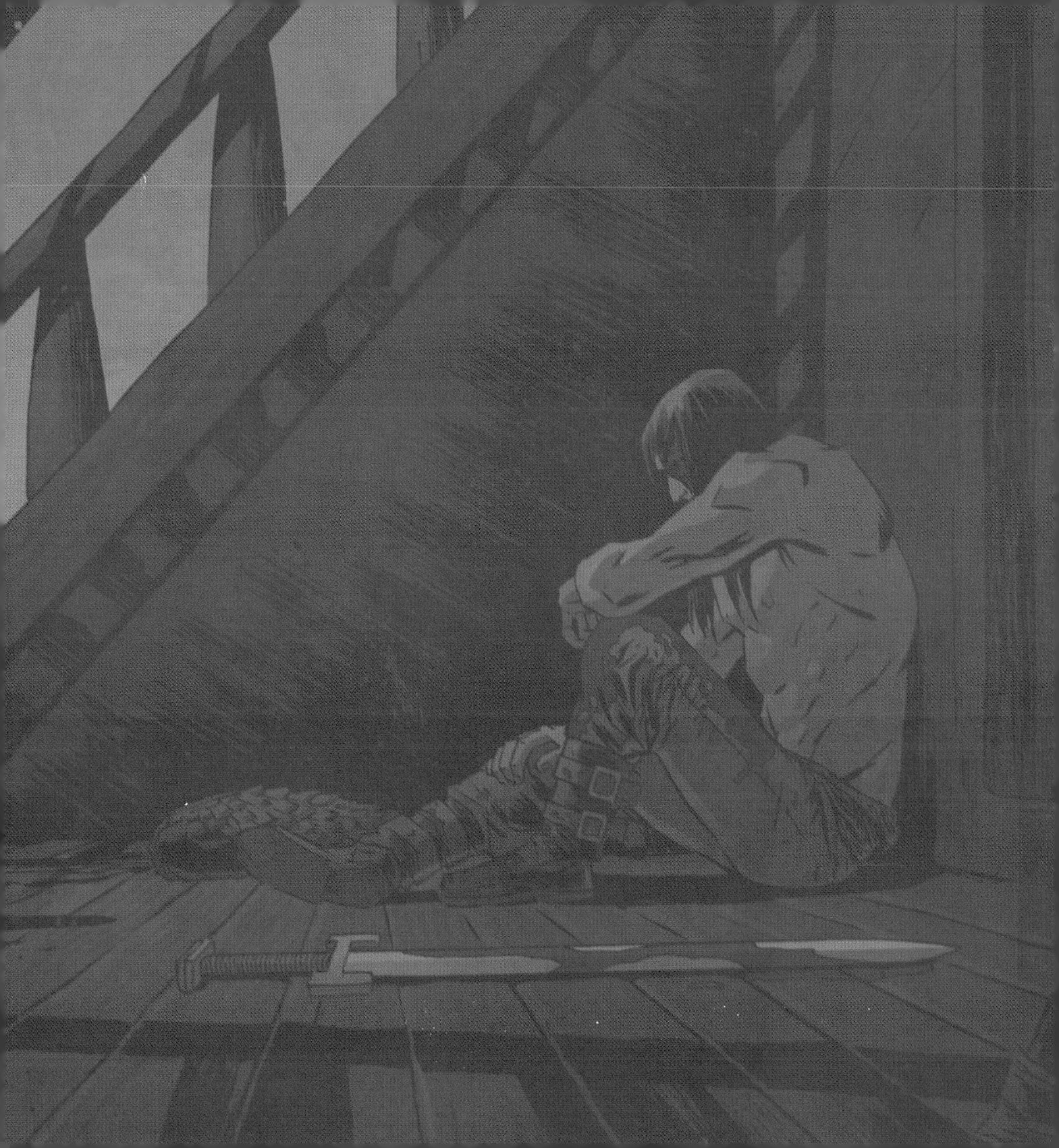

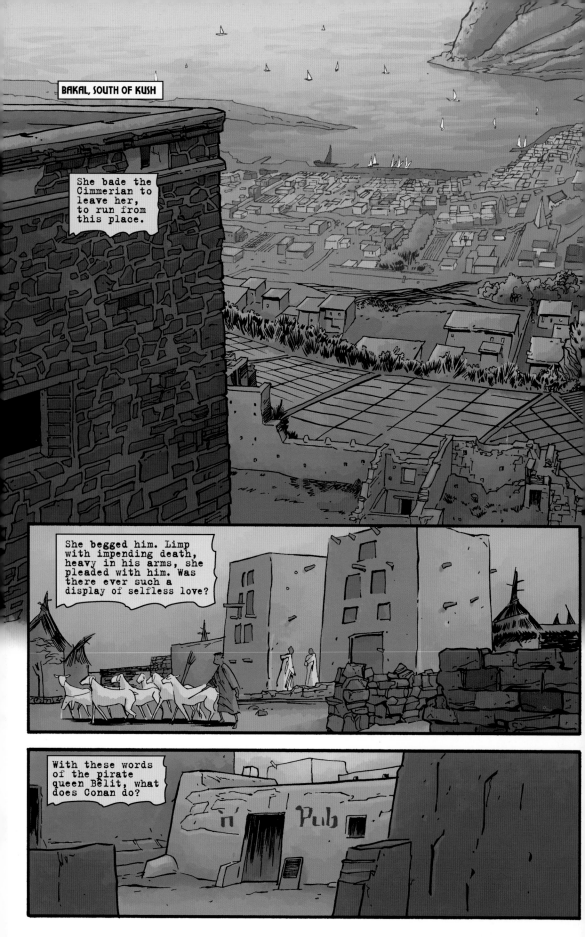

BAKAL, SOUTH OF KUSH

She bade the Cimmerian to leave her, to run from this place.

She begged him. Limp with impending death, heavy in his arms, she pleaded with him. Was there ever such a display of selfless love?

With these words of the pirate queen Bêlit, what does Conan do?

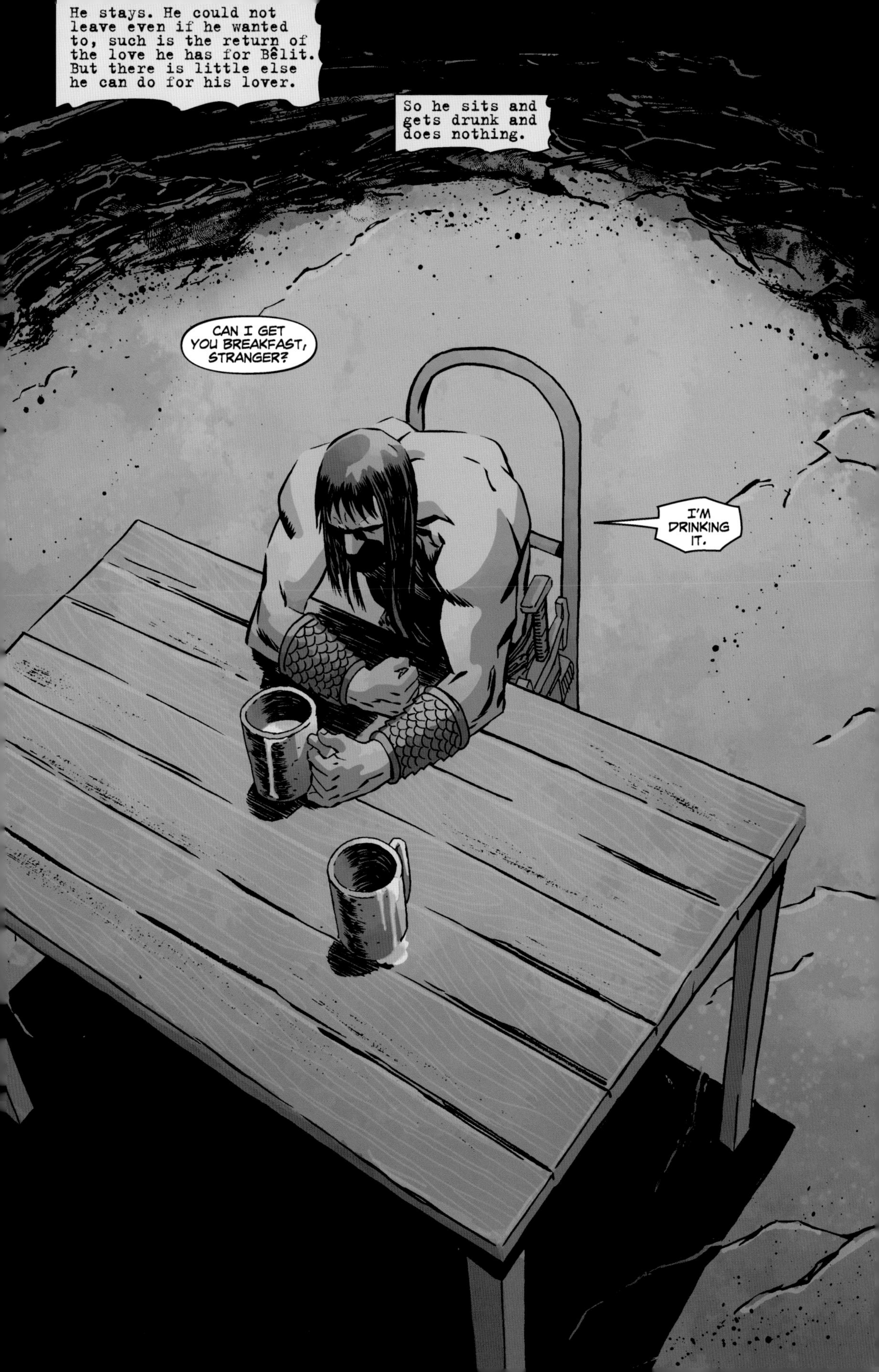
He stays. He could not leave even if he wanted to, such is the return of the love he has for Bêlit. But there is little else he can do for his lover.
So he sits and gets drunk and does nothing.
CAN I GET YOU BREAKFAST, STRANGER?
I'M DRINKING IT.

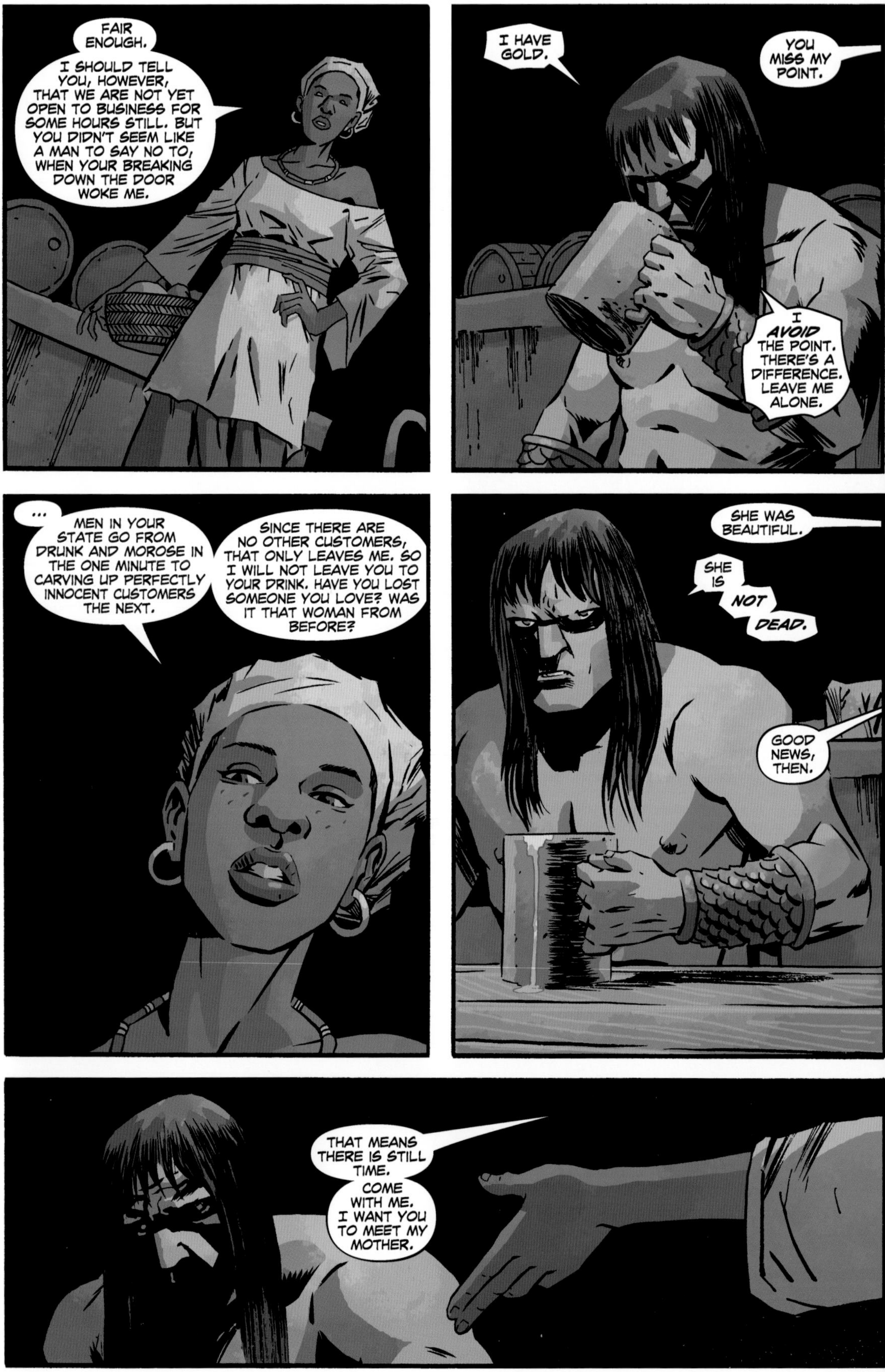

FAIR ENOUGH.
I SHOULD TELL YOU, HOWEVER, THAT WE ARE NOT YET OPEN TO BUSINESS FOR SOME HOURS STILL. BUT YOU DIDN'T SEEM LIKE A MAN TO SAY NO TO, WHEN YOUR BREAKING DOWN THE DOOR WOKE ME.
I HAVE GOLD.
YOU MISS MY POINT.
I *AVOID* THE POINT. THERE'S A DIFFERENCE. LEAVE ME ALONE.
...
MEN IN YOUR STATE GO FROM DRUNK AND MOROSE IN THE ONE MINUTE TO CARVING UP PERFECTLY INNOCENT CUSTOMERS THE NEXT.
SINCE THERE ARE NO OTHER CUSTOMERS, THAT ONLY LEAVES ME. SO I WILL NOT LEAVE YOU TO YOUR DRINK. HAVE YOU LOST SOMEONE YOU LOVE? WAS IT THAT WOMAN FROM BEFORE?
SHE WAS BEAUTIFUL.
SHE IS *NOT DEAD.*
GOOD NEWS, THEN.
THAT MEANS THERE IS STILL TIME.
COME WITH ME. I WANT YOU TO MEET MY MOTHER.

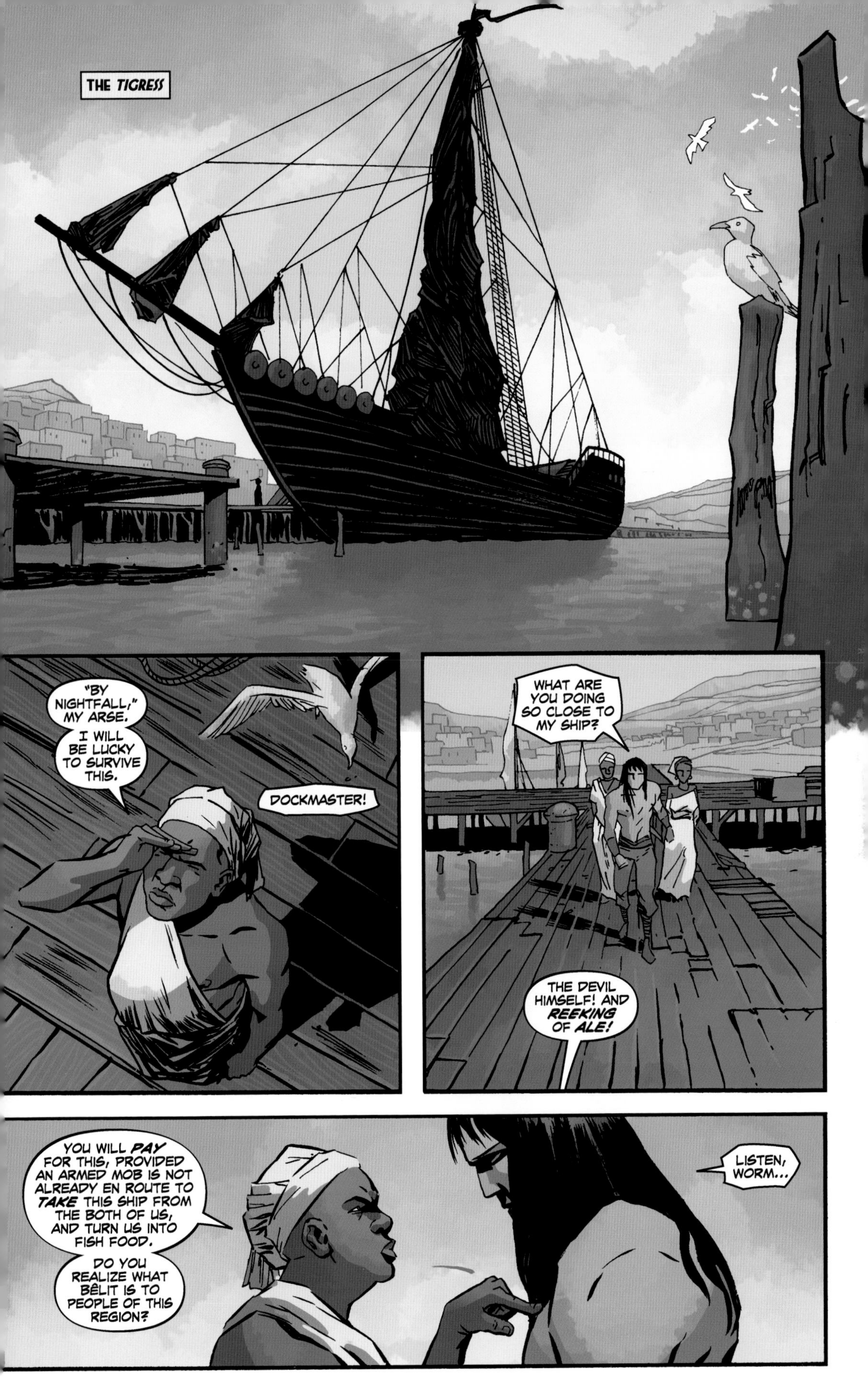
THE TIGRESS
"BY NIGHTFALL," MY ARSE. I WILL BE LUCKY TO SURVIVE THIS.
DOCKMASTER!
WHAT ARE YOU DOING SO CLOSE TO MY SHIP?
THE DEVIL HIMSELF! AND REEKING OF ALE!
YOU WILL PAY FOR THIS, PROVIDED AN ARMED MOB IS NOT ALREADY EN ROUTE TO TAKE THIS SHIP FROM THE BOTH OF US, AND TURN US INTO FISH FOOD.
DO YOU REALIZE WHAT BÊLIT IS TO PEOPLE OF THIS REGION?
LISTEN, WORM...

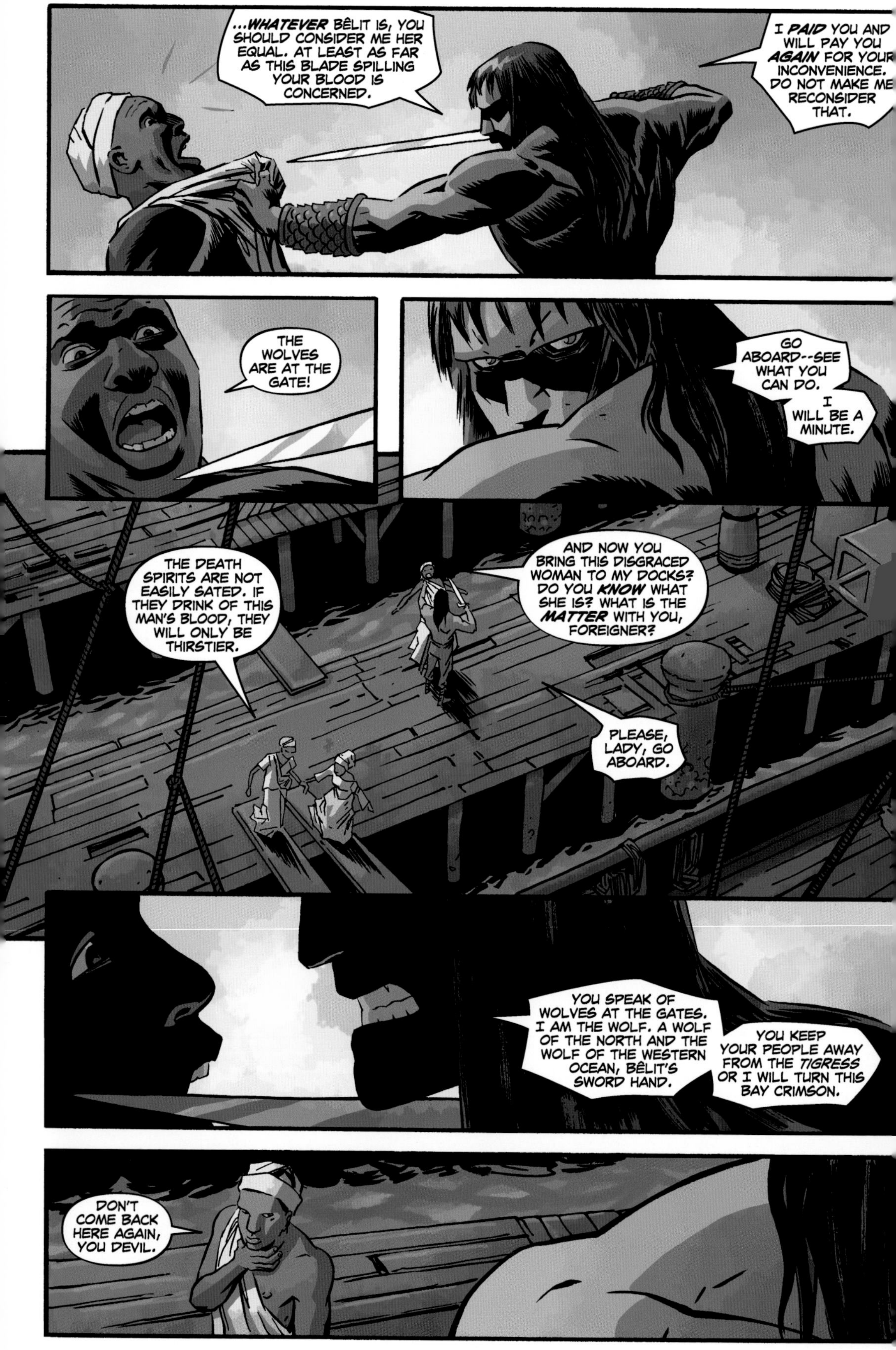
...WHATEVER BÊLIT IS, YOU SHOULD CONSIDER ME HER EQUAL. AT LEAST AS FAR AS THIS BLADE SPILLING YOUR BLOOD IS CONCERNED.
I PAID YOU AND WILL PAY YOU AGAIN FOR YOUR INCONVENIENCE. DO NOT MAKE ME RECONSIDER THAT.
THE WOLVES ARE AT THE GATE!
GO ABOARD--SEE WHAT YOU CAN DO.
I WILL BE A MINUTE.
AND NOW YOU BRING THIS DISGRACED WOMAN TO MY DOCKS? DO YOU KNOW WHAT SHE IS? WHAT IS THE MATTER WITH YOU, FOREIGNER?
THE DEATH SPIRITS ARE NOT EASILY SATED. IF THEY DRINK OF THIS MAN'S BLOOD, THEY WILL ONLY BE THIRSTIER.
PLEASE, LADY, GO ABOARD.
YOU SPEAK OF WOLVES AT THE GATES. I AM THE WOLF. A WOLF OF THE NORTH AND THE WOLF OF THE WESTERN OCEAN, BÊLIT'S SWORD HAND.
YOU KEEP YOUR PEOPLE AWAY FROM THE TIGRESS OR I WILL TURN THIS BAY CRIMSON.
DON'T COME BACK HERE AGAIN, YOU DEVIL.

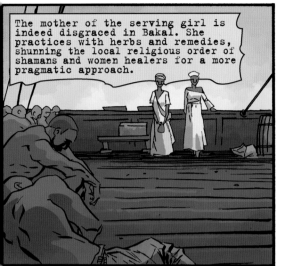

The mother of the serving girl is indeed disgraced in Bakal. She practices with herbs and remedies, shunning the local religious order of shamans and women healers for a more pragmatic approach.

YOU CAN HELP...STEEP THIS IN WATER-- IT DOES NOT HAVE TO BE HOT...

She diagnoses quickly, and with a surety of action that gives Conan hope.

SHE INSTRUCTS ME TO PLAY *NURSEMAID,* CONAN...

LISTEN TO HER, N'GORA.

I ALWAYS THOUGHT I WOULD DIE IN BATTLE.

INSTEAD I SHALL DIE FETCHING TEA.

I DON'T SEE A DYING MAN WHEN I LOOK AT YOU, MY FRIEND...

...JUST A WISEASS.

HEH, TRUE. WHERE HAVE YOU BEEN, CONAN?

I HAD ORDERS OF MY OWN.

BUT I CHOSE TO DISOBEY THEM.

WHERE IS N'YAGA?

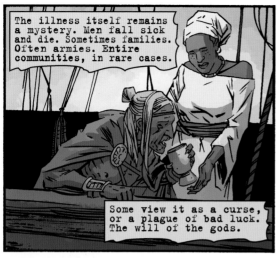

The illness itself remains a mystery. Men fall sick and die. Sometimes families. Often armies. Entire communities, in rare cases.

Some view it as a curse, or a plague of bad luck. The will of the gods.

But true to the mocking nature of the gods, they hide the cures in plain sight. The secrets of life lie locked in Mother Nature, and it takes a clever man to unlock them. Or a clever woman.

BARBARIAN, YOU FRIGHTEN AWAY THE GIRLS.

N'YAGA.

WHAT IS "THE DEATH"? YOU USED THOSE WORDS AS THE CREW OF THE *TIGRESS* FELL SICK.

YET I DO NOT BELIEVE WE WILL DIE HERE.

AH.

SO WHAT IS "THE DEATH"?

HAS SHE NOT TOLD YOU...?

NOOOOO!

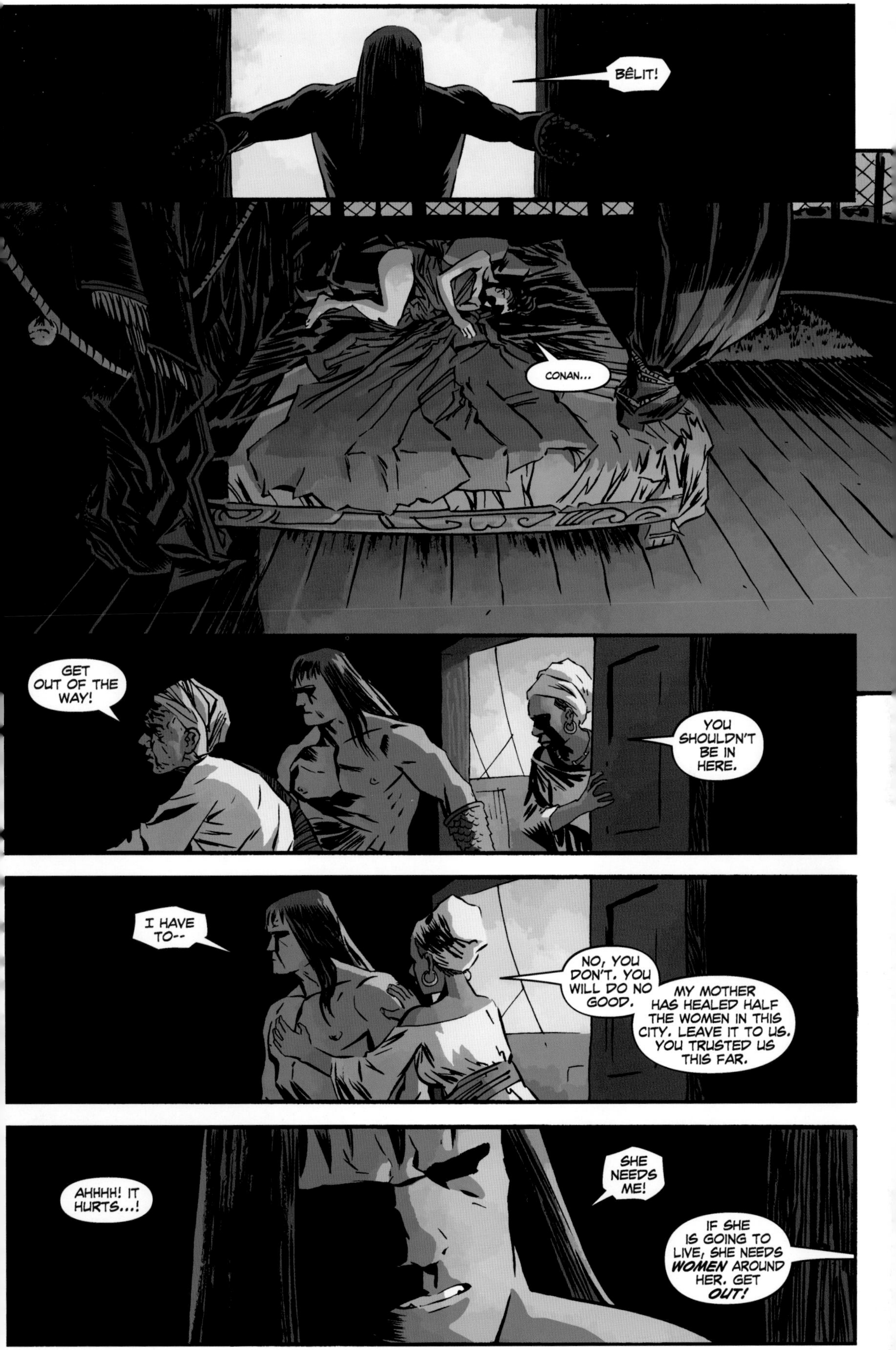
BÊLIT!
CONAN...
GET OUT OF THE WAY!
YOU SHOULDN'T BE IN HERE.
I HAVE TO--
NO, YOU DON'T. YOU WILL DO NO GOOD.
MY MOTHER HAS HEALED HALF THE WOMEN IN THIS CITY. LEAVE IT TO US. YOU TRUSTED US THIS FAR.
AHHHH! IT HURTS...!
SHE NEEDS ME!
IF SHE IS GOING TO LIVE, SHE NEEDS *WOMEN* AROUND HER. GET *OUT!*

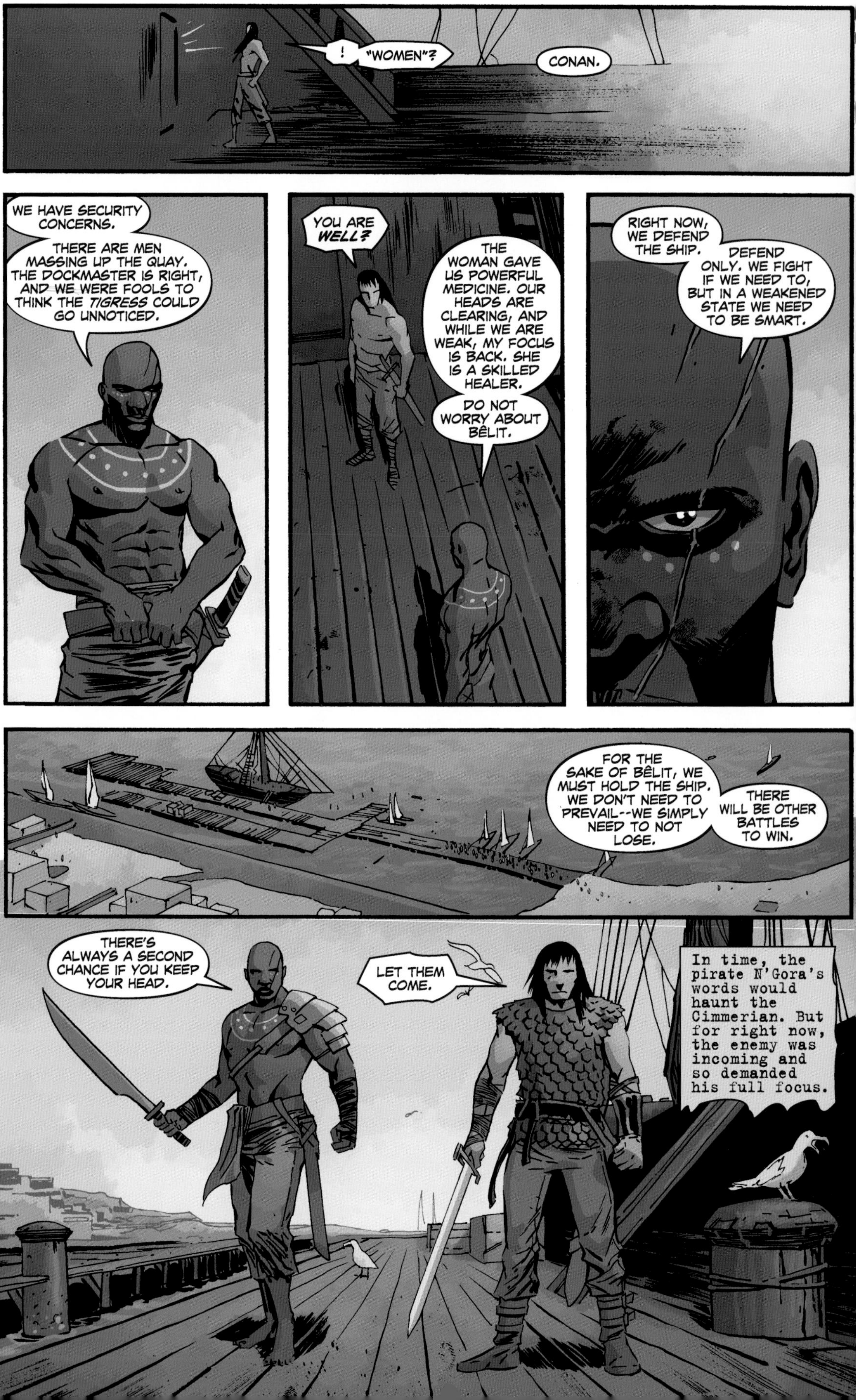
!
"WOMEN"?
CONAN.
WE HAVE SECURITY CONCERNS.
THERE ARE MEN MASSING UP THE QUAY. THE DOCKMASTER IS RIGHT, AND WE WERE FOOLS TO THINK THE *TIGRESS* COULD GO UNNOTICED.
YOU ARE *WELL?*
THE WOMAN GAVE US POWERFUL MEDICINE. OUR HEADS ARE CLEARING, AND WHILE WE ARE WEAK, MY FOCUS IS BACK. SHE IS A SKILLED HEALER.
DO NOT WORRY ABOUT BÊLIT.
RIGHT NOW, WE DEFEND THE SHIP.
DEFEND ONLY. WE FIGHT IF WE NEED TO, BUT IN A WEAKENED STATE WE NEED TO BE SMART.
FOR THE SAKE OF BÊLIT, WE MUST HOLD THE SHIP. WE DON'T NEED TO PREVAIL--WE SIMPLY NEED TO NOT LOSE.
THERE WILL BE OTHER BATTLES TO WIN.
THERE'S ALWAYS A SECOND CHANCE IF YOU KEEP YOUR HEAD.
LET THEM COME.
In time, the pirate N'Gora's words would haunt the Cimmerian. But for right now, the enemy was incoming and so demanded his full focus.

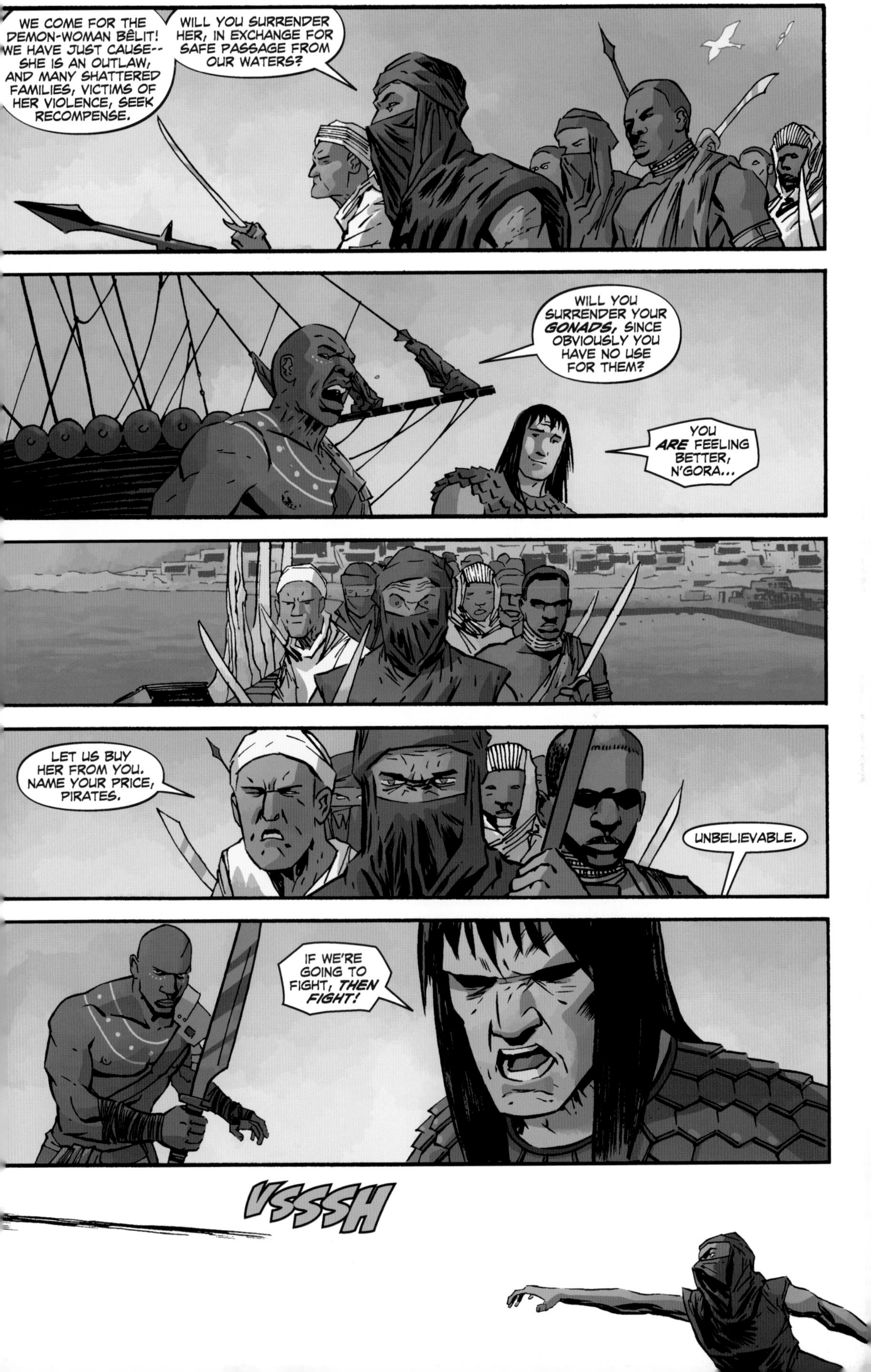
WE COME FOR THE DEMON-WOMAN BÊLIT! WE HAVE JUST CAUSE-- SHE IS AN OUTLAW, AND MANY SHATTERED FAMILIES, VICTIMS OF HER VIOLENCE, SEEK RECOMPENSE.
WILL YOU SURRENDER HER, IN EXCHANGE FOR SAFE PASSAGE FROM OUR WATERS?
WILL YOU SURRENDER YOUR GONADS, SINCE OBVIOUSLY YOU HAVE NO USE FOR THEM?
YOU ARE FEELING BETTER, N'GORA...
LET US BUY HER FROM YOU. NAME YOUR PRICE, PIRATES.
UNBELIEVABLE.
IF WE'RE GOING TO FIGHT, THEN FIGHT!
VSSSH

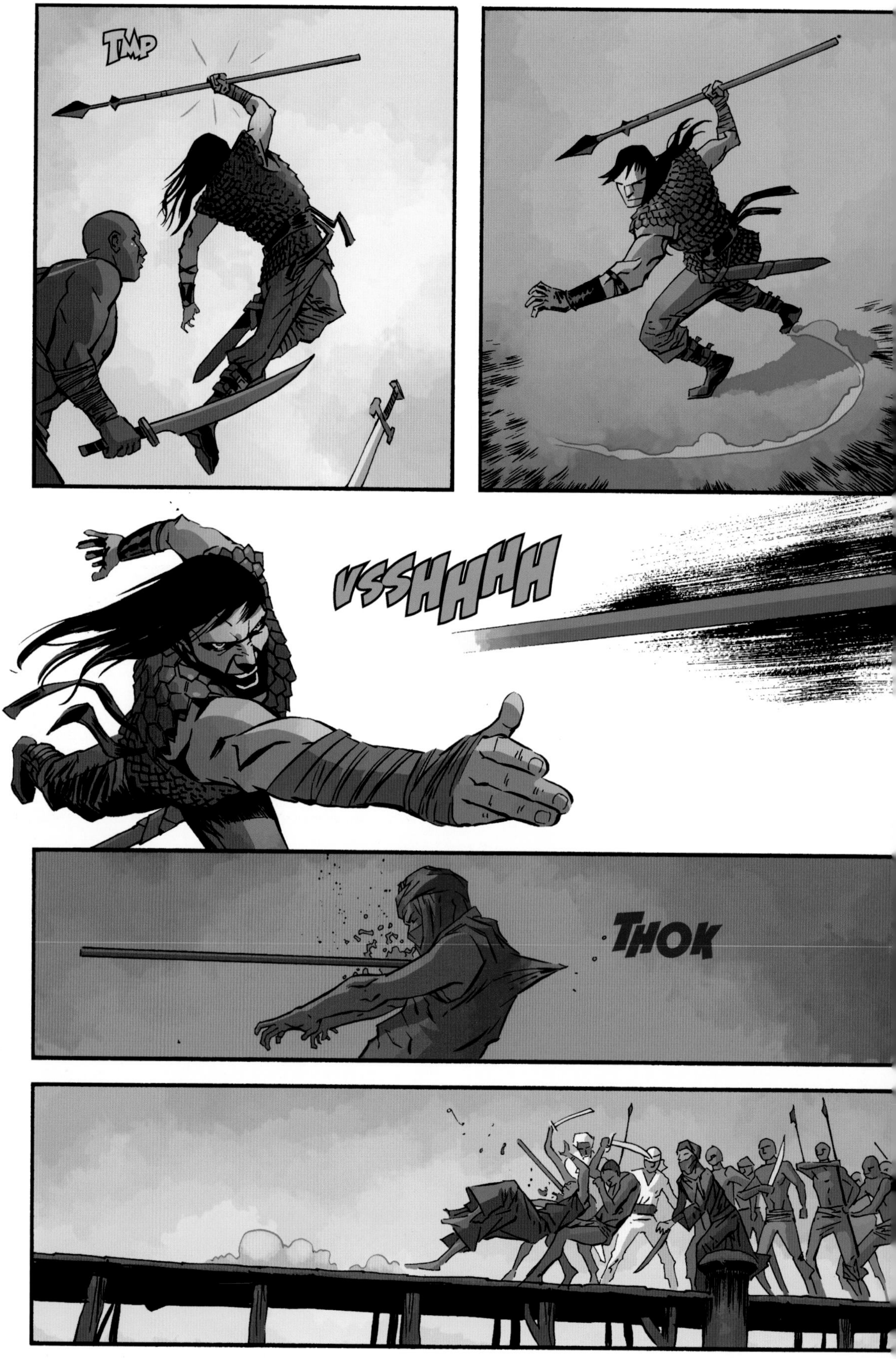
TMP
VSSHHHH
THOK

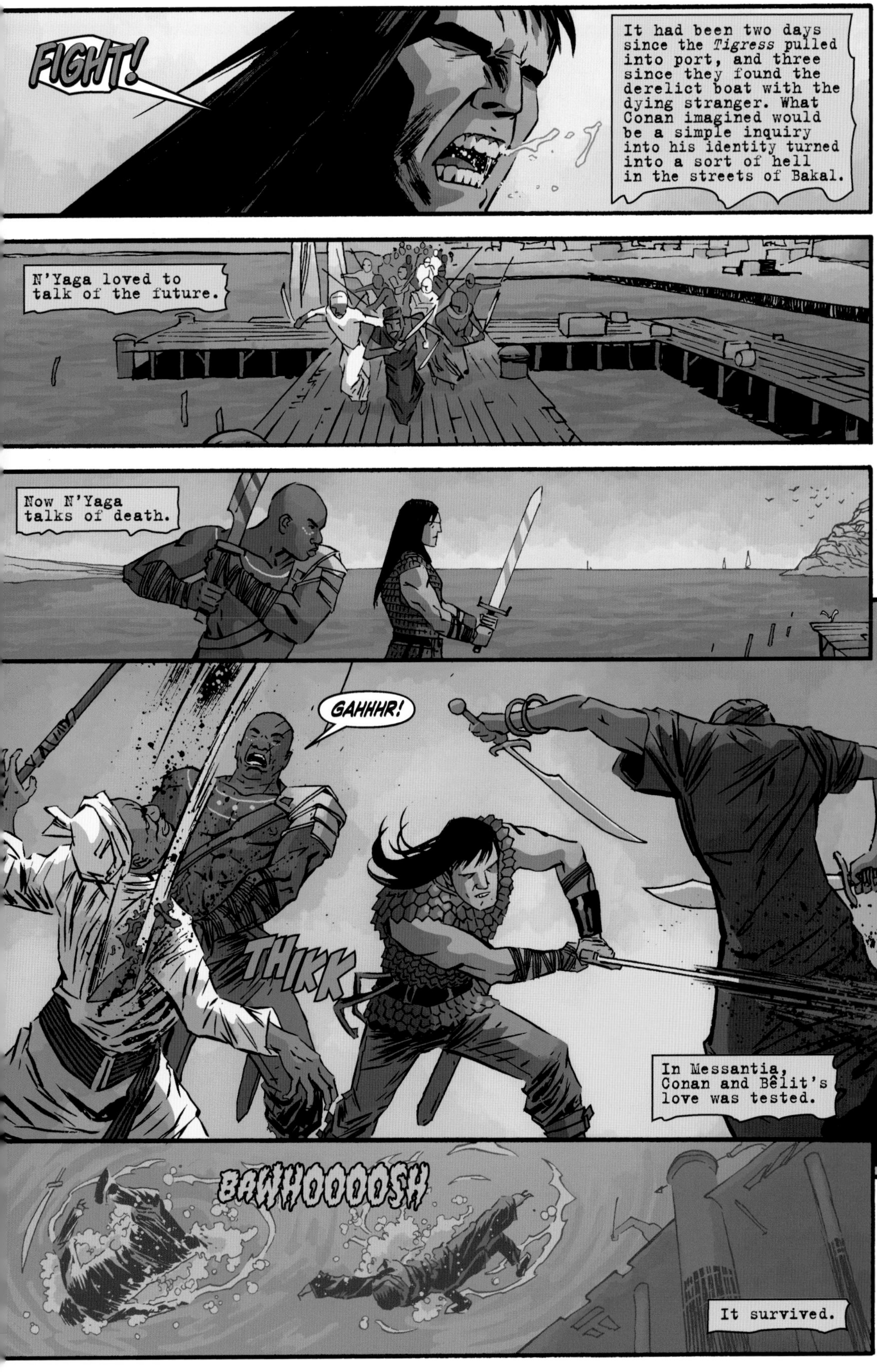
FIGHT!
It had been two days since the *Tigress* pulled into port, and three since they found the derelict boat with the dying stranger. What Conan imagined would be a simple inquiry into his identity turned into a sort of hell in the streets of Bakal.
N'Yaga loved to talk of the future.
Now N'Yaga talks of death.
GAHHHR!
THIKK
In Messantia, Conan and Bêlit's love was tested.
BAWHOOOOSH
It survived.

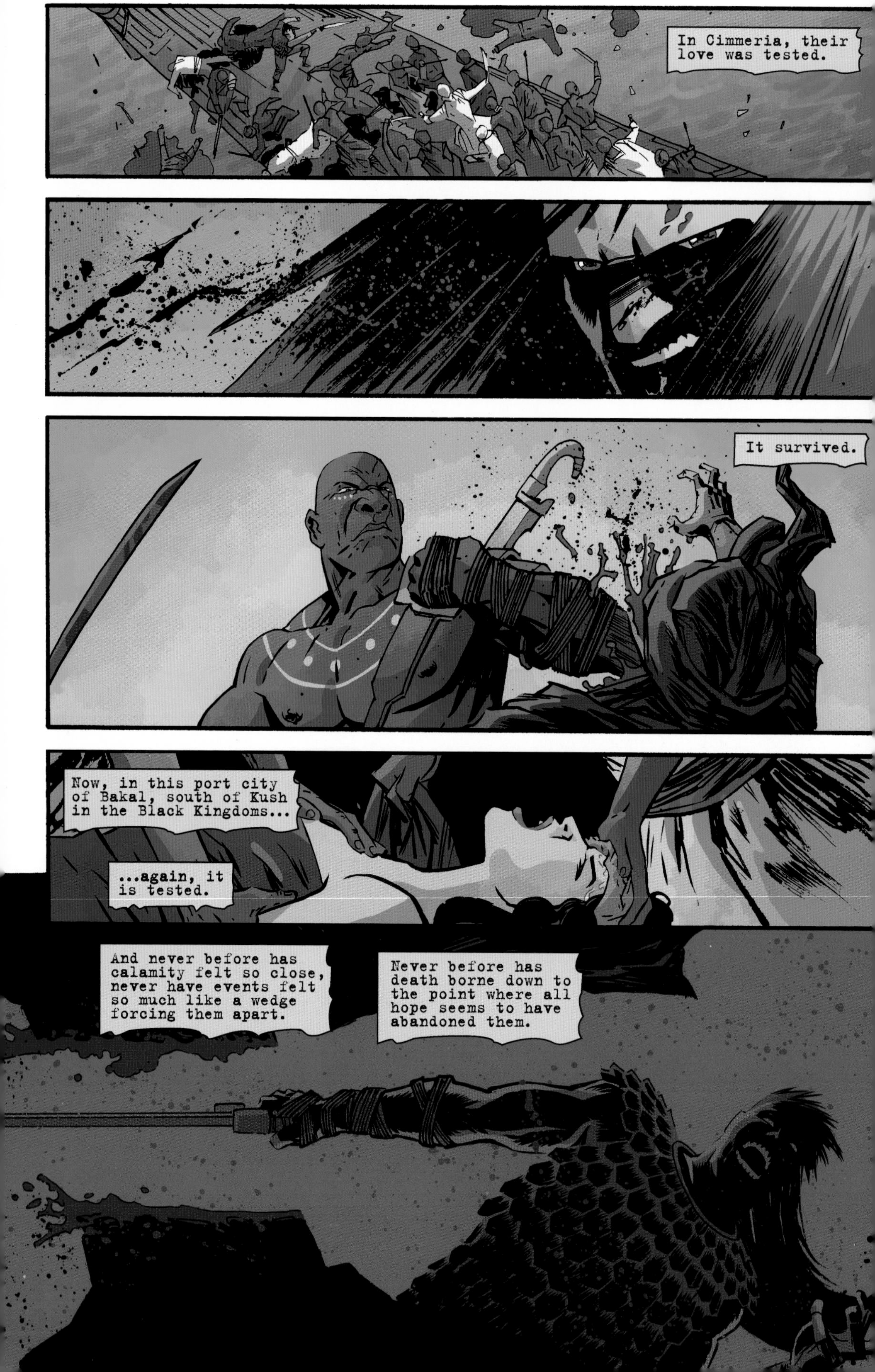
In Cimmeria, their love was tested.
It survived.
Now, in this port city of Bakal, south of Kush in the Black Kingdoms...
...again, it is tested.
And never before has calamity felt so close, never have events felt so much like a wedge forcing them apart.
Never before has death borne down to the point where all hope seems to have abandoned them.

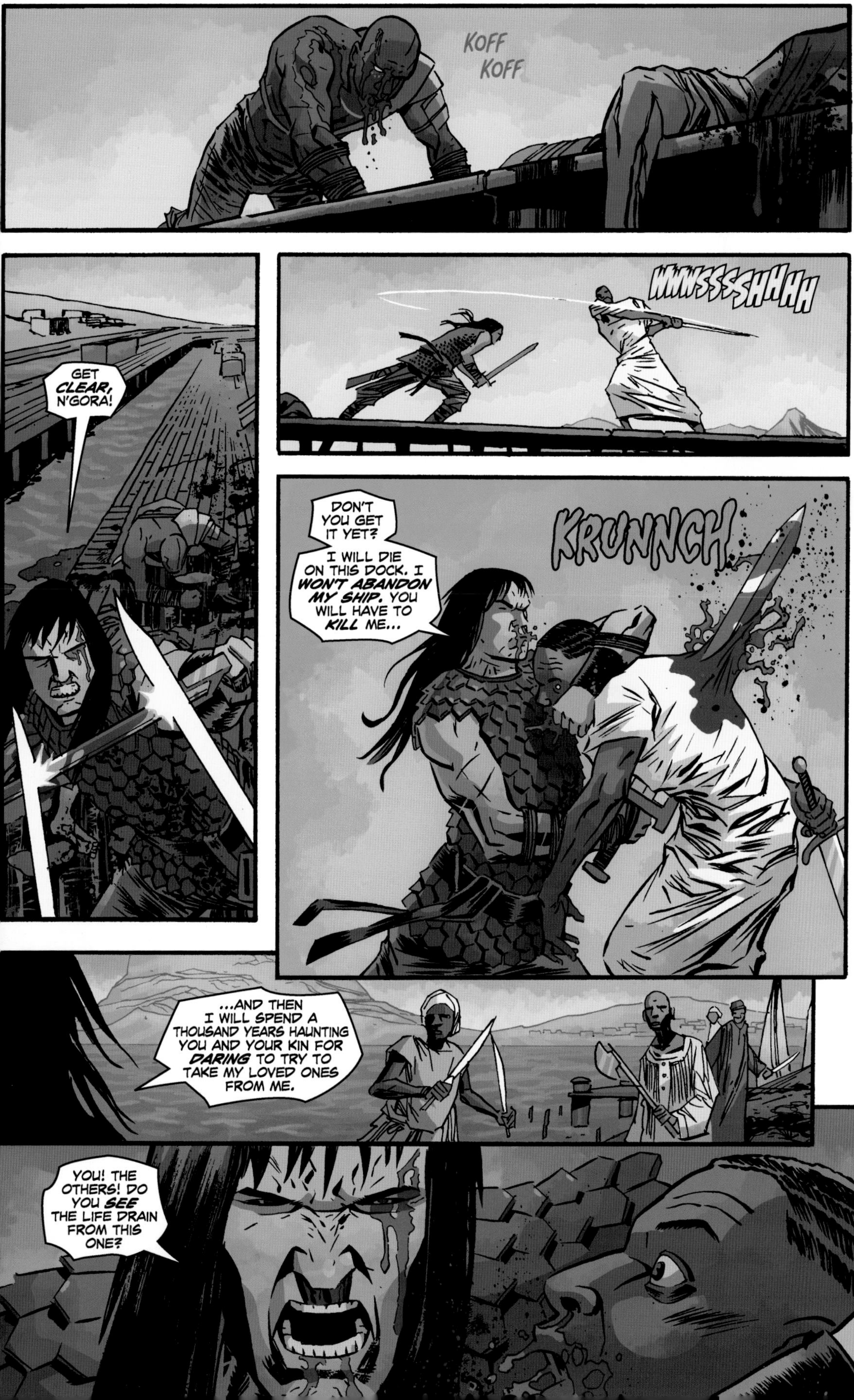
KOFF KOFF
GET CLEAR, N'GORA!
WWWSSSSHHHH
DON'T YOU GET IT YET?
I WILL DIE ON THIS DOCK. I WON'T ABANDON MY SHIP. YOU WILL HAVE TO KILL ME...
KRUNNCH
...AND THEN I WILL SPEND A THOUSAND YEARS HAUNTING YOU AND YOUR KIN FOR DARING TO TRY TO TAKE MY LOVED ONES FROM ME.
YOU! THE OTHERS! DO YOU SEE THE LIFE DRAIN FROM THIS ONE?

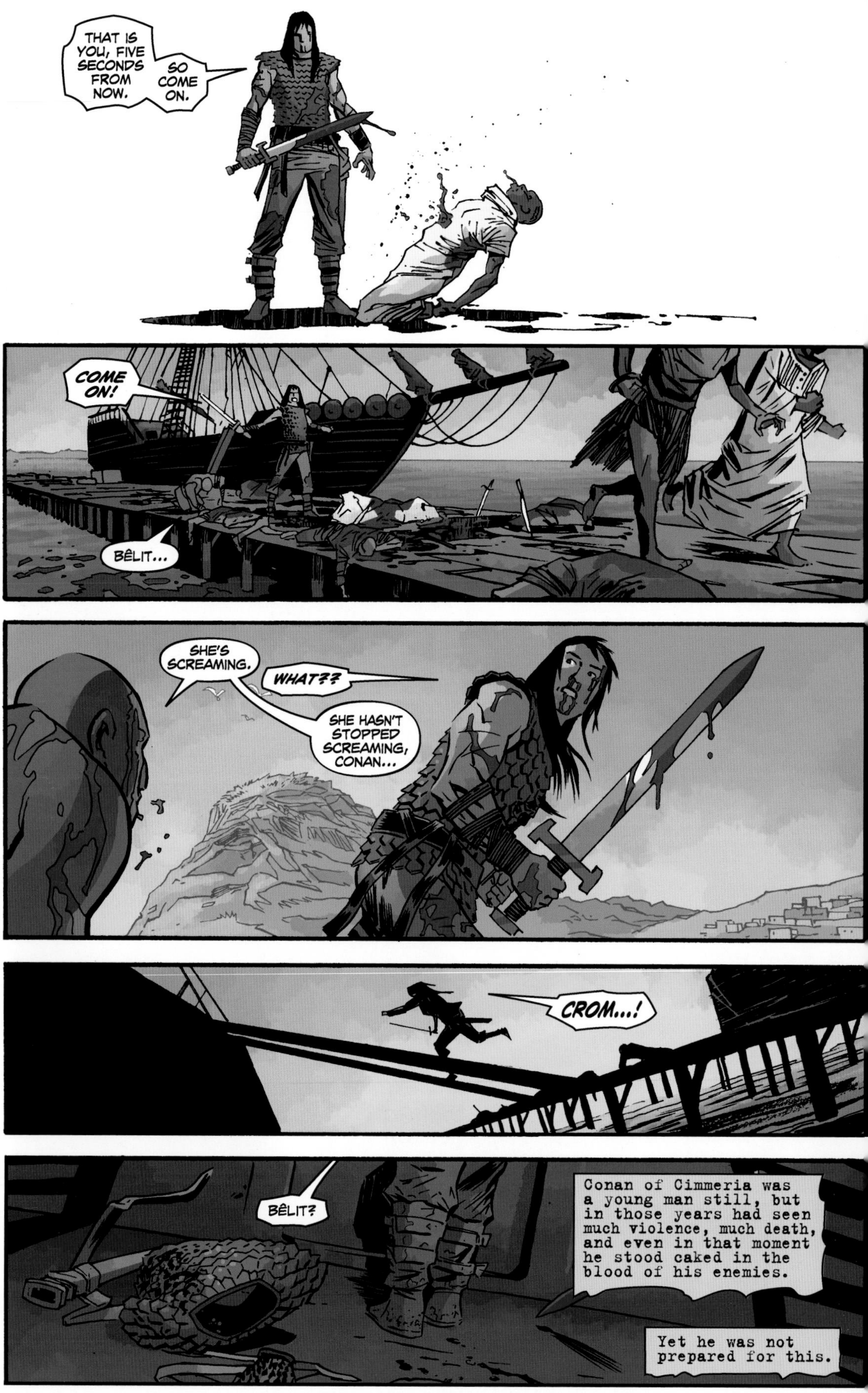
THAT IS YOU, FIVE SECONDS FROM NOW.
SO COME ON.
COME ON!
BÊLIT...
SHE'S SCREAMING.
WHAT??
SHE HASN'T STOPPED SCREAMING, CONAN...
CROM...!
BÊLIT?
Conan of Cimmeria was a young man still, but in those years had seen much violence, much death, and even in that moment he stood caked in the blood of his enemies.
Yet he was not prepared for this.

The screaming came back, as the battle lust faded. It was primal, a sound he could not imagine coming from the body of the woman he loved.

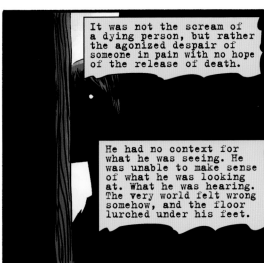

It was not the scream of a dying person, but rather the agonized despair of someone in pain with no hope of the release of death.

He had no context for what he was seeing. He was unable to make sense of what he was looking at. What he was hearing. The very world felt wrong somehow, and the floor lurched under his feet.

He would follow Bêlit to the ends of the earth...

...but he could not will himself to enter that room.

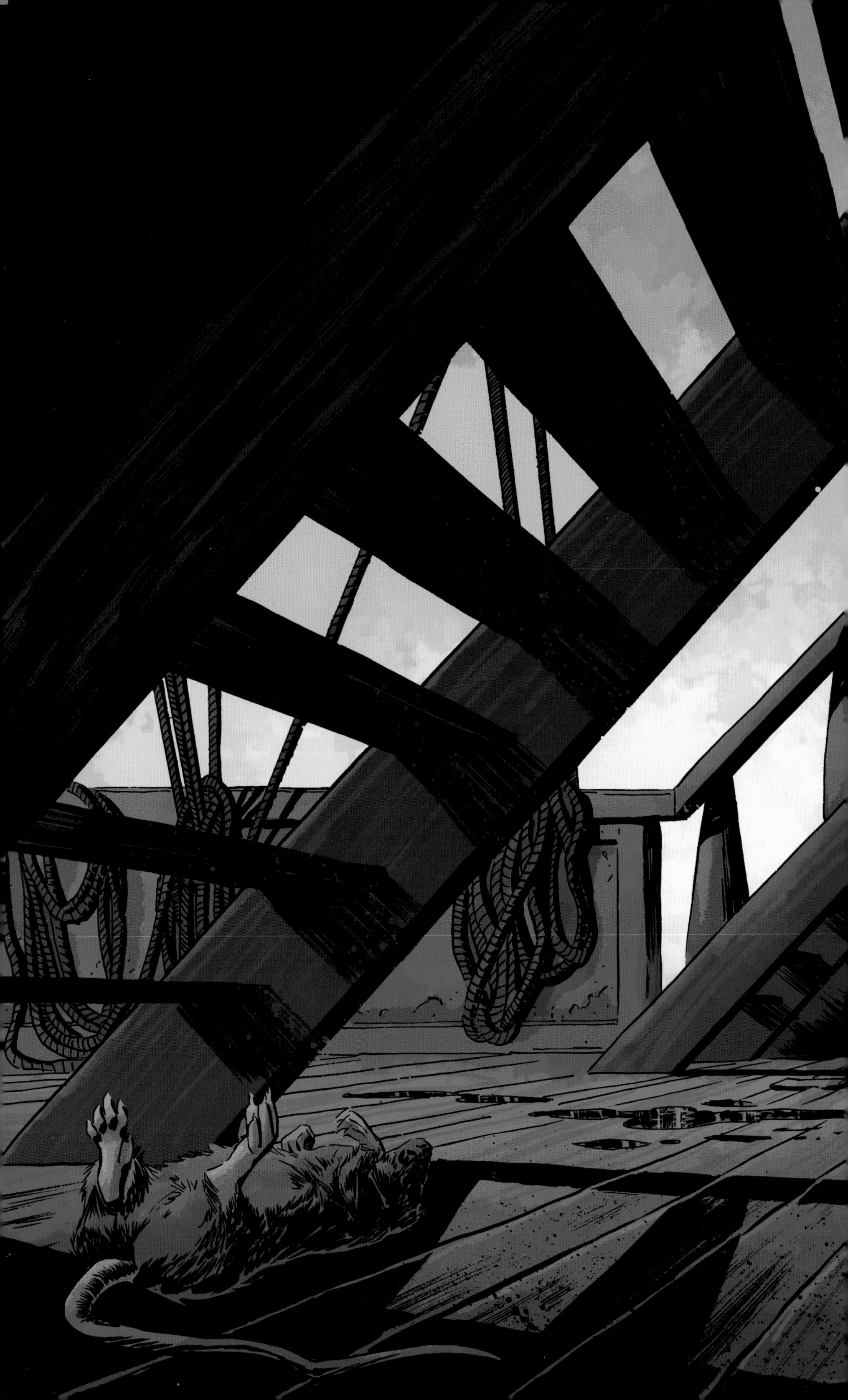

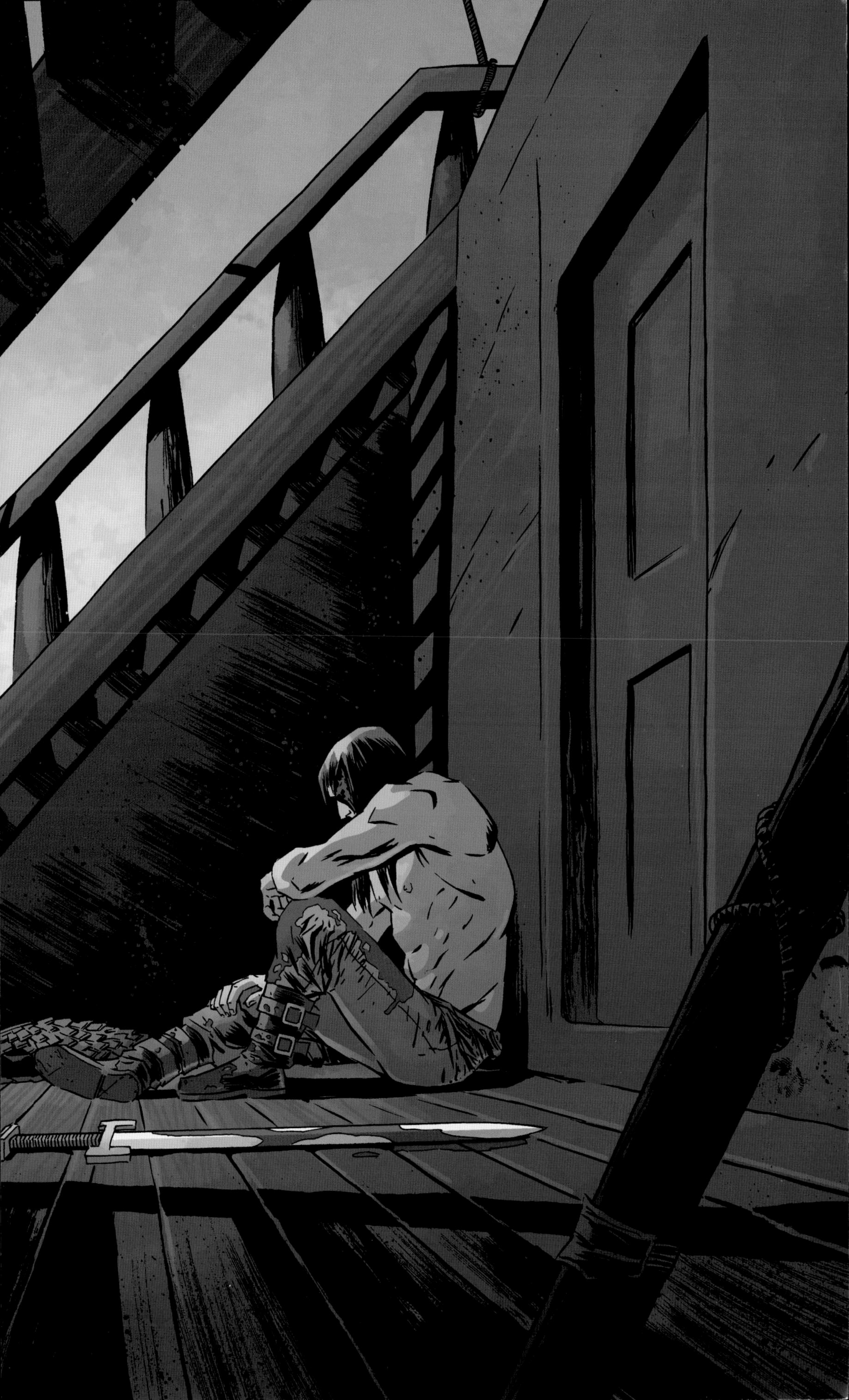

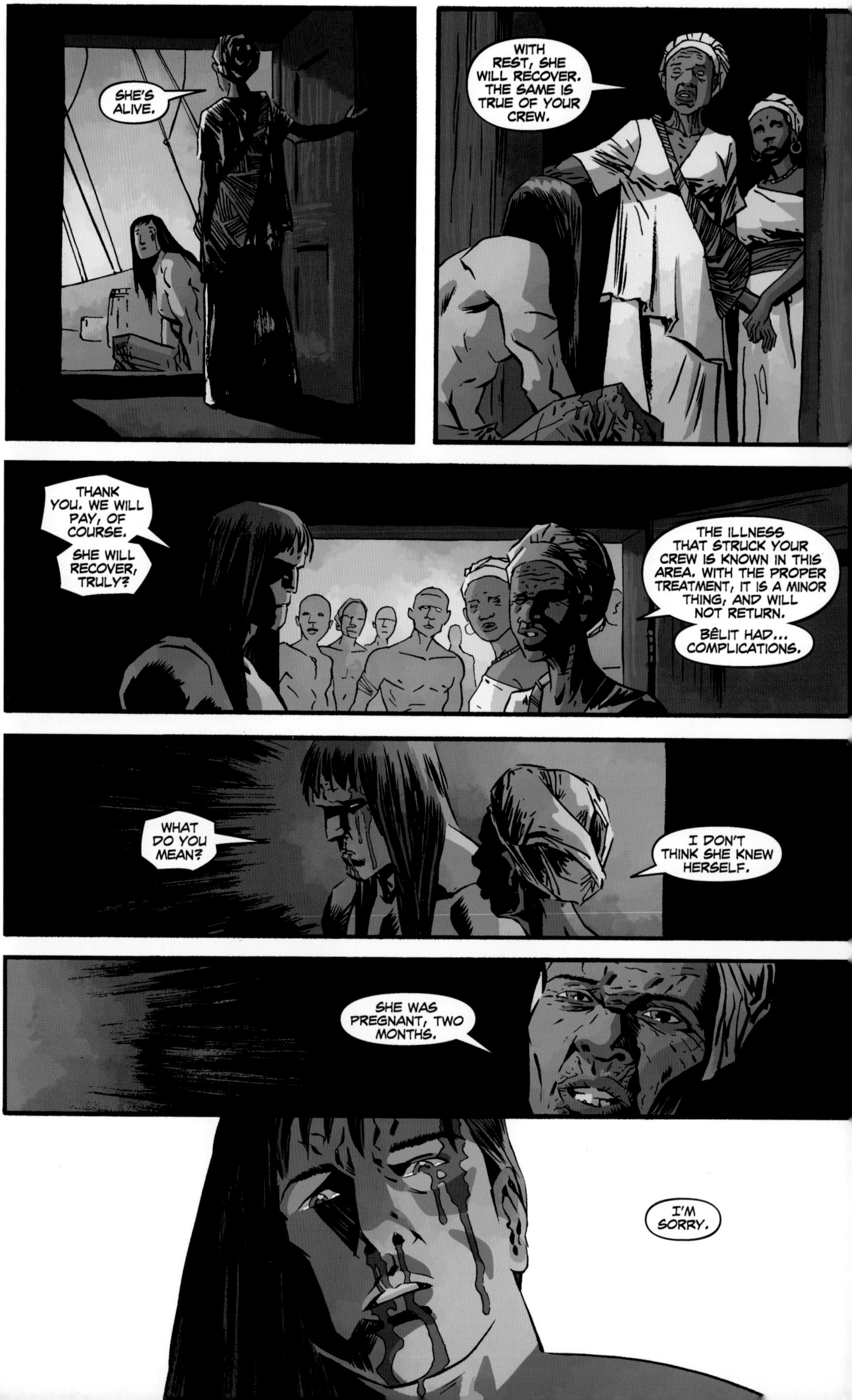
SHE'S ALIVE.
WITH REST, SHE WILL RECOVER. THE SAME IS TRUE OF YOUR CREW.
THANK YOU. WE WILL PAY, OF COURSE.
SHE WILL RECOVER, TRULY?
THE ILLNESS THAT STRUCK YOUR CREW IS KNOWN IN THIS AREA. WITH THE PROPER TREATMENT, IT IS A MINOR THING, AND WILL NOT RETURN.
BÊLIT HAD... COMPLICATIONS.
WHAT DO YOU MEAN?
I DON'T THINK SHE KNEW HERSELF.
SHE WAS PREGNANT, TWO MONTHS.
I'M SORRY.

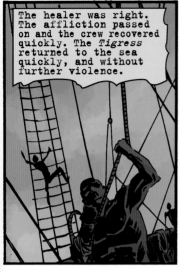

The healer was right. The affliction passed on and the crew recovered quickly. The *Tigress* returned to the sea quickly, and without further violence.

The feeling amongst the crew was similar to having pulled through a bad dream. The memory of those last few days was unclear, and so, in time, completely forgotten.

If they were aware of what happened in Bêlit's cabin...

...it was not spoken of. Indeed, above decks life quickly returned to normal.

Below, there too was little talking, but for different reasons.

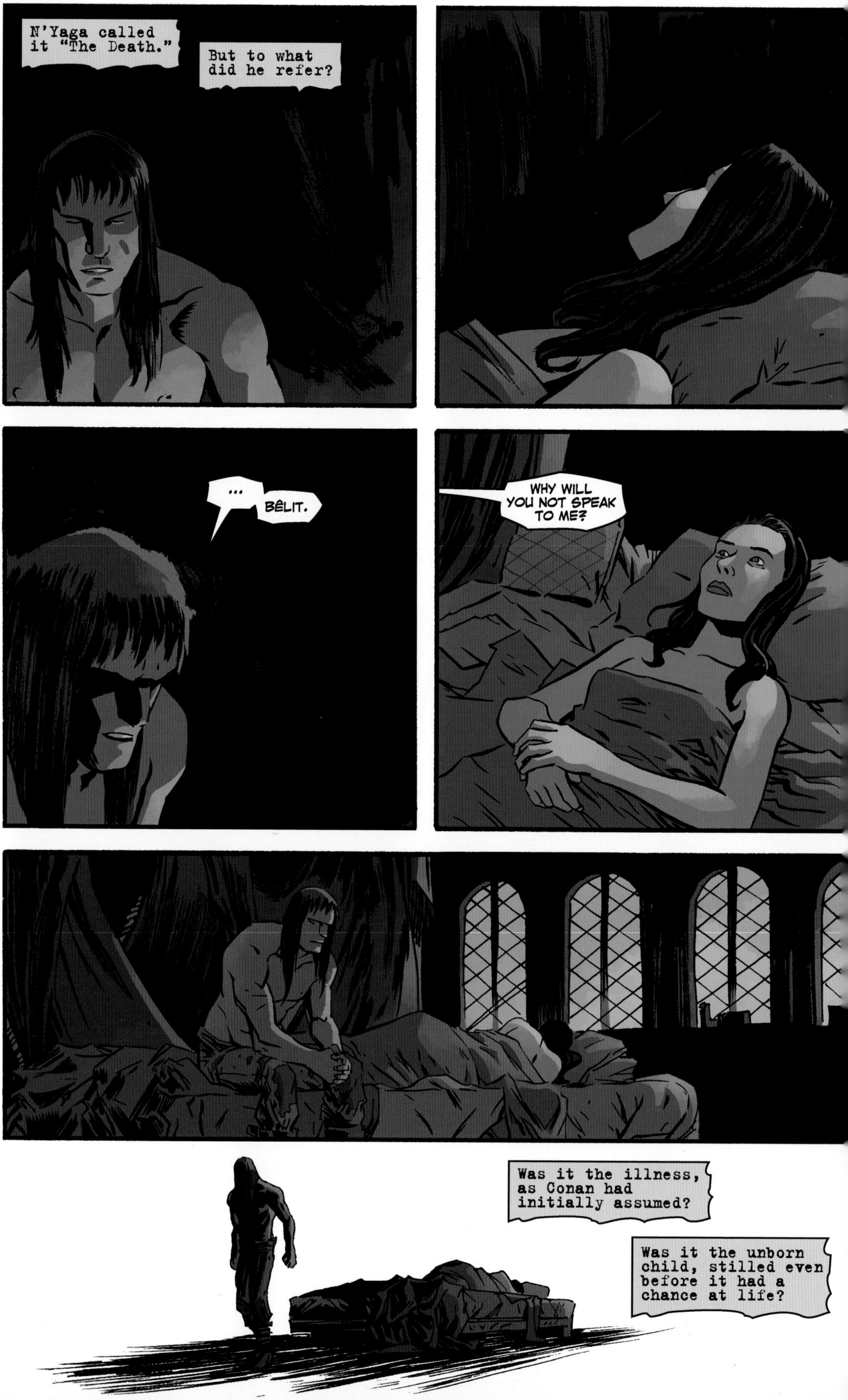
N'Yaga called it "The Death."
But to what did he refer?
...
BÊLIT.
WHY WILL YOU NOT SPEAK TO ME?
Was it the illness, as Conan had initially assumed?
Was it the unborn child, stilled even before it had a chance at life?

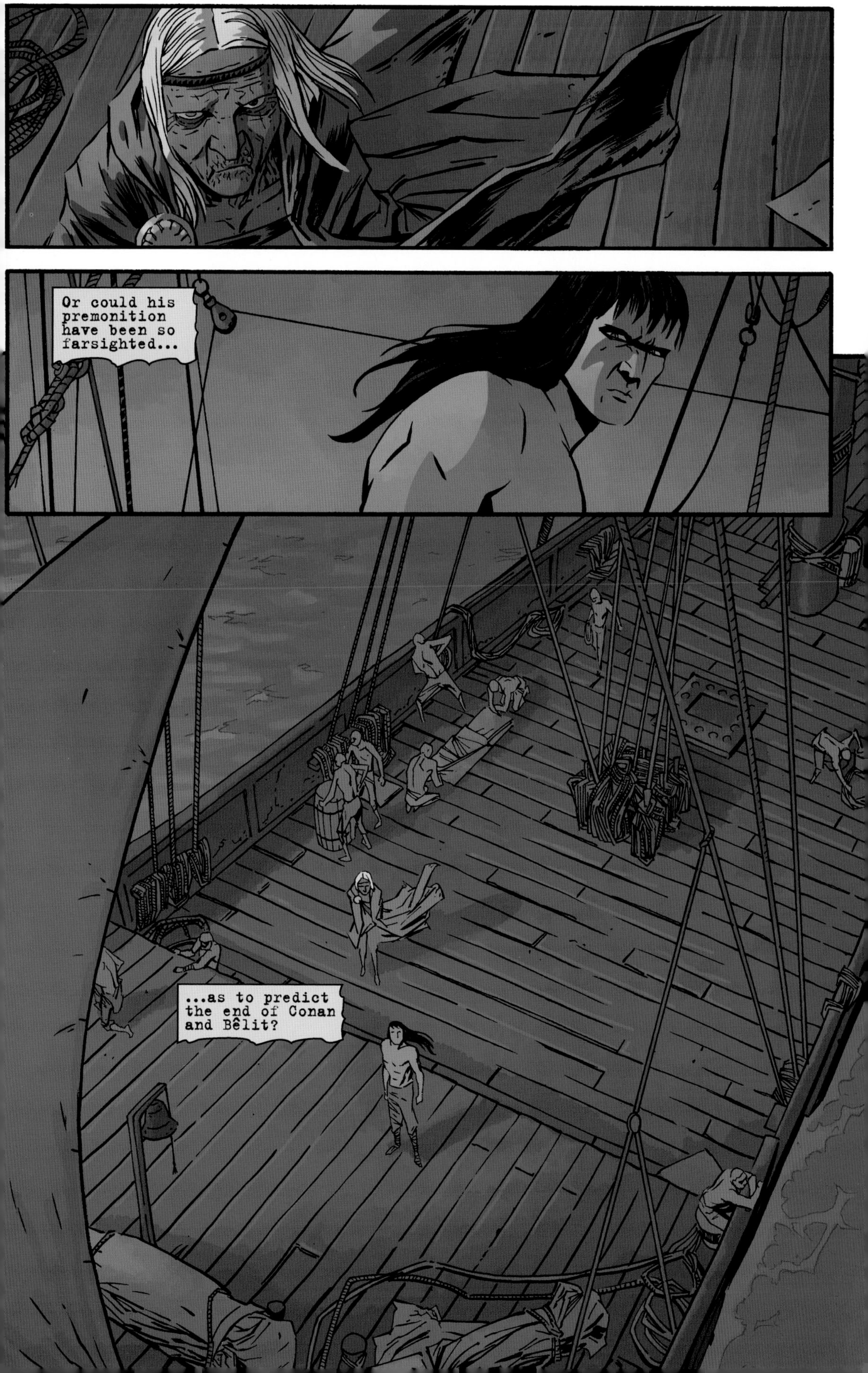
Or could his premonition have been so farsighted...
...as to predict the end of Conan and Bêlit?